# The Coordination of BRICS Development Strategies Towards Shared Prosperity

# The Coordination of BRICS Development Strategies Towards Shared Prosperity

Editors

**WANG Linggui**
**ZHAO Jianglin**
Chinese Academy of Social Sciences, China

World Scientific

NEW JERSEY · LONDON · SINGAPORE · BEIJING · SHANGHAI · HONG KONG · TAIPEI · CHENNAI · TOKYO

*Published by*

World Scientific Publishing Co. Pte. Ltd.
5 Toh Tuck Link, Singapore 596224
*USA office:* 27 Warren Street, Suite 401-402, Hackensack, NJ 07601
*UK office:* 57 Shelton Street, Covent Garden, London WC2H 9HE

**Library of Congress Cataloging-in-Publication Data**
Names: Wang, Linggui, editor. | Zhao, Jianglin, editor.
Title: The coordination of BRICS development strategies towards shared prosperity /
    edited by Linggui Wang (Chinese Academy of Social Sciences, China) and
    Jianglin Zhao (Chinese Academy of Social Sciences, China).
Description: New Jersey : World Scientific 2019. | Includes bibliographical references.
Identifiers: LCCN 2019014022 | ISBN 9789811200991 (hardcover)
Subjects: LCSH: BRIC countries--Economic policy. | BRIC countries--Foreign economic relations. |
    BRIC countries--Economic conditions--21st century. | Economic development--BRIC countries.
Classification: LCC HC59.7 .C644 2019 | DDC 338.9009172/4--dc23
LC record available at https://lccn.loc.gov/2019014022

**British Library Cataloguing-in-Publication Data**
A catalogue record for this book is available from the British Library.

Copyright © 2020 by World Scientific Publishing Co. Pte. Ltd.

*All rights reserved. This book, or parts thereof, may not be reproduced in any form or by any means, electronic or mechanical, including photocopying, recording or any information storage and retrieval system now known or to be invented, without written permission from the publisher.*

For photocopying of material in this volume, please pay a copying fee through the Copyright Clearance Center, Inc., 222 Rosewood Drive, Danvers, MA 01923, USA. In this case permission to photocopy is not required from the publisher.

For any available supplementary material, please visit
https://www.worldscientific.com/worldscibooks/10.1142/11299#t=suppl

Desk Editors: Anthony Alexander/Lixi Dong

Typeset by Stallion Press
Email: enquiries@stallionpress.com

# Preface

The word "BRIC" first originated from a foreign minister's meeting between Brazil, Russia, India and China during the 2006 General Assembly of the United Nations. The concept was based on an idea brought forth by a chief economist from Goldman Sachs and extended into an international economic body. In 2010, with the joining of South Africa, BRIC became BRICS. From 3 to 5 September, as the 9th BRICS summit opened in Xiamen, China, the curtains opened in the second golden decade of development. It is from this that the idea for this book evolved.

In the joint effort of the member states, BRICS countries have successfully cooperated for 10 years. From an investment concept in economic report to the arena of global governance, to becoming a shiny placard in cooperation between emerging markets and developing countries, BRICS countries achieved significant cooperation in politics, economy, security and cultural affairs. As the field of cooperation of BRICS countries expands, from unilateral to bilateral, from single to multi dimensional, from trade and investment in the beginning to tourism, finances, culture and science, from trade to enterprises and global governance reform negotiations, from governmental communications to party communications to think tank, culture, science, technology, education and legislative communications, from domestic issues to negotiations on international issues, from bilateral to multilateral cooperation, the BRICS cooperation has become an important force in stimulating world economic

vi  *Preface*

growth, perfecting global governance and making international relations about people's welfare.

At present, the international situation is complicated. Under the shadow of an international financial crisis, all countries around the world are having a hard time and the BRICS countries are no exception. They face many complicated and harsh challenges in further development. How should BRICS countries further strengthen cooperation and continue to be front-runners of pushing global governance? How should they stay unshaken by storms, undisturbed by discords and unobstructed by difficulties, continue constructing and strengthening a partnership that maintains world peace, enhances joint development, publicizes multilateral civilization and increases global economic governance, in order to achieve greater development?

In this process where challenges can be turned into opportunities, pressure can be changed to motivation, from Ufa to Goa to Xiamen, BRICS cooperation increases in height, especially needs leadership from the five countries to frequently visit each other, hear each other's opinions and consider the world's situation from the perspective of the other countries.[1] "Strengthening cooperation with BRICS countries has always been a priority in Chinese diplomatic relations. China will keep strengthening cooperation with BRICS countries and increase economic growth, complete cooperation framework and produce more results, in order to bring benefits for the people and contribute more to world peace and development".[2] BRICS countries will definitely "lead cooperation with an open mind, promote development according to economic rules, fully exploit the 'golden rules' of dialogue, exercise the political wisdom of 'finding common ground while admitting differences', establish the 'path of confidence' with BRICS cooperation and make BRICS cooperation into the origin of new ideas in global governance'. When President Xi Jinping was attending an informal BRICS leadership meeting in Turkey on 15 November 2015, he pointed out that "the world needs to have a new

---

[1] Chen Zhongwei, The Development and the Trend of BRICs Cooperation, *The CPPCC Paper*, 13 June 2017.

[2] Xi Jinping, "Cooperation and Development", in *Xijinping: The Governance of China*, (Foreign Language Press), 2014, p. 326.

view on the makeup of the BRICS".[3] On 7 July 2017, Xi Jinping made a conclusion speech while presiding at an informal meeting of BRICS leadership conference in Hamburg, bringing out the four "unwavering".[4] The 9th BRICS summit in Xiamen, China became a new starting point for BRICS countries to step up to a whole new level and took the BRICS cooperation into the key development stage for a second decade.

"BRICS research project" is one of the key projects of the National Institute for Global Strategy of the Chinese Academy of Social Sciences. In the long term, we have followed the principle of "setting foot on domestic matters, using foreign experiences to advertise domestic affairs, closely follow and pay attention to commentary from foreign strategic think tanks on BRICS development, as a grassroots research path and method". On 14 May 2017, chairman of board of directors Cai Fang brought forth a five-point suggestion to more than 200 directors of strategic think tanks and experts on how to promote joint research project on the Belt and Road Initiative during the "think tank parallel forum" in the "Belt and Road Forum for International Cooperation". He said that the first requirement was to jointly plan topics and promote joint research. Each think tank has its own specialty field and can contribute wisdom to Belt and Road construction in all ways. Through joint research, we can find common interests, which can help the execution of Belt and Road Initiative to be close to reality and the people. The second requirement was to establish a sharing mechanism for academic results. Periodic or a periodic strengthening of academic exchange is one of the best ways of keeping the interaction between think tanks. It helps deepen understanding and exchange of ideas. The third requirement was to share cultivation of talents. We should encourage visiting of researchers and cultivation of post-doc candidates between think tanks. The visits and exchanges can be short term or long term, with the goal of cultivating special talents interested in research on Belt and Road. The fourth requirement was to jointly publish results. The form of publishing joint research reports can enable people to take calls on important concerns and produce vast societal

---

[3]*Xinhuanet*, Xi Jinping's speech at the informal meeting of the leaders of BRICs, 16 November 2015.

[4]*Xinhuanet*, Xi Jinping's speech at the informal meeting of the leaders of BRICs, 7 July 2017.

**viii** *Preface*

influence, which is beneficial to pushing government decision. The fifth requirement was to hold periodic joint conferences and establish a daily contact mechanism. Conference is the most direct way of strengthening communication and is helpful in generating new ideas and suggestions. On the contrary, daily contact is necessary. We are gradually accumulating experience in this field.

He also stated that "In pushing Belt and Road, we first need to communicate, know what each other are worried about, what each other need, in order to have cooperation. We hope to establish a think tank alliance, a think tank net. In this alliance, in this net, what we need to do is to better serve our research to practice, to have Belt and Road better serve to China's and the world's development in all aspects." In this alliance, this net, people can survive together, gather ideas, and form a mechanism of long-term cooperation through people exchanges, cooperative research and information exchanges. We can have interaction and communication at least in the field of academia and build it as an example of people connecting along the Belt and Road.[5] This is also the origin of us paying attention to strengthening contact and integration with BRICS think tanks and treat joint research as an important channel of research. It's the realization and forum of the "opening up and establishing think tanks" concept brought forth by chairman Cai Fang and can be an exploration and attempt of our research work that serves our domestic fellowmen.

On 8–9 June 2017, the first BRICS think tank forum with Guangming Think Tank and University of International Relations was held in Beijing. The forum was titled "2017 BRICS Think-Tanks Forum — The coordination of BRICS Development Strategies: Way to Shared Prosperity" and invited about 50 government officials and experts from BRICS' main think tanks to discuss the cooperation and development of the BRICS countries in the next 10 years to come. This book is a presentation of the joint research and sharing of the exchange of viewpoints.

In the future, National Institute for Global Strategy think tank is willing to conduct scientific and deep joint research with think tanks from BRICS countries and other experts and scholars on the future

---

[5]Cai Fang's speech at a Think Tank Forum on 14 May 2017.

developmental route of BRICS mechanism, to support BRICS countries to "keep deepening partnership for a brighter future" with our wisdom. At the same time, in this process, we can also form a good "partnership" with BRICS think tanks and together we can push for a "bright future" of think tank cooperation. This is our wish and one of our academic goals.

# About the Editors

**Wang Linggui** Senior Research Fellow, Executive Vice Chairman of Board of Directors and Secretary General of National Institute for Global Strategy (NIGS), Chinese Academy of Social Sciences (CASS) since the end of 2015. His major study covers China's Belt and Road Initiative, China's global strategy, counter-terrorism issue, Middle East issue, and others. During the period of his position, he published about 400 works as papers, books and reports. Some of his works were awarded by CASS and some government institutions. He also acts as the chief of several important governmental study projects.

**Zhao Jianglin** Senior Research Fellow, Deputy Secretary of National Institute for Global Strategy (NIGS), Chinese Academy of Social Sciences (CASS). Her research areas cover International Economics, China's Belt and Road Initiative, and others. During the period of her position, she has published papers, books and reports and also acted as the chief of study projects.

# Contents

*Preface*                                                                    v

*About the Editors*                                                         xi

Chapter 1    Deepen BRICS Partnership for a Brighter Future        1
             *Wang Linggui and Zhao Jianglin*

Chapter 2    Opportunities and Challenges for BRICS
             Countries: The International Environment
             and Policy Outlook for BRICS Countries              21
             *Roberto Abdenur*

Chapter 3    BRICS and the Changing International System          29
             *Alexander Lukin*

Chapter 4    The Role and Place of BRICS in the Context
             of Globalization                                    35
             *Boris Guseletov*

Chapter 5    Are the BRICS Nations Ready for a New Era?          45
             *Zhu Caihua*

Chapter 6    Difficulties and Path of BRICS Countries'
             Structural Reform                                   57
             *Huang Maoxing*

xiv  *Contents*

Chapter 7  Dynamics from BRICS Countries — A Perspective
on BRICS Development Strategies: Prospects
and Issues                                                    67
*Vinod Anand*

Chapter 8  Brazil's Participation in BRICS Cooperation
Mechanism: Strategic Consideration and
Analysis of Results                                          77
*Zhou Zhiwei*

Chapter 9  Brazil in the BRICS After Davos 2017: Coordinating
Development Strategies in a New Epoch                        95
*Ana Flávia Barros Platiau and
Jorge Gomes do Cravo Barros*

Chapter 10  Balance of Power and International Trade: The
Perception of the Brazilian Public Opinion
about China and BRICS                                       109
*Amancio Jorge de Oliveira and Janina Onuki*

Chapter 11  Coordinating BRICS Strategies: A Russian Point
of View and Suggestions                                     121
*Georgy Toloraya*

Chapter 12  South Africa Beware the BRIC Bearing BRICS,
as the Soothsayer Hath Warned Caesar "Beware
the Ides of March!"                                         135
*Matlotleng Matlou*

Chapter 13  Seeking Sino–India Development Coordination
under the Belt and Road                                     155
*Lin Minwang*

Chapter 14  The Development and Future of BRICS
Countries — BRICS: Toward Multipolarity
and Global Governance                                       169
*Bali Ram Deepak*

*Contents* **xv**

Chapter 15    The BRICS: An Attractive and Compelling
Alternative to Global Governance                                179
*Tony Karbo*

Chapter 16    Policy Suggestions on the Coordination
of BRICS Strategies                                             193
*Renato Galvao Flores*

Chapter 17    Soft Power, Inter-cultural Communication and
Inter-civilizational Dialogue as Main Strategies
of Development of International Cooperation                     203
*Guseynova Innara Alyevna*

Chapter 18    A New Type of South–South Cooperation and
BRICS New Development Bank                                      211
*Zhu Jiejin*

Chapter 19    The Coordination of BRICS Development Strategies:
Way to Common Prosperity — Sum of 2017 BRICS
Think Tanks Forum and International Conference                  217
*Wei Siying*

*Index*                                                                        229

# Chapter 1

# Deepen BRICS Partnership for a Brighter Future

Wang Linggui and Zhao Jianglin

*National Institute for Global Strategy (NIGS), CASS, Beijing, P. R. China*

## Introduction

How BRICS is different from other cooperative organizations in the world is that it started out as a concept in investment and later transformed into a complex concept that includes politics, economy, security and culture. Since the first BRICS leadership summit in 2006, even though there have been multiple challenges, the BRICS countries have achieved great developments in multiple fields, past many layers and in mechanization, and have become the BRICS power in global governance and put in efforts to promote justice and fairness, openness and tolerance in world development. On 7 July 2017, when President Xi Jinping was presiding over an informal conference of BRICS leadership in Hamburg, he brought forth the four "unwavering" declaratives on the future development of BRICS cooperation.[1] The four unwavering declaratives reveal the historical responsibilities and cooperation goals BRICS countries should shoulder in order to input their own efforts for the development of developing countries and joint development of the world.

---

[1] *Xinhuanet*, Xi Jinping's speech at the informal meeting of leaders of BRICS, 7 July 2017.

## Status and Function of BRICS in World Economic Layout

Because of the BRICS countries' perspective status in their regions, their own abilities and importance in the world, they have transformed from an economic concept into a compound concept. This chapter tends to discuss more of their economic cooperation, and so the evaluation of the BRICS' international status is mainly focused on an economic aspect.

The BRICS countries are distributed in Asia, Africa, Europe and Latin America. In 2016, their total population took up about 41.9% of the world's population and about 22.4% of the world's GDP. From establishment to 2016, they contributed more than 50% to the growth of the world economy. In recent years, the change in status of BRICS countries in world economy can be shown from the following aspects.

First, there's a relatively rapid growth of overall abilities. In 2016, the GDP of the BRICS reached 16,848 billion USD, taking up 22.6% of world's GDP in 2015, up from 6.6% in 1980, demonstrating an increase of 20% points in 35 years (Table 1). In 2015, the economic prowess of BRICS has surpassed the European Union and was close to the US.

Table 1.    BRICS GDP in world's share (unit: billion dollars, %).

|  | 1980 | 1990 | 2000 | 2005 | 2010 | 2015 | 2016 | 2022 | 2016 |
|---|---|---|---|---|---|---|---|---|---|
| World | 100.0 | 100.0 | 100.0 | 100.0 | 100.0 | 100.0 | 100.0 | 100.0 | 75,278 |
| Developed nations | 75.8 | 78.2 | 79.2 | 76.3 | 65.5 | 60.5 | 61.2 | 55.7 | 46,076 |
| G7 | 61.7 | 63.7 | 65.1 | 59.9 | 49.9 | 46.4 | 47.1 | 42.7 | 35,447 |
| US | 25.7 | 25.5 | 30.4 | 27.5 | 22.7 | 24.3 | 24.7 | 23.8 | 18,569 |
| EU | 34.1 | 31.4 | 26.4 | 30.4 | 25.8 | 22.0 | 21.8 | 18.8 | 16,408 |
| BRICS | 6.6 | 5.6 | 8.2 | 10.8 | 18.2 | 22.6 | 22.4 | 26.6 | 16,848 |
| Brazil | 1.4 | 2.0 | 1.9 | 1.9 | 3.4 | 2.4 | 2.4 | 2.7 | 1,799 |
| China | 2.7 | 1.7 | 3.6 | 4.9 | 9.2 | 15.1 | 14.9 | 17.7 | 11,218 |
| India | 1.7 | 1.4 | 1.4 | 1.8 | 2.6 | 2.8 | 3.0 | 3.9 | 2,256 |
| South Africa | 0.7 | 0.5 | 0.4 | 0.5 | 0.6 | 0.4 | 0.4 | 0.4 | 294 |
| Russia | — | — | 0.8 | 1.7 | 2.5 | 1.8 | 1.7 | 1.8 | 1,281 |

*Source*: International Monetary Fund.

From the estimates of the International Monetary Fund, it will surpass the US in 2020.

Second, the openness of the BRICS is increasing day by day, and their influence on the world is increasing continuously. The status shift of BRICS in world trade is notable, especially in imports. The scale of products imported by BRICS from the world went up from 9.9% in 2005 to 15.3% in 2015 and service product imports went up from 8.5% to 15.4%. The increase of status of developing countries in world import mainly comes from BRICS (Tables 2 and 3). As for capital flow, in the past, the BRICS mainly attracted foreign investment, and now the countries are increasing their investments in other countries. BRICS attracted 768.5 billion USD foreign investment in 2005, and it went up to 2,372.5 billion USD in 2015, increasing 3.1 times. At the same time, investment scale from the BRICS went up from 313.1 billion USD to 1,745.4 billion USD,

Table 2. BRICS product import and export and world percentage (unit: 100 million USD, %).

| | Export | | | | Import | | | |
|---|---|---|---|---|---|---|---|---|
| | 2016 | 2005 | 2015 | 2016 | 2016 | 2005 | 2015 | 2016 |
| World | 159,564 | 100.0 | 100.0 | 100.0 | 161,415 | 100.0 | 100.0 | 100.0 |
| Developing countries | 69,645 | 36.3 | 44.6 | 43.6 | 66,014 | 31.8 | 42.0 | 40.9 |
| Transitioning countries | 4,459 | 3.4 | 3.2 | 2.8 | 3,746 | 2.2 | 2.3 | 2.3 |
| Developed countries | 85,460 | 60.4 | 52.2 | 53.6 | 91,654 | 66.0 | 55.7 | 56.8 |
| EU | 52,702 | 38.3 | 32.1 | 33.0 | 51,131 | 37.8 | 30.7 | 31.7 |
| G7 | 52,015 | 38.5 | 32.1 | 32.6 | 59,430 | 44.1 | 36.4 | 36.8 |
| US | 14,546 | 8.6 | 9.1 | 9.1 | 22,514 | 16.1 | 13.9 | 13.9 |
| BRICS | 29,044 | 12.1 | 19.1 | 18.2 | 23,730 | 9.9 | 15.3 | 14.7 |
| Brazil | 1,853 | 1.1 | 1.2 | 1.2 | 1,435 | 0.7 | 1.1 | 0.9 |
| China | 20,982 | 7.3 | 13.8 | 13.1 | 15,874 | 6.1 | 10.1 | 9.8 |
| India | 2,640 | 0.9 | 1.6 | 1.7 | 3,591 | 1.3 | 2.4 | 2.2 |
| Russia | 2,818 | 2.3 | 2.1 | 1.8 | 1,914 | 1.2 | 1.2 | 1.2 |
| South Africa | 751 | 0.5 | 0.5 | 0.5 | 916 | 0.6 | 0.6 | 0.6 |

*Source*: UNCTAD.

**4** *Wang Linggui & Zhao Jianglin*

Table 3. BRICS service import and export and percentage against the world's (unit: 100 million USD, %).

| | Export | | | | Import | | | |
|---|---|---|---|---|---|---|---|---|
| | 2016 | 2005 | 2015 | 2016 | 2016 | 2005 | 2015 | 2016 |
| World | 48,793 | 100.0 | 100.0 | 100.0 | 47,974 | 100.0 | 100.0 | 100.0 |
| Developing countries | 14,357 | 23.1 | 29.9 | 29.4 | 18,177 | 28.4 | 38.4 | 37.9 |
| Transitioning countries | 1,069 | 2.0 | 2.2 | 2.2 | 1,265 | 2.6 | 3.0 | 2.6 |
| Developed countries | 33,366 | 74.9 | 67.9 | 68.4 | 28,533 | 69.0 | 58.6 | 59.5 |
| EU | 20,211 | 47.9 | 41.3 | 41.4 | 17,896 | 43.9 | 36.7 | 37.3 |
| G7 | 19,452 | 44.3 | 39.9 | 39.9 | 16,355 | 43.0 | 33.8 | 34.1 |
| US | 7,524 | 14.1 | 15.4 | 15.4 | 5,031 | 11.7 | 10.3 | 10.5 |
| BRICS | 4,685 | 7.0 | 9.8 | 9.6 | 7,398 | 8.5 | 15.4 | 15.4 |
| Brazil | 333 | 0.6 | 0.7 | 0.7 | 637 | 0.9 | 1.5 | 1.3 |
| China | 2,085 | 3.0 | 4.5 | 4.3 | 4,530 | 3.2 | 9.2 | 9.4 |
| India | 1,618 | 2.0 | 3.2 | 3.3 | 1,337 | 2.3 | 2.6 | 2.8 |
| Russia | 505 | 1.1 | 1.1 | 1.0 | 744 | 1.6 | 1.9 | 1.6 |
| South Africa | 144 | 0.4 | 0.3 | 0.3 | 150 | 0.5 | 0.3 | 0.3 |

*Source*: UNCTAD.

going up 5.6 times. The percentage of investment scale against that of the world went up from 2.6% to 7% (Table 4).

Third, BRICS countries are still in a development phase, not yet in the developed economies' phase. Right now, the average per capita GDP in BRICS countries is below 10,000 USD, of which Brazil, China and Russia are above 8,000 USD. Judging from World Bank's standards, they are already at the medium-high income level. South Africa's is above 5,000 USD, thus making it a medium-income country, and India's is less than 2,000 USD, making it a medium-low income country (Table 5).

Fourth, the domestic development within BRICS is unbalanced. Judging from per capita GDP, the difference in the development level within the BRICS countries is increasing. From 2020, Brazil, China and Russia will enter the beginning level of a high-income country, while South Africa and India will maintain their medium and medium-low income levels, respectively. At the same time, the urbanization rate differs greatly within BRICS (see Table 5), from 32.4% in India to 84.2% in

*Deepen BRICS Partnership for a Brighter Future*  **5**

Table 4.   BRICS investment flow from 2005 to 2015.

| | Inward flow (100 million USD) | | Outward flow (100 million USD) | | Inward flow (%) | | Outward flow (%) | |
|---|---|---|---|---|---|---|---|---|
| | 2005 | 2015 | 2005 | 2015 | 2005 | 2015 | 2005 | 2015 |
| World | 114,574 | 249,832 | 118,565 | 250,449 | 100.0 | 100.0 | 100.0 | 100.0 |
| Developing countries | 26,355 | 83,744 | 11,878 | 52,963 | 23.0 | 33.5 | 10.0 | 21.1 |
| Transitioning countries | 2,563 | 6,014 | 1,426 | 3,078 | 2.2 | 2.4 | 1.2 | 1.2 |
| Developed countries | 85,657 | 160,074 | 105,261 | 194,408 | 74.8 | 64.1 | 88.8 | 77.6 |
| EU | 43,744 | 76,354 | 50,245 | 93,327 | 38.2 | 30.6 | 42.4 | 37.3 |
| G7 | 56,655 | 102,008 | 76,047 | 134,190 | 49.4 | 40.8 | 64.1 | 53.6 |
| US | 28,180 | 55,880 | 36,380 | 59,828 | 24.6 | 22.4 | 30.7 | 23.9 |
| BRICS | 7,685 | 23,725 | 3,131 | 17,454 | 6.7 | 9.5 | 2.6 | 7.0 |
| Brazil | 1,779 | 4,860 | 758 | 1,814 | 1.6 | 1.9 | 0.6 | 0.7 |
| China | 2,721 | 12,209 | 572 | 10,102 | 2.4 | 4.9 | 0.5 | 4.0 |
| India | 432 | 2,823 | 97 | 1,390 | 0.4 | 1.1 | 0.1 | 0.6 |
| Russia | 1,786 | 2,584 | 1,392 | 2,520 | 1.6 | 1.0 | 1.2 | 1.0 |
| South Africa | 967 | 1,249 | 310 | 1,628 | 0.8 | 0.5 | 0.3 | 0.7 |

*Source*: UNCTAD.

Table 5.   BRICS per capita income level and urbanization ratio.

| | Per capita GDP (USD) | | Population (million) | Urbanization ratio (%) |
|---|---|---|---|---|
| | 2016 | 2020 | 2016 | 2016 |
| Brazil | 8,727 | 11,538 | 206 | 84.2 |
| China | 8,113 | 10,644 | 1,383 | 57.9 |
| India | 1,723 | 2,358 | 1,309 | 32.4 |
| Russia | 5,261 | 5,925 | 56 | 73.2 |
| South Africa | 8,929 | 11,981 | 143 | 63.9 |

*Source*: UNCTAD and International Monetary Fund.

Brazil, which shows there's still a large room for cooperation among BRICS countries. Judging from technology innovation, the innovation efficiencies of China and India rank higher than the total rank (see Table 6), especially China which ranks third in the world. In comparison, the other

## 6 *Wang Linggui & Zhao Jianglin*

Table 6.    2017 global innovation index.

| Country | Total rank | Efficiency rank |
| --- | --- | --- |
| Switzerland | 1 | 2 |
| Sweden | 2 | 12 |
| The Netherlands | 3 | 4 |
| US | 4 | 21 |
| Britain | 5 | 20 |
| Denmark | 6 | 34 |
| Singapore | 7 | 63 |
| Finland | 8 | 37 |
| Germany | 9 | 7 |
| Ireland | 10 | 6 |
| South Korea | 11 | 14 |
| Japan | 14 | 49 |
| China | 22 | 3 |
| Russia | 45 | 75 |
| South Africa | 57 | 97 |
| India | 60 | 53 |
| Brazil | 69 | 99 |

*Source*: The Global Innovation Index 2017, WIPO.

BRICS countries rank behind the world average, even countries like South Africa and Brazil. This means that not only do South Africa and Brazil have limited future development potential but also that if the present structure is not changed, the imbalance of BRICS inner development will keep increasing.

Fifth, the future development potential of BRICS is huge. Since the 1990s, BRICS countries' economic growth is higher than global level, developing countries, developed countries and other categories (Table 7). In the future, BRICS countries can be expected to maintain a sustainable economic growth rate that excels beyond that of other countries or regions.

Table 7. BRICS GDP growth rate from 1992 to 2016 (unit: %).

| | 1992–1995 | 1995–2000 | 2000–2005 | 2005–2010 | 2010–2015 | 2016 |
|---|---|---|---|---|---|---|
| World | 2.6 | 3.4 | 2.9 | 1.9 | 2.5 | 3.1 |
| Developing countries | 5.2 | 4.3 | 5.4 | 5.9 | 4.7 | |
| Transitioning countries | −9.9 | 1.5 | 6.6 | 3.6 | 1.7 | |
| Developed countries | 2.4 | 3.2 | 2.1 | 0.5 | 1.5 | 1.7 |
| G7 | 2.3 | 3.0 | 2.0 | 0.2 | 1.6 | 1.5 |
| US | 3.3 | 4.4 | 2.6 | 0.4 | 2.1 | 1.6 |
| EU | 1.9 | 3.0 | 1.8 | 0.5 | 0.9 | 2.0 |
| BRICS | 4.0 | 4.8 | 7.0 | 8.0 | 5.7 | |
| Brazil | 5.1 | 1.7 | 2.8 | 4.3 | 0.5 | −3.6 |
| China | 12.7 | 8.5 | 9.8 | 11.2 | 7.8 | 6.7 |
| India | 6.8 | 5.8 | 7.0 | 7.9 | 6.7 | 6.8 |
| Russia | −9.0 | 1.2 | 6.2 | 3.1 | 1.3 | 0.3 |
| South Africa | 2.6 | 2.5 | 3.8 | 2.9 | 2.1 | −0.2 |

*Source*: UNCTAD.

## Status and Characteristics of BRICS Cooperation

Even though the BRICS countries have characteristics of their own, one common element they share is that they are all influential countries in their own regions and can have a constructive effect in these areas. This influence of economic and political status made BRICS countries steady forces in global governance, making them supporting powers in changing the imbalance and difference of global economic and political development. For a long time, the main forces of global politics and economy were concentrated in Europe and the US, and developing countries had limited chances in the global political economic order. As the BRICS concept was formed, global traditional political and economic order are shifting to new directions, trying to win more outside support and creating new cooperation mechanisms to structure a starting point for BRICS countries' motivation and cooperation.

From the first summit in 2006 till now, BRICS has lasted for over 10 years. From topic design and mechanism building to practical operation, BRICS countries have made great achievements. Table 8 lists the main topics discussed by BRICS in former summits and the main achievements. The main characteristics of BRICS cooperation are described in the following.

First is the steadiness of BRICS cooperation. Even though in the past 10 years BRICS countries were shrouded by all manner of rumors and criticism, such as the theory of "diminishing colors", they have been "sharpening a sword in 10 years" and kept pushing on with cooperation to go deeper and become steadier step by step. In concept, BRICS insists development first, focuses on energy in developing economy and improves people's lives; in principle, they insist on openness, tolerance, cooperation and win–win, focusing on structuring a mechanism and cooperation structure that covers all aspects and is multilayered; in terms of moral aspects, they support international justice and fairness, striving to have a voice in important international and regional issues. At present, BRICS has already become an international model that holds great importance and has pushed for global governance reform and promotes the presentation and voice of emerging market economies and developing countries (Niu Haibin, 2013). As President Xi Jinping pointed out on 15 July 2014 when he was attending the sixth BRICS leadership meeting in Brazil, BRICS countries jointly voiced their opinions on many important international and regional questions and contributed to promoting world economy growth and completing global economic governance, pushing for democratization of international relations and thus became an important force in international relations as well as active construction of international system.

Second, BRICS is stepping toward mechanization. Since the leaders of China, Russia, India and Brazil first met in June 2009, BRICS has completed the transition from a virtual economics concept to an international cooperation platform. At present, members of BRICS come from Asia, Europe, Africa and America, and there are a total of 28 cooperation mechanisms, 14 of which are at the ministerial level and nine at the high

Table 8. Fruits of past BRICS summits.

| Time | Place | Topic | Result |
|---|---|---|---|
| June 2009 | Yekaterinburg, Russia | International situation, G20, reform of international financial organizations, food security, energy security, climate change, BRICS dialogue, cooperation and future development direction. | Joint Statement of the BRIC Countries' Leaders in Yekaterinburg; approval of BRIC Joint Statement on Global Food Security. |
| April 2010 | Brasilia, Brazil | International situation, international financial crisis, G20 affairs, climate change. Discussion of specific matters to push for BRIC cooperation and coordination. | Published the BRIC leaders joint statement. Brazil also held entrepreneur's forum, consortium banks, cooperation forums and think tank conferences. |
| April 2011 | Sanya, China | International situation, international economic and financial affairs, development, BRICS cooperation. | Published the Sanya Declaration and Action Plan. South Africa made its first official appearance. China also held BRICS think tank meeting, BRICS bank cooperation mechanism annual meeting and financial forum, BRICS industrial and commercial forum and BRICS economic and trade ministerial meeting. |
| March 2012 | New Delhi, India | Discussion of global governance and sustainability centered around "BRICS for global stability, security and prosperous partnership". | Published the Delhi Declaration and Action Plan, discussed the possibility of establishing a BRICS development bank, signed Master Agreement on Extending Credit Facility in Local Currency under BRICS Interbank Cooperation Mechanism, as well as the BRICS Multilateral Letter of Credit Confirmation Facility Agreement. |

(Continued)

Table 8. (*Continued*)

| Time | Place | Topic | Result |
|---|---|---|---|
| March 2013 | Durban, South Africa | Discussion of world economic situation, global economic governance, **BRICS** cooperation and strengthening cooperation with African countries centered around the theme of "**BRICS** and Africa: Partnership for Development, Integration and Industrialization". | First round of BRICS leadership conferences. Published the Durban Declaration and Action Plan, signed multiple cooperation documents, decided to set up the BRICS Development Bank and Emergency Reserve Arrangements, declared to set up the BRICS Business Council and think tank council. |
| July 2014 | Fortaleza, Brazil | Discussion of **BRICS** future cooperation plan and present issues in political and economic areas centered around the theme "Inclusive Growth: Sustainable Solutions". | Second round of BRICS leadership conferences. Published the Fortaleza Declaration and Action Plan, the five leaders witnessed and signed the establishment of BRICS Development Bank and emergency reserve arrangements. |
| July 2015 | Ufa, Russia | Discussion of issues in global political and economic fields and **BRICS** cooperation surrounding the theme of "**BRICS** Partnership — a Powerful Factor of Global Development". | Published the Ufa Declaration and action plan, as well as guiding documents like The Strategy for BRICS Economic Partnership. |
| October 2016 | Goa, India | Building responsive, inclusive and collective solutions. | Published the Goa Declaration, signed multiple cooperation agreements, committing to joint action against terrorism and economic crimes like tax evasion and money laundering. |

*Source*: Han Yiyuan (2016).

official level, five from other fields, forming a multi-rail, broad-region, multiple-layered united profit body that covers multiple levels, such as leadership summit, financial commissioners, young diplomats and media representatives, concerning economists, grassroots representatives, government officials and groups from society and political bureaus. BRICS pushed for the establishment of a New Development Bank and arrangements for emergency fund reserves and as two multilateral financial organizations gradually became established and operations began falling in place. BRICS complemented and improved the multi-lateral cooperation mechanism and international development organizations under the Bretton Woods System. The establishment and operation of BRICS leadership meeting mechanism not only helps these countries to improve influence and cohesion but also provides a chance for coordination and a platform of exchanges for developing countries to unite their viewpoints and gain recognition when participating in global governance.

Third, BRICS countries can cooperate in a variety of fields. Right now, some of the fields include economy, fiscal policies, finances, agriculture, education, health, technology, culture, drug ban, statistics, tourism, think tanks, friendly cities and local government cooperation. These fields reflect the interest of BRICS countries and the regions they represent as well as developing countries' interest. Of course, under the current cooperation foundation and motivation, BRICS countries cannot cover all cooperation fields and need to make choices, which lead to development of cooperation in each field being unbalanced — some fields have achieved great things while other fields have not. All in all, BRICS countries achieved more development in mechanization of financial field, which originates from the BRICS high-level agreement on fighting global risks, especially financial risks (Xu Chao, 2015). They cope with development risks brought by the outside world to BRICS countries and even developing countries through their own efforts and hope to win development opportunities by self-constructing new mechanisms. Furthermore, there can be multiple goals of BRICS cooperation, which leads to BRICS not having development in accordance with the cooperation extended. As regional influential countries, and even global influential countries, BRICS identity decided the countries cooperate with multiple goals. They need to satisfy their own interests and demands for political and economic development. Second, they represent their respective regions and demand the international society for regional members' economic and social development. Third, they represent developing countries and hope to win more international development space for developing countries. Because of these multiple goals, it was shown that BRICS countries cooperate in complexity. When the three goals are in agreement, BRICS countries can push for faster cooperation. But when the five countries cannot reach an agreement for some cooperation goal, then the difficulty of cooperation increases.

## Main Questions Faced by BRICS Cooperation

The main questions BRICS countries face are from within, not the outside, or they are not shown on the outside.

First, BRICS countries are still exploring their directions and need to make clear their cooperation goals and direction, which lead to uncertainty in cooperation. At present, the trend of global economic recovery is still weak, global trade and investment are down, the price of large commodities keeps fluctuating, and the deep-level conflicts that triggered the international financial crisis are still unresolved. Some countries exercise policies that are more and more inward bound, protectionism is on the rise and "anti-globalization" thoughts are surging. Geopolitical elements are complicated; traditional and untraditional security risks are mingled; and global challenges are more apparent, such as terrorism, infectious diseases and climate change. BRICS countries are faced with the complex, harsh outside environment. Against this background, how BRICS countries should define themselves in the next decade of cooperation and how they should create an open world are questions that need to be solved urgently.

Second, it's difficult to coordinate the limitation of investment of cooperation resources from the BRICS countries, and the complexity of the issues needs to be solved immediately. On the one hand, some global issues are already laid out in front of the BRICS countries, such as how to exercise their perspective advantages, strengthen economic cooperation, cultivate global market and complete global value chain? How to sustain a spirit of tolerance, push for tolerance of different social systems, reflections of different cultures and civilizations, and mutual benefit of different development mode? How to keep the spirit of cooperation, take care of each other, seek economic growth for each country and provide motivation for perfecting global governance? How to insist on a win–win spirit, to care for the benefit of other countries as pursuing benefits for one's own, to push for a path where countries can cooperate and mutually benefit? These global issues need to be faced and solved by BRICS countries. On the other hand, the economic prowess of the BRICS countries is not enough to face global difficulties. From both financial investment and investment of other cooperation resources, BRICS countries are still distant from solving these issues.

Third, the spillover effect of BRICS countries is mainly focused in their respective regions, not within the five countries or around the world. Therefore, the influence of BRICS countries and input are unmatched, which can make BRICS countries unmotivated about pushing for cooperation. It can be seen from Figure 1 that the concentration index of BRICS trading products and regional dispersion index are more similar to the level of developing countries, and they need to transition toward

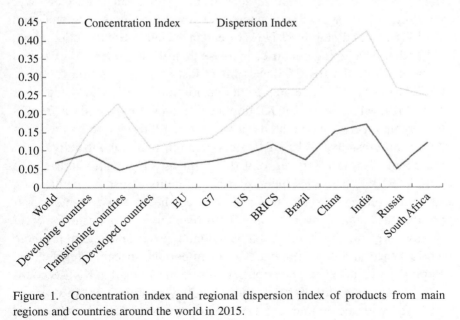

Figure 1. Concentration index and regional dispersion index of products from main regions and countries around the world in 2015.

*Source*: UNCTAD.

developed countries; on the one hand, they need to diversify their products and lower concentration points, and on the other hand, they need to lower their dispersion index and spread their influence to the rest of the world. Only in this way can they have a significant influence on the world and have motivation to increase consistency and coherence in dealing with global issues.

Fourth, reach an international governance system that's to the advantage of developing countries in direction and rule. At present, BRICS countries are actively trying to change the existing international system, but which system exactly suits the development needs of BRICS countries? How should BRICS countries adjust to the existing international system? In the future development process, how should they jointly increase the representation of emerging economies in global governance, push for quotient reform of IMF and design a new quotient formula that reflects the proportion of these countries' GDP against the world economy? How to realize the political and economic "two-wheel drive" to be the world's economic engine, as well as a shield of international peace? How to learn lessons from history, ditch the Cold War mindset, refuse a zero-sum game and jointly maintain regional and world peace and stability? How to enhance South–South cooperation, help other developing countries increase their development abilities and help them ride the BRICS development fast train? A solution for all of these issues is closely related to the positioning of BRICS. As early as July 2014, when president Xi Jinping was attending the sixth BRICS leadership meeting, he pointed out while being interviewed by the Latin American press that "The BRICS cooperation is not about individuals, it's about placing effort on joint development of global countries. As long as BRICS countries increase political mutual trust, concentrate on strategic common ground, make their voices heard and give more proposals, they can contribute more positive energy to pushing world economy grow, improve global economic governance and promote world peace and development." In an important speech, President Xi Jinping made further explanations on this point saying that BRICS countries should "increase macroeconomic policy coordination, in order to push for wide economic and trade market, vast financial circulation, and large connections of basic infrastructure and vast cultural communications, to walk the front lines of international open cooperation, to actively play a leadership role on the global arena."[2]

Fifth, the strategic trust bottleneck between BRICS countries has not been breached, and there's still no essential breakthrough in many fields of cooperation. There's lack of strategic mutual trust between some BRICS countries, which has become the main obstacle in BRICS countries' coordination in exerting influence. Some researches show that BRICS influence in global economy is far less than its economic prowess. Therefore, the construction of BRICS partnership in the future stems not only from their development need but also from the need to jointly voice their concerns. President Xi Jinping pointed out that we need to regard BRICS relationship as "good friends, brothers and partners who treat each other with honesty", we should also deepen friendship and cooperation, "to treat the implementation of The BRICS Economic Partnership Strategy as an opportunity to deepen economic cooperation in all regions, promote competition of BRIC countries. We need to construct, maintain and develop the new BRICS development bank and emergency reserve arrangements, to provide powerful insurance for the economic development of developing countries. We need to strengthen cultural and people-to-people exchanges, build a steady public foundation for BRICS cooperation. We need to expand and steady BRICS 'friend circle,' keep openness, tolerance, strive for joint development."[3]

## Future Direction of BRICS Cooperation

Based on the above analyses, the trends of future cooperation direction of BRICS countries are as follows.

First, the BRICS countries need to reevaluate and reposition their self-cooperation, especially their periodic cooperation goals. Even though the countries have been cooperating for more than 10 years, there's one important question that has not yet been answered: Why are the BRICS countries cooperating. Is it born out of a concept, or is there necessity for cooperation? According to common knowledge, the more common

---

[2] *Xinhuanet*, Xi Jinping's speech at the eighth meeting of the BRICS leaders, 17 October 2016.
[3] *Ibid.*

interests countries have, the more the motivation they have for cooperation. BRICS countries differ greatly in their domestic affairs; even though they have about the same broad goals on development issues, they lack common consensus on development mode. In the future, how should BRICS countries strengthen coordination on development mode and can they have supplementary cooperation on development strategy? Combing through these issues is not only beneficial to making sure of BRICS countries' development goal from the inside but also beneficial to establishing a complete BRICS image from the outside.

Second, the BRICS countries will keep a steady cooperation mechanism. The next 10 years mark the second decade of BRICS cooperation. How to develop the existing BRICS mechanism and whether there needs to be new content in the mechanism in the future are some points each BRICS country needs to consider. Questions include whether BRICS should be developed into an official international organization, whether there needs to be a secretariat, whether there needs to be an expansion, etc. Judging from the present, keeping a steady cooperation mechanism is most beneficial to BRICS countries. Under the current situation, where interest framework is uncertain, if BRICS countries blindly follow the path of a strong mechanism, it will lead to more prominent domestic conflicts, diminishing BRICS' united voice toward the outside world. Furthermore, mechanization depends on the increase of strategic mutual trust between BRICS members. As of now, some members are engaged in more competition than cooperation, and mechanization cannot be further pushed. Finally, mechanization can be realized in some areas and gradually expanded into others. Therefore, it should be a gradual process.

Third, BRICS countries will push for new development modes. Right now, the world has entered the phase of the fourth industrial revolution, but BRICS countries have not finished their tasks from previous industrial revolutions. How should they coordinate and balance the development differences among themselves? The exploration of a BRICS development mode not only helps development of BRICS countries themselves but is also beneficial in promoting coordinated development among the countries, eventually providing an example of cooperation for the world. Therefore, President Xi Jinping stated in his speech that BRICS should "hold up a flag of development, combined with carrying out 2030 sustainable development's agenda and fruits of the G20 Hangzhou summit, strengthen South–North dialogue and South–South cooperation, to inject new motivation into international development cooperation with new mindset, new ideas and new actions, to pioneer new space and push global economy to have stronger, sustainable, balanced and tolerant growth."[4]

Fourth, the BRICS countries need to create a basic power that participates in global economic governance. Just and fair global governance is the necessary condition for realizing the countries' collective development. As early as the fifth meeting between the BRICS leadership in Durban, South Africa on 27 March 2013, President Xi Jinping has pointed out in his speech, "We are from five countries on four continents and have come together to construct and partnership and to realize the goal of collective development. We have come together to push for democratization of international relations and pushing for peace and stability. Peace, development, cooperation and mutual win are our common wish and responsibility." In recent years, BRICS countries have achieved great things in maintaining global justice (Pan Xingming and Zhou He, 2015). However, hegemonic politics and unjust international political and economic order still restrain new emerging countries and developing countries from pursuing development. Therefore, President Xi Jinping restated China's position and attitude, saying "We should continue to be the participants, propellants and leaders of global governance reform, pushing international order to develop in a more just and logical direction, keep increasing the representation and say of emerging market countries and developing countries. We will continue to be guardian's of international peace, insist on following, principle and rules of international relations, to deal with issues according to the rights and wrongs of the issues themselves, release positive energy and push for construction of new international relations that focuses on cooperation and win–win."[5]

Fifth, the BRICS countries need to gradually increase strategic mutual trust in cooperation. In the future, the level of strategic mutual trust will be increased to a great extent. This came partly as a result of cooperation.

---

[4] *Ibid.*
[5] *Ibid.*

Strategic mutual trust is the premise of BRICS cooperation and development. At the same time, future development and cooperation will further push for BRICS' mutual trust. Cooperation is beneficial to eliminating misunderstanding and misjudgments and can increase the power of mutual trust. Second is the method of cooperation. Sometimes lack of ways to realize strategy can easily lead to lack of strategic mutual trust. Therefore, there's the necessity to increase the level of strategic mutual trust through multiple cooperation methods and channels. Third is the process of cooperation. Through this process, BRICS countries develop understanding toward each other and the handling of bottom line, which can help them expand the border of cooperation under the premise of maintaining their respective profits.

## China's Push and Outlook toward BRICS Cooperation

At present, the BRICS cooperation mechanism is going through a historic transition from a capitalist market investment concept to international political strategic power, transitioning from economic governance-oriented dialogue forums to an all-aspect negotiation mechanism that focuses on both politics and economy. China is willing to strengthen the establishment of BRICS partnership, pushing BRICS to become steady supporters of globalization, becoming open and cooperative powers.

In the past 10 years, China actively participated in BRICS cooperation, including sending positive cooperation proposals, and invested in BRICS bank construction, signing all sorts of agreements (Zhao Kejin, 2014). In the future, China will keep pushing for BRICS construction:

First, China will keep pushing for a global governance system, especially reform of economic governance. As to global governance issues the BRICS countries face, President Xi Jinping proposes to "Strengthen negotiation and communication on large international issues and regional hotspots, pushing for political solutions of hot issues, join hands to face global issues like natural disasters, climate change, infectious diseases and terrorism. We should voice together, call for international society to increase input, and should take practical actions, pushing for solution of real issues, to solve conflicts from the roots and contribute to the security and order of international society."[6]

Second, China will push for negotiation on a commonly acknowledged development mode within the BRICS. Development is the main issue faced by BRICS countries; exploring a new development mode needs effort from all five countries. At present, the five countries are all working hard in this aspect. China will also be dedicated to the exploration of pushing for a common development mode.

Third, China will keep holding a flag of openness. Historic and present experiences from both China and foreign countries have shown that opening up is the essential way of realizing prosperity. In the new age, if BRICS countries want to create a new development pole of world economy, they need to follow the objective rule of history development, follow the development trend of this era, push for structural reform, innovate the growth method, construct an open economy and advocate against all forms of protectionism. China will place some effort in pushing for more openness and making great contributions.

Fourth, China will stabilize the existing results of cooperation. On 16 October 2016, president Xi Jinping gave an important speech titled "stabilize confidence and develop together" at the eighth BRICS leadership conference in Goa, India centered on "creating an effective, tolerant and common solution". He positively commented on the results of the past 10 years of BRICS cooperation and brought forth five proposals on strengthening BRICS cooperation. Some commentaries pointed out that President Xi Jinping's speech reflected the BRICS countries' wish of stabilizing confidence, increasing the morality, decreasing the sufferings and increasing the ability to solve difficulties together. This shows that in the face of global economic dilemma, BRICS countries have the ability to turn challenges into opportunities and turn pressure into motivation, to push for cooperation in more practical matters and keep pushing for exploitation of world economy and financial reform.

Fifth, China will actively push for establishment of global peace. At the eighth BRICS summit held in Goa, India on 16 October 2016, President Xi Jinping pointed out, "We need to maintain international

---

[6] *Ibid.*

peace and justice, maintain world peace and stability. Right now, the world is not peaceful, global threats and challenges keep rising. BRICS should love peace, treasure peace, help all countries around the world achieve a peaceful and stable social environment, help people around the world to live peacefully and happily, that is our common wish", "peace, development, cooperation and mutual benefit are our common wish and responsibility" (Xi Jinping, 2014).

BRICS countries are a unity with common interests, also a unity that will move forward and take actions together. The key words of "deepening BRICS partnership for a brighter future" provide the direction and path for the BRICS cooperation. The cooperation development process in the last 10 years has shown that the five emerging countries are willing and able to provide new motivation for future cooperation; at the same time, they have wisdom and confidence to establish a cooperation example for developing countries.

## References

Han Yiyuan (2016) BRICS cooperation development process and outlook. *International Study Reference*, Volume 11.

Niu Haibin (2013) The evaluation and prospects of the cooperation of BRICS. *Journal of East China Normal University*.

Xi Jinping (2014) Cooperation and Development, *Xijinping: The Governance of China* (Foreign Language Press).

Xu Chao (2015) Financial cooperation of BRICS: Causes, influence and prospects. *Foreign Theoretical Trends*.

# Chapter 2

# Opportunities and Challenges for BRICS Countries: The International Environment and Policy Outlook for BRICS Countries

Roberto Abdenur

*CEBRI — Brazilian Center for International Relations, Rio de Janeiro, Brazil*

## The International Context

The current international context makes the BRICS group all the more relevant and important.

The United States, the country responsible for the creation of the so-called liberal international order following the Second World War, with institutions like the UN, the FMI and the World Bank, finds itself now on a course of retrenchment toward a narrow-minded, backward-looking, nationalistic posture.

The new American government has become the object of growing concerns for the international community on a series of topics.

The international trading system is at stake, as the US espouses a protectionist and mercantilist attitude and seems decided to backtrack on earlier free-trade agreements such as NAFTA, and to confront countries such as Germany and China, with which it has sizeable deficits in bilateral trade.

The Western alliance, based on previous solid engagements between the US and Europe, is being frayed as President Trump shows disregard for the European Union as a deep integration project, supports BREXIT and seems to wish that other member countries will follow the example of the United Kingdom. Likewise, NATO is being weakened by Trump's decision to prioritize financial considerations over security commitments as such. The future of the EU is put into doubt as a consequence of BREXIT and the emergence of political forces hostile to globalization and the Union's deep integration project with elements of supra-nationalism.

In Europe, as a matter of fact, new extremist, xenophobic political forces pose a threat to the very basic ideals and principles of open societies and to the continuation of forward-looking integration projects. Recent elections in countries like the Netherlands, Austria and France have resulted in the victory of candidates committed to liberal democracy and regional integration, but the results have also shown that the movements hostile to political and social pluralism have risen to a new, unprecedented level of influence. Those forces are bound to last over time, and the threat they embody cannot be ignored.

Europe is also being challenged by mass migrations as a result of civil conflicts in Syria and other countries. This new situation is having a disruptive effect on the socio-political structures of several countries. New social tensions and political fissures and cleavages have emerged.

The decision taken by President Trump to pull out of the Paris Agreement requires even more action by other major countries to continue combating climate change.

BRICS countries are all deeply committed to the Paris Agreement and to the efforts to develop clean energy and lower the dependence on fossil fuels. China has become a model country that heavily — and successfully — invests in new, carbon-free forms of energy, like wind and solar, besides nuclear.

The new US foreign policy moves steadily away from multilateral engagements of all sorts. The WTO, the fundamental pillar of the international trading system, is at risk of seeing the US fail to abide by well-established norms and procedures. There are even those who fear a plain withdrawal from the WTO by the US, which would entail extremely serious damage to the rules-based, open and transparent international trading system.

*Opportunities and Challenges for BRICS Countries* **23**

The UN itself may face serious reductions in its availability of financial and human resources for important activities, such as peace-keeping and aid to refugees, as a result of drastic reductions in the US government budget for international endeavors.

Trump's decision to withdraw from the Transpacific Trade Partnership — taken without even a minimum of reflection and analysis — is a counter-productive move, as it deprives the US of the possibility to establish a whole new network of trade and investment connections with Asia. President Obama's "pivot to Asia" now lacks its economic pillar.

It is now up to Asian countries themselves to fill the vacuum thus created, by launching innovative trade and economic projects among themselves. China has taken the lead with the Belt and Road Initiative and the Regional Comprehensive Economic Partnership, in addition to the Asian Infrastructure Development Bank.

Other initiatives, including some launched by Russia and its neighbors, will contribute to new development impulses in Central Asia. Likewise, India is a central player in the trade and integration projects in Southern Asia.

Away from Asia, Brazil and South Africa are engaged in moving forward with their respective regional integration schemes. In the case of Mercosul, free-trade negotiations with the European Union are moving forward. The result will hopefully establish an interesting intercontinental trade arrangement.

The vast Eurasian space will become more integrated as some of those projects create new, dynamic linkages between Asia and far-away Europe.

As we see, big geopolitical changes are taking place in the world at large, and not just as a result of measures taken by the new American government.

These changes bring about new opportunities for the BRICS, both in terms of their, so to say, internal cooperation and in regards to their international role as a group. This new scenario offers us exciting new possibilities, but it also entails growing responsibilities. BRICS countries must now stand up to defend multilateralism as the only means to ensure adequate levels of global governance. In a world where more and more issues become global problems, the international community cannot afford the luxury of passivity and fragmentation in tackling those challenges.

**24** *Roberto Abdenur*

To put it shortly, the long US strategic shadow is shrinking. It does not anymore reach practically the whole of the planet. It is up to other nations and groupings to fill the vacuum thus generated.

## Policy Suggestions

The BRICS group has evolved remarkably over a relatively short period of time. It has proven its worth during several instances in which the coordination of positions among the member states has had an impact on important issues discussed in various international fora, such as the G20, the WTO, the IMF and the World Bank.

The BRICS have demonstrated an extraordinary capacity to congregate around common positions. Although the group does not seek confrontation with other groups, it has succeeded in developing joint forms of action which make possible significant gains to their interests in the context of decision-making processes in major international negotiations.

Although a certain level of progress has been achieved in what refers to the internal cooperation among the member countries — with eight summits held so far and the creation of numerous working groups, seminars and other forms of dialogue — there is still much to be done in order to foster their common development. The level of interaction between the BRICS still falls short of what would be desirable.

Interestingly, the internal dynamics of the group has generated a big number of initiatives, but so far there is a relatively low level of contacts between their societies. It is true that important steps have been taken in what has to be done with academic, business and diplomatic communities. But the overall level of mutual knowledge and understanding is still rather low. The BRICS societies remain relatively remote from each other.

With the exception of China, which enjoys a high level of trade and investments with the other members, intra-BRICS trade, for instance, is still very low. Tourism has been facilitated through some visa-waiver agreements, but still there is a lack of initiatives aimed at stimulating people-to-people contacts.

In regards to the BRICS economic development, there is a common challenge faced by all five countries — the difficulty to overcome the

*Opportunities and Challenges for BRICS Countries*  **25**

so-called middle-income trap. Fast growth and urbanization enabled the BRICS countries to successfully complete the early stages of their economic development. But history shows that very few developing countries have succeeded in becoming truly developed, advanced high-income economies. Despite the difficulties inherent in their respective economic development, all BRICS countries do have the means to free themselves from the middle-income trap. But it is clear that this task will be made more feasible if the BRICS countries increase their overall level of cooperation on trade, investment and public policies in general. The BRICS group can indeed play a useful role in fostering each country's development.

This having been said, there follows a series of specific suggestions in terms of policymaking by the BRICS:

- China has successfully launched the Asian Infrastructure Investment Bank (AIIB). It is bound to significantly increase the availability of much-needed resources for infrastructure. Asia alone needs 26 trillion dollars for infrastructure by 2030 if it is to avoid major roadblocks in its development. It would make sense for the AIIB to work hand in hand with the World Bank and also the various regional development banks. In what has to be done with Brazil, it would be good to have AIIB and both the InterAmerican Bank (IDB) and Corporación Andina de Fomento (CAF) engaged in cofinancing of projects. It would also make sense for AIIB to work with major national development banks, such as Banco Nacional de Desenvolvimento Economico e Social (BNDES) in Brazil. It would also be good if all companies from BRICS can have the opportunity to participate in projects carried out in other countries.
- Another extremely important initiative by China is the OBOR project. It will involve an enormous amount of investments. It would be good if OBOR projects are open to the participation of other BRICS countries.
- As regards the Regional Comprehensive Economic Partnership (RCEP), an initiative still in the making, it would be good if at the end of the day it is open to some form of linkage with other regional integration groups, such as MERCOSUL in South America.

26 *Roberto Abdenur*

- Another successful initiative, the New Development Bank (NDB) is bound to play an important role in terms of BRICS cooperation and joint action. Its emphasis on infrastructure financing should not make it oblivious of the need to tackle poverty and environmental issues which are of great significance to all member countries and to other countries as well.
- The Goa Declaration states that the BRICS share "a common vision of ongoing profound changes in the world as it transitions to a more just, democratic and multi-polar international order". The current international context doesn't seem to be developing onto a more just and democratic order, even if it is indeed becoming more multipolar. Drastic new developments such as BREXIT and the election of Donald Trump in the US and the narrowly nationalistic trends in Europe are leading to a retrenchment toward inward-looking, protectionist governments. At the same time, even if the world is not deglobalizing, the fact is that the process of globalization has slowed down, which is not beneficial to emerging and developing countries. So it is now important for the BRICS countries to raise their voice in favor of globalization and free trade and against protectionism and attempts by stronger nations to prevail in bilateral negotiations with developing countries. It is also desirable that the BRICS countries join forces against unilateral postures, by defending the WTO as the cornerstone of a rules-based, open, transparent and non-discriminatory multilateral trading system, with development at its core.
- The BRICS countries consider that development and security are closely interrelated and play a decisive role in support of sustainable peace in the world at large. The BRICS countries have been active in UN peace-keeping operations. It makes sense for them to launch initiatives aimed at sharing experiences and perfecting their capabilities in peace-keeping. This would be a new area for their coordination and cooperation efforts, strengthening their voice on major international security issues. It also makes sense for the BRICS countries to continue their engagement in the efforts to reform the UN and expand the Security Council, so as to make it more efficient and representative.
- BRICS should actively support the G20 Action Plan on the 2030 Agenda for Development, as decided at the G20 Hangzhou summit,

so as to extend their support to less-developed, poorer countries, particularly in Africa. This would be in line with the BRICS broader commitment to work against poverty and inequality and to seek more inclusive ways for international development cooperation. BRICS should continue the practice of coordinating positions on G20 issues, along with the goal of improving global governance and reducing asymmetries between well-established powers and emerging countries.

- It is a welcome development that the Renminbi (RMB) has been included in the basket of currencies of the IMF special drawing rights. It would be good if the RMB is used more broadly, not just for trade with China but also for trade between the other member countries.

- The BRICS are net donors of technical cooperation. It makes sense for them to seek more cooperation between their respective agencies and other entities dedicated to technical cooperation with other countries. Special attention should be given to agriculture as a priority area for cooperation with less-developed, poorer countries, particularly in Africa.

- A major issue faced by BRICS is corruption. This is a serious problem of all of them. It makes sense, therefore, for the BRICS governments to cooperate in an active way both in sharing experiences and best practices and in efforts to recover assets obtained through corruption and deposited in financial institutions of another BRICS country. The establishment of the BRICS Anti-Corruption Working Group was a very positive step. It is to be expected that the working group will play a relevant role in furthering intra-BRICS cooperation in this serious matter.

- In order to increase intra-group trade, it would be desirable for the BRICS countries to negotiate trade agreements, even if on a somewhat limited basis (that is, accords that would fall short of full-fledged free trade agreements). But even in the absence of such agreements, it would make sense for the governments to try and reduce or eliminate specific barriers to trade within the group, on an *ad hoc* basis.

- The dialogue among think tanks and the activities of the Academic Forum have become powerful tools for increasing the contacts between the BRICS societies. Think tanks also serve to identify ways and means for greater coordination and cooperation within the group and to deepen the study and analysis of issues relevant to the group. The contacts among think tanks should occupy a position of priority in the group's activities.

- Finally, it draws attention to the fact that the latest summit statement — the Goa Declaration — has more than 100 paragraphs, covering a great number of topics. This seems to be excessive. It might make sense for future meetings to concentrate on a more limited list of subjects, so as to have more focus and a greater sense of priorities.

# Chapter 3

# BRICS and the Changing International System

Alexander Lukin

*Department of International Relations, National Research University, Higher School of Economics, Moscow, Russia*

*Center for East Asian and Shanghai Cooperation Organization Studies, Moscow State Institute of International Relations (MGIMO University), Moscow, Russia*

The collapse of the Soviet Union in the early 1990s caused a fundamental change to the long-standing system of international relations that was based on the confrontation between two centers of power. Although back in the Soviet era some researchers noted a trend toward a multipolar world, as the leading states in each region grew in power, the Soviet Union's sudden departure from the scene left a vacuum. Although many states, even outside the Western world, disliked the Soviet Union and even criticized it, its absence left many states, especially larger ones, wary of a certain threat. That threat stemmed, first, from the instability in the international situation resulting from the end of a bipolar system that had guaranteed a certain order, and second, from the possibility that the one remaining center of power, now freed from any external checks and balances, might encroach on the interests of others.

30  *Alexander Lukin*

Thus, when the United States celebrated its victory in the Cold War and Francis Fukuyama declared the "end of history", China, India, Brazil and many other countries of Asia, Africa and South America viewed that development with some uneasiness. Had the US shown restraint, subsequent events might have unfolded somewhat differently, but under Bill Clinton, and to a greater extent George W. Bush, Washington set out to secure that victory and achieve world dominance for the United States. Europe either could not or would not pursue an independent course and, as always, kept in line with Washington's policy.

Under these circumstances, the disgruntled states have begun building bridges between each other. That cooperation was not initially directed against the West because all of the participants in that process were largely tied to the Western system and valued their collaboration with it. However, they looked for ways to coordinate their positions on those aspects of the new Western-dominated world that did not suit them. That desire led to the creation or strengthening of institutions and groups in which Western states did not participate: ASEAN and various formats of associated cooperative endeavors, SCO, CELAC and, of course, BRICS.

Of these groups, BRICS — not formally an organization — has attracted the most interest. There are several reasons for this. First, the group brings together the largest and most influential non-Western countries. Second, it is not a regional but a global group that claims to represent the entire "South", or more broadly, the entire non-Western world. Third, BRICS actively puts forward its own initiatives as an alternative to Western projects for organizing the global economic and political order.

Interestingly, the real BRICS (originally BRIC), although borrowing the name invented by a Goldman Sachs' economist Jim O'Neil, has in fact developed in a very different manner. The basis for this cooperation was not economic similarities but geopolitics. This can clearly be seen from the process of the group's creation. The BRICS which comprised major non-Western states that represented various continents where they were natural leaders took its current form by stages. Its origin can be seen in the two decades of Sino–Russian rapprochement based on the unity of geopolitical interests. Without it, BRICS could have hardly come into being. Later, the Russia–China–India (RIC) cooperation model emerged demonstrating that India has joined the process. RIC then turned into BRIC with the inclusion of Brazil (formally, RIC still exists, but it became passive after the emergence of BRIC), and the final step was the turning of BRIC into BRICS after South Africa joined the group.

BRICS gains geopolitical significance by offering its own views on the processes at work in the world. One of the main topics BRICS addresses is the need to reform the global economy. The BRICS member states strongly propose increasing the representation of non-Western countries in international financial institutions, but are met with fierce resistance from the traditional masters of global finance. It was this disappointment that BRICS experienced in its attempt to reform the World Bank and IMF and put them on more equitable footing that led the group to create its own development bank and pool of currency reserves. While these institutions might not offer a comprehensive alternative to existing international financial institutions, they should help correct their pro-Western bias and provide non-Western states with an alternative when choosing the source for their financial development and in the event of a serious economic crisis.

So the reform of the global financial system is the most important of the group's four strategic interests. Its other goals are of strengthening the central role of the UN Security Council in the international system, making maximum use of the complementary nature of the member states' economies in order to accelerative economic development and modernizing the social sphere and economic life of those countries. As we can see, only some of these goals are purely economic in nature.

Recent international events, especially the Ukrainian crisis, US policy in the South China and the inclusion of Montenegro into NATO, show that despite Trump's coming to power, the West will continue — and with greater persistence than ever — to build a unipolar world model, pulling an ever greater number of satellites into its foreign policy orbit and demanding conformance in both their foreign and domestic policies, saddling them with what the West calls "international" and even "universal" standards. Many states in the non-Western world view this approach as a new wave of colonialism that substitutes the ideological slogan of "democracy" for "more advanced culture", but retains the same methods and goals. Of course, such circumstances will only increase the desire of the non-Western world to increase its mutual coordination.

## 32    *Alexander Lukin*

BRICS unite very different countries, and their disagreements with the West have different historical and political basis. But what they have in common is not the subject of disagreements but their very existence and a strong will to resist any form of diktat. It is important for BRICS that this time the united "North" chose to criticize one of its members. This will strengthen BRICS solidarity.

The BRICS countries present a new approach to international relations. It is called differently in individual countries, but the idea is very similar. It manifests itself in such concepts as multipolar, or polycentric, world in Russia and China, the Chinese idea of "和而不同" (creating harmony while maintaining diversity), Indian concepts of "cooperative pluralism" and "unity in diversity" and Brazilian foreign policy concepts of "autonomy through distance", "autonomy through participation" and "autonomy through diversification". They all express a similar worldview: the world should not be dominated by one power or one set of ideas, but by many countries and civilizations which cooperate with each other and treat each other with respect.

The freezing of the activities of G8 by the West as one of the sanctions against Russia accelerated the creation of the two poles within G20. While earlier Russia being a member of both G20 and G8 could soften disagreements, now there are two clear poles within G20: Purely Western G7 and BRICS which will represent all other parts of the world.

The Ukrainian crisis will only further consolidate BRICS. It has shown that the group is moving in the right direction and should strengthen its efforts to coordinate its actions in order to provide a real alternative to Western efforts to impose a unipolar world structure. That activity by BRICS will go a long way toward creating a truly multipolar world structure.

For its part, Russia has an even greater interest in cooperation within the BRICS framework. This is not only because Moscow is seeking support in its confrontation with the West but also for the deeper reason that the complete breakdown of mutual trust with the West, the West's sanctions and its attempt to use economic leverage to apply political pressure as well as Russia's actions in response have given greater impetus to the process of Russia turning toward the non-Western world that had already begun before the current crisis. Given that the sanctions are unlikely to be repealed in the foreseeable future, Asian and South American states will gradually replace Europe as the exporters of many goods, especially food and agricultural products. Russia's hydrocarbon exports are gradually moving in the direction of China and the Asia-Pacific region. Russian political elite are beginning to understand that they cannot achieve the strategic goal of developing Siberia and the Far East without cooperating with their neighbors in Asia. On the whole, Europe and the United States are beginning to be viewed as unreliable partners who are ready to sacrifice economic ties for the sake of political pressure at any moment. Thus, not only ideology but also objective circumstances and economic interests compel Russia to shift its attention to other regions. What's more, developing deeper cooperation with political and economic leaders in those regions, such as the BRICS member states, will become the key focus of Russian foreign policy.

# Chapter 4

# The Role and Place of BRICS in the Context of Globalization

Boris Guseletov

*The Institute of Europe, Russian Academy of Sciences,
Moscow, Russia*

## Introduction

BRICS countries contribute to the elaboration of a new economic system based on financial sources and trade markets. These countries have great potential to become a new pole of political and economic influence, free from geopolitical calculation to impose their social models and political standards.

BRICS is an important place to discuss problems of international politics and world economy. Brazil, Russia, India, China and South Africa are interested in a dynamic economic cooperation into this group.

## The BRICS Character Traits

BRICS is an international group of countries which includes Brazil, Russia, India, China and the South African Republic. The formation of the BRICS group reflects the tendency toward the formation of a multipolar system of international relations and the growth of mutual economic dependence of its member countries. Now, the BRICS countries are one of the main driving forces in the global economic development. First, the prerequisite for the unification of these countries was the high potential for further growth, as well as the desire to combine available resources with the aim of gaining more weight in the international arena.

Initially, the BRICS group was formed with the aim of political interaction, and economic cooperation between them was not envisaged. However, the development of the group has shown that the interaction between countries would not be limited to the political sphere. At the moment, BRICS is actively developing cooperation in the fields of economy, finance and trade.

BRICS countries were also helped by the common goals and long-term interests. First, the member countries of the group made a bet on strengthening their positions and becoming full-fledged players in the world arena. At the end of the "cold" war between Russia and the United States, the governments of Brazil, Russia, India and China began to carry out economic and political reforms to allow their countries to reach a new level of development. In order to become more competitive, these countries simultaneously focused on education, attracting foreign investment and stimulating domestic consumption and entrepreneurial activity.

Today the BRICS countries are one of the fastest growing economies in the world. The BRICS ambitions have good objectives: BRICS countries account for 26% of the land area, 43% of the population, about 15% of world trade, 40% of wheat production, 50% of pork production, 30% of poultry and beef production and 32% of arable lands. Russia, China and India possess 5.190 nuclear warheads. Their economies, over the past 10 years have grown 4.2 times (while the economies of developed countries have grown only by 61%).

Moreover, it should be noted that the nominal GDP of BRICS is about 18.5% (including PPP — 26.7%) of the global indicator.

Table 1, compiled based on the global competitiveness rating 2011–2012, shows the positions of the five countries under consideration in different categories.

From Table 1, it can be seen that at present the member countries of the BRICS group differ significantly in terms of economic development and established political traditions. At the same time, despite several distinctive features, the BRICS countries show similarity in high rates of economic growth and a high level of investment attractiveness, and their

*The Role and Place of BRICS in the Context of Globalization* **37**

Table 1.   The role of BRICS in the different fields of activities.

| Category | Brazil | Russia | India | China | SAR |
|---|---|---|---|---|---|
| Territory | 5 | 1 | 7 | 3 | 25 |
| Population | 5 | 9 | 2 | 1 | 25 |
| GDP (nominal) | 7 | 8 | 10 | 2 | 28 |
| Export | 18 | 11 | 16 | 1 | 36 |
| Import | 20 | 17 | 11 | 2 | 34 |
| Gold and currency reserves | 7 | 3 | 6 | 1 | 33 |
| Number of armed forces | 14 | 5 | 3 | 1 | 59 |
| Number of Internet users | 5 | 7 | 4 | 1 | 44 |

*Source*: The Global Competitiveness Index 2011–2012.

economies are in many ways complementary. In particular, the Russian economy is closely linked to the extraction of energy and hydrocarbon resources, while China's economy is linked to relatively cheap labor in the production of goods, India's economy is associated with the production of IT as well as cheap intellectual resources, South Africa's economy is linked to natural resources and Brazil's economy is linked with agricultural products and electricity, which gives them opportunities for further cooperation.

Many leading economists interested in the future of BRICS study the potential of these countries, and because of their research, optimistic forecasts are made regarding their future development and interaction with developed countries. For example, Jim O'Neill, an analyst at Goldman Sachs, in his article on the BRICS wrote that even the most optimistic forecasts did not imply such a significant and rapid growth in the economies of these countries. If in the late 20th century the USA and Japan were the key sources of the development of the world economy, then in the 21st century BRICS countries replaced them.

According to the forecasts of the World Bank, it is expected that by 2025 the economies of the BRICS countries will be equivalent to half of the economies of the Big Six, and by 2040 those will exceed.

At the BRICS summit, held in the summer of 2014 in the cities of Fortaleza and Brasilia, Brazil, Russia, India, China and South Africa, on behalf of the developing countries, said that the current system of inter-country interaction and cooperation no longer met the new challenges and

## 38  Boris Guseletov

needs of the 21st century and expressed their readiness to serve as the basis for a new world order.

## The Geopolitical Priorities of BRICS Group Development

Today, the activities of the group are more political than economic. The participating countries adhere to a common point of view on the need for the existence of several major centers of power in the world. Proceeding from this, they intend to create a counterbalance to the policy of the USA. Importantly, Russia and China are in the same position when it comes to this issue.

Since 2009, the established group has continued to strengthen its influence in the international arena, and taking into account the tasks and objectives set by the group, it is necessary to include the representative of Africa in the organization. At the third BRIC summit, the South African Republic (South Africa) joined the group, which undoubtedly increased the capabilities of all member countries. South Africa is the leader among African countries in terms of GDP and direct investment and also has various natural resources. In addition, South Africa is the only country in Africa that is part of the G20. According to the Minister of International Relations and Cooperation of South Africa, "BRICS can play a decisive role in strengthening the influence of developing countries on the changing global political, economic and financial architecture. It is called to become more fair and balanced. BRICS unites the most energetically developing states of the planet against the backdrop of economic decline in America and Europe."

The political influence of BRICS is determined by the fact that for today, member countries are members of various organizations. Brazil, India and China, together with South Africa and Mexico, are G7 partners. All BRICS countries are members of the G20 group. Russia and China are partners in the Framework of the Shanghai Cooperation Organization (SCO). Brazil is a member of MERCOSUR.

As for the development of foreign policy and foreign economic relations, the BRICS countries have different priorities in this matter.

For example, if Russia is one of the important economic and trade partners of the European Union, which accounts for about 48% of the volume of foreign trade, China is most interested in developing relations with the Asia-Pacific region, India with South Asia and Brazil with the Western Hemisphere, in particular, with the USA and Latin American countries.

In addition to strengthening their positions in the economic and political arena, BRICS countries expressed their desire to strengthen their positions in international organizations, such as the UN, OECD and the IMF.

As for the Organization for Economic Cooperation and Development (OECD), at the moment, none of the BRICS countries has become a member. All five BRICS countries participate in negotiations on their inclusion in the organization. However, the OECD predicts a slowdown in the economies of Brazil, Russia, India, China and South Africa in the future, which significantly reduces their attractiveness for the organization.

In the framework of cooperation with the IMF, the BRICS countries are unhappy with the distribution of votes and require a review of the number of quotas. After all, it's no secret that at the moment the USA has the largest share of votes in the IMF — 17%. The countries of Europe have about a third of the votes. The BRICS countries, whose total share, after reviewing the quotas and accession of South Africa, increased to 14.799%, only 0.2% of the votes are missing before the blocking package.

Thus, it can be said that the interaction of the BRICS countries is multilateral and affects various areas. In particular, as mentioned above, the BRICS countries are successfully cooperating to strengthen their influence in leading international organizations, such as the IMF, the UN and the OECD. In addition, BRICS makes every possible attempt to reduce its dependence on the world's leading economies, such as the US and the EU. One of the most effective way is to use national currencies in conducting cross-country operations, as well as the prospect of creating a single supranational currency in the future.

In general, the further active cooperation of the countries with the embodiment of the conceived projects will allow consolidating the existing status of this alliance, and in the future even to increase the political and economic influence in the world arena.

## The Main Problems of Development and Internal Interaction of the BRICS Countries

Cooperation within the BRICS is not homogeneous because there are many differences between Brazil, Russia, India, China and South Africa, not only economic but also political and cultural. In addition, there are significant differences in financial systems: the financial systems of China and India are more closed than Russia, Brazil and South Africa, which makes it difficult to develop a unified approach to economic activity.

To the above differences, we can add a geographical factor which can negatively affect the further development of the group. The distance of the countries located on three different continents creates certain difficulties in the field of logistics and can seriously complicate the process of trade between countries.

In addition to the above problems, the fact that the member countries have different views on the further development of the world system gives greater uncertainty to the future of the BRICS. The fact that BRICS members are strategic competitors on several issues raises the question of their fundamental compatibility. For example, Russia and India are a potential obstacle to China's establishment of domination in the Asian region.

Also, there is an asymmetry in the internal indicators of the BRICS countries. Now, one of the most acute problems is demography. China and India are suffering from overpopulation, while Russia and, especially, South Africa, on the contrary, suffer from a lack of population. Only in recent years, in these countries, the birth rate has not much exceeded the death rate.

The global financial crisis has had a different impact on the economies of countries: the Russian economy experienced the most negative impact, while China was least affected by the crisis. Accordingly, the consequences of the crisis may lead to further strengthening of the differentiation of economic indicators of the BRICS countries.

Also, Brazil, Russia, India, China and South Africa are united by common problems related to the need for modernization and economic and social life of countries, the most serious of which are high inflation and underdeveloped infrastructure.

In addition, the key factor in the dissociation is that BRICS is not an official international organization, now. The group does not have a permanent secretariat or the main executive body, and the decisions taken during the discussions are not binding.

As we can see, a lot of differences and difficulties existing between the BRICS countries make the process of working out a single common solution or speaking with a common position an extremely difficult task.

However, the BRICS countries have many cohesive factors, which cannot be forgotten, but we should also remember that there are some problems in building relationships and developing a unified strategy for further interaction.

## Prospects for the Strategic Development of the Group of BRICS Countries

BRICS as an "informal group" has existed for more than 10 years, and the issue of its further development is becoming increasingly controversial. In relation to the grouping, there are different points of view: some believe that BRICS can become the basis of a new world order, others believe that the unification of countries is symbolic and not capable of exerting a significant influence on world processes, while others consider the group mainly as an anti-Western coalition.

As discussed earlier, there are many factors that contribute to both rallying and disengagement of the grouping. Regarding further prospects for the development of the grouping, at the moment it is difficult to make an unambiguous assessment. The BRICS countries are currently taking joint efforts to develop the organization according to a positive scenario.

According to the BRICS statement made on 29 March 2012, further work within the association will focus primarily on reviving global growth, revising quota values in the IMF and supporting the growth of emerging economies.

Another interesting nuance is that the issue of further expansion of the BRICS has been increasingly raised in recent years. The countries mentioned as potential candidates for joining the group include Iran, Indonesia, South Korea, Mexico and Turkey. It is worth noting that countries such as Mexico and South Korea have sufficient economic potential to be ranked as BRICS.

42  *Boris Guseletov*

However, the further expansion of the grouping is not advisable now. The organization has already sufficient representativeness, and reckless expansion can lead to even greater disunity and ineffective coordination of the association. In addition, the criteria for joining new members and requirements for indicators of their economies have not been developed so far. The BRICS countries are yet to complete the process of formation, and now it is more important for them to develop ties within the grouping than to grow in breadth.

In recent times, a growing interest in BRICS from Western Europe is seen. It is not excluded that in the future this interest can materialize in attempts to coordinate positions with the other BRICS countries in various areas. It can help Western Europe to sustain political and economic dependence on the United States.

While the BRICS manage to avoid confrontation with the West and opposing the "North" to "South". However, much will depend on the worsening crises of global economy and the struggle for natural resources. In the meantime, the philosophy of BRICS and its practical politics complicate predictions about its role in the future geopolitical situation.

In addition to the issue of further expansion, one of the key issues currently faced by the BRICS countries is the search for the necessary actions to make the global financial system more stable. To achieve this goal, the creation of the BRICS Development Bank, which helps developing countries in the event of difficult situations, can help.

Also in the near future, there is a plan to increase the areas of cooperation between the BRICS countries. In particular, we are talking about joint projects in the production of high-tech products, namely, in the military-technical sphere, in the field of helicopter and missile construction, as well as in the nuclear industry. Table 2 provides information on the development of the BRICS countries.

As can be seen, the prospects for the BRICS countries are very large because, in aggregate, for 2012 the share of production of high-tech products is 10.6% higher than that in the EU countries.

In addition, all countries are in favor of further increase in trade turnover with each other, and mainly with the use of national currencies. As was discussed earlier, the first steps in this direction have already been taken by Russia and China.

*The Role and Place of BRICS in the Context of Globalization* **43**

Table 2. Dynamics of the BRICS countries share in the world production of high-technology products.

| Country and country's groups | 1985 | 1990 | 1995 | 2000 | 2005 | 2012 |
|---|---|---|---|---|---|---|
| Brazil | 2.0 | 1.9 | 1.8 | 1.5 | 1.4 | 2.3 |
| Russia | 0.1 | 0.1 | 0.5 | 0.2 | 0.6 | 1.4 |
| India | 0.3 | 0.3 | 0.4 | 0.3 | 0.6 | 0.9 |
| China (including Hong Kong) | 3.1 | 2.3 | 2.6 | 4.1 | 10.0 | 23.9 |
| SAR | | | 0.1 | 0.1 | 0.1 | 0.1 |
| Total: BRICS | 5.5 | 4.6 | 5.4 | 6.2 | 12.7 | 28.6 |
| For comparison: | | | | | | |
| EU | 24.3 | 29.2 | 24.2 | 21.6 | 25.3 | 18.0 |
| NAFTA | 44.9 | 33.7 | 31.2 | 37.8 | 32.8 | 29.7 |

*Source*: National Science Board (2010, Appendix: Tables 6.5; 2014, Appendix: Tables 6.7).

As we can see, at the moment there are many areas of common ground between Brazil, Russia, India, China and South Africa. Moreover, their number is constantly growing. All BRICS countries are interested in strengthening and expanding cooperation and express their readiness to make joint efforts in achieving the set goals. At the moment, it is very important that these countries move from statements to real actions and begin to implement their plans. If they manage to do this, the BRICS group will have all chances for a further successful existence.

Speaking of the BRICS as a whole, we can say that the group's potential is able to change the alignment of forces in the world and overcome such problems as significant differences in the level of economic development, in the field of political and ideological principles, leading to a mismatch of interests on a number of issues, and also the difference in the financial systems of the countries in question, structures of their economies and priorities for the development of foreign economic and foreign policy relations.

However, despite all the difficulties, one cannot ignore the significant progress in the interaction of countries and their obvious desire to develop further cooperation. The BRICS countries occupy a unique position, and the unification of efforts and further cooperation will give them the chance to take a worthy place in the international system. Although earlier the BRICS countries were associated, first of all, with crises and high risks, at the moment they show stable annual growth and are considered as promising emerging markets and serious rivals in the world arena along with current global players.

## References

Chitour, C. E. (2012) Les BRICS et la construction du nouveau monde (BRICS countries and the construction of the new world). *Le Grand Soir.*

Economic Research from the GS Financial Workbench — Dreaming With BRICs: The Path to 2050. Electronic recourse. URL: http://www.goldmansachs.com/korea/ideas/brics/99dreaming.pdf.

National Science Board. (2010) *Science and Engineering Indicators 2010.* (Appendix: Tables 6.5). Two volumes (National Science Foundation, Arlington, VA).

National Science Board. (2014) *Science and Engineering Indicators 2014.* (Appendix: Tables 6.7). Two volumes (National Science Foundation, Arlington, VA).

# Chapter 5

# Are the BRICS Nations Ready for a New Era?

Zhu Caihua

*Institute of Foreign Trade Studies, Chinese Academy of International Trade and Economic Cooperation, MOFCOM, P. R. China*

## Introduction

With more than 20% of the global economy and over 40% of the world's population, the BRICS nations, including Brazil, Russia, India, China and South Africa, have drawn much attention of the world to their large, sometimes fast-growing economies and significant influence on regional affairs, or even global affairs. Now, the world is changing rapidly and unfolding itself as a new era before us. This chapter is trying to answer the following three questions: First, what defines the new era? Second, what are the implications of this new era for the BRICS nations? Thirdly, what can BRICS cooperative mechanism do in this new era?

## What Defines the New Era?

The new era is mainly shaped by two disruptive forces: one is globalization, or reglobalization mainly driven by rising anti-globalization force; the other is technological disruption arising from the two revolutions: the fourth industrial revolution and the new energy revolution.

## An era of reglobalization

The core issue of the past globalization can be attributed to incompatible relationship between growing interdependence among countries and increasing imbalance, especially imbalance in technology, industries, trade and income across the globe. The main reason behind this imbalanced globalization is that the economy is being globalized while, without a global government, politics is being nationalized. The accumulation of this paradox resulted in such hallmark events as Brexit and Donald Trump's election as the US president, indicating the introduction of a new era of reglobalization. Globalization is now under great question. The main issues to be addressed in the process of reglobalization will include over-globalization of financial services and under-globalization of infrastructure, divergence of economic performance among countries, rising inequality within countries and across countries, social integration challenges amid immigration and job pressure, climate change and other ecological issues, and so on and so forth.

To make the planet more secure, sustainable and equitable in the process of reglobalization, a variety of actors — states authorities, intergovernmental organizations (IGOs), NGOs, businesses, academia, civil society and even individuals — should play their due roles in properly managing the process. The only way to address the above issues is to encourage innovative and constructive thinking and ideas which may guide the process of reglobalization in a more inclusive and tolerant manner rather than in a manner of leaving people and nature behind.

## An era of fourth industrial revolution

The world economy had been greatly driven by the first three industrial revolutions represented, respectively, by water-and-steam-power-led mechanization, electric-power-led mass production and electronics-and-information-technology-led automation in production. The Fourth Industrial Revolution, characterized by a fusion of technologies that is blurring the lines between the physical, digital and biological spheres, is unfolding at an unexpected speed. Now, an unprecedentedly connected world is taking shape. Possibilities of connectivity will be multiplied by emerging technology breakthroughs in fields such as artificial intelligence (AI), robotics, the Internet of Things (IoT), autonomous vehicles, 3D printing, nanotechnology, biotechnology, materials science, energy storage quantum computing, etc. As a result, there will be a radical shift in the way people produce, distribute and consume. Here are some major impacts of this revolution.

First, production will be more efficient. According to French industrial system thinker, Olivier Scalabre[1] (2016), the new round of technological innovation will boost industrial productivity by 1/3. Factories will be smaller and more flexible. Scale customization will help produce better and smarter products. Instead of size, consumer proximity is becoming the new norm. Rules of competition will be shifted from low-cost to innovation.

Second, due to radical shifts in the world's production pattern, International trade growth on merchandise will slow down or even cease to grow. However, service trade will embrace a spring of growth. Similarly, massive investment in cross-border production will become lukewarm while investment in services and R&D will have a big surge. Therefore, globalization will be under a new era in which the East to West trade flows will be replaced by regional trade flows — East for East, West for West.

Third, in job market, according to a study[2] by the University of Oxford, as many as 47% of US jobs could be completely wiped out by automation over the next 20 years or so. However, this is not the full story of labor market. The real challenge automation poses is not that the United States is running out of work, but that many of those jobs are not good jobs and many citizens cannot qualify for the good jobs that are being created. According to David Autor, in the past 37 years, the United States embraced an increasingly polarized job market. On the one hand, employment growth is robust in high-education and high-wage jobs such as doctors and nurses, programmers and engineers, marketing and sales managers; similarly, employment growth is also robust in many low-skill

---

[1] Olivier Scalabre, The *Next Manufacturing Revolution Is Here*, TED Talk Show, May 2016. http://www.ted.com/ talks/olivier_scalabre_the_next_manufacturing_revolution_is_here.
[2] Carl Benedikt Frey, Michael Osborne, *The Future of Employment*, http://www.oxfordmartin.ox.ac.uk/publications/ view/1314.

and low-education jobs such as food services, cleaning, security, home health aids. Simultaneously, employment is shrinking in many middle-education, middle-wage and middle-class jobs (such as blue-collar production positions and white-collar clerical positions). This polarized labor market has resulted in the shrinking size of middle class and has caused enormous domestic political stresses in the US.

Fourth, the fourth industrial revolution will also have far-reaching impact on developing countries. So far, 1.3 billion people (17% of the world's population) still lack electricity; 4 billion (56% of the world's population) have no access to Internet. These figures actually tell us that many developing countries have not even touched upon the second and third industrial revolutions. Questions then follow: When robots begin to substitute for cheap labor as the costs of new technology come down (Right now they are just substituting for middle-class in developed economies), can developing countries still follow the same development path as many countries like China did before? How long will this path be available before automation begins to substitute for labor worldwide? Maybe the time left for developing countries is not much because production of those labor-intensive goods traditionally produced in developing economies are not shifting back to developed economies. For example, Nike began to employ Flyknit in 2012 to produce shoes and saved a lot of labor working on the assembly lines.

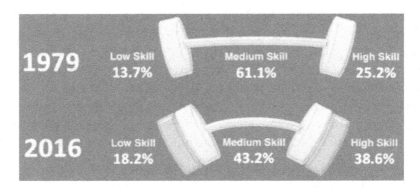

Figure 1. Share of US workers in low-, medium- and high-skill occupations: 1979 and 2016.
*Source*: David Autor, Will Automation Take Away All Our Jobs? https://www.ted.com/talks/david_autor_why_are_there_still_so_many_jobs.

## An era of new energy revolution

More and more countries realized that renewable energy is the smarter, cleaner path forward and are putting policy in place to make it happen. For example, in 2014, China announced to peak its greenhouse gas emissions by around 2030 and boost the share of non-fossil fuels in primary energy consumption to around 20% by 2030. In the same year, India committed to 175 GW of renewable energy by 2022 to provide electricity to every citizen in India. In 2017, India announced a new plan that every car sold in India from 2030 will be electric. This gradual switch to electric vehicles across India would decrease carbon emissions by 37% by 2030. Also in 2017, China confirmed to push ahead with plans that will see alternative fuel vehicles account for at least one-fifth of the 35 million annual vehicle sales projected by 2025. These ambitious plans to use renewable energy in energy mix carried out by many major economies like China and India have brought about good news to global warming. As shown in Figure 2, due to renewable energy and energy efficiency effort, carbon emissions peaked in 2014 — even though the economy continued to grow.

In this regard, the future is quite bright. As shown in Figure 3, new generation of cheaper, smaller and better batteries — a key ingredient in the global energy revolution, has seen the trend price drop. Tesla Motors, for instance, plans to have its Gigafactory running in 2017 and expects

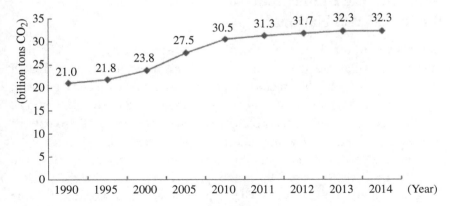

Figure 2. Global $CO_2$ emissions from energy use: 1990–2014.
*Source: The IEA.*

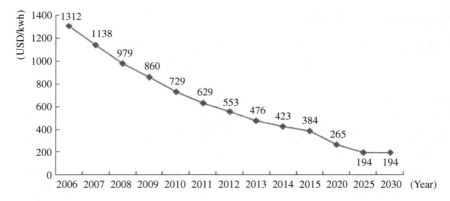

Figure 3. Battery price drop.
*Source*: http://cleanenergycanada.org/trackingtherevolution-global/2015/.

its batteries will be 30% cheaper than average prices today and hit USD 210/kwh.

But for those oil firms and oil-exporting countries, this is not totally good news because they will face an uncertain future! Especially this new energy revolution will require a fast economic transformation for Russia whose economy depends too much on fossil energy industry.

## What are the Implications of This New Era for the BRICS Nations?

The above are the three main aspects of a disruptive new era. The next question is what are the implications of this new era for the BRICS nations? Of course this means opportunities and challenges as well. Opportunities mainly reside in rising market in the BRICS nations. Challenges are always concerned with the question whether these nations can escape middle-income trap in this disruptive new era.

Due to decades of fast economic growth and increasing income of the people, the BRICS nations have now gradually grown into the world's important consumption base. The gap between their average income per capita (in purchasing power parity-adjusted US dollars) and that of the United States narrowed significantly between 2002 and 2014.

For instance, in China and Russia, per capita income as a share of that in the United States increased by about 13 percentage points and 26 percentage points, respectively, during that period. China, for example, imported 1.96 trillion USD of goods in 2014 from the rest of the world, only next to the United States (2.41 trillion USD). In the next decade, according to an OECD report, as shown in Table 1, 85% of growth in middle-class population will come from developing Asia (mainly India and China). Similarly, more than 80% of growth in demand will come from developing Asia. By 2050, developing Asia will overtake lion's share of the Global Middle Class consumption.

This growing consumption market not only represents the upward power on the global stage for the BRICS nations to have more say in managing global and regional affairs in the process of reglobalization but also is an important asset for the BRICS nations to catch up in the new industrial revolution and new energy revolution because the market-driven globalization and technological progress can only thrive the world economy through serving the market to the best. Where there is market, there is profit. That's the real market rule. The growing consumption market will help the BRICS nations boost their own technological innovations in almost all fields and let them have their footprints in the new industrial revolution. In terms of challenges, the BRICS nations, with different economic and industrial structures, have different economic problems, but face one thing in common — the issue of

Table 1. Numbers (millions) and share (%) of the global middle class.

|  | 2009 | 2020 | 2030 |
|---|---|---|---|
| North America | 338 (18%) | 333 (10%) | 322 (7%) |
| Europe | 664 (36%) | 703 (22%) | 680 (14%) |
| Central and South America | 181 (10%) | 251 (8%) | 313 (6%) |
| Asia-Pacific region | 525 (28%) | 1,740 (54%) | 3,228 (66%) |
| Sub-Saharan Africa | 32 (2%) | 57 (2%) | 107 (2%) |
| Middle East and North Africa | 105 (6%) | 165 (5%) | 234 (5%) |
| World | 1,845 (100%) | 3,249 (100%) | 4,884 (100%) |

*Source*: Kharas (2010).

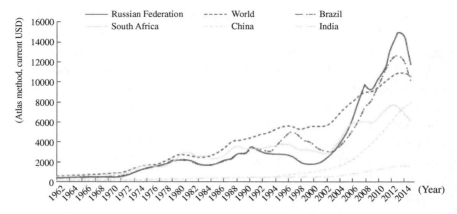

Figure 4. GNI per capita for the BRICS nations: 1962–2015 (Atlas method, current USD).

*Source*: World Bank Data, updated on 26 May 2017.

middle-income trap.[3] As shown in Figure 4, all the BRICS nations still rank in middle-income group according to the World Bank's criterion. Though Russia and Brazil once escaped the trap (Russia in 2012, 2013 and 2014, and Brazil in 2012 and 2013), now they have come back to the middle-income rank again due to economic turbulence worldwide. It is an extremely difficult era for the BRICS nations to escape the middle-income trap because these countries are now squeezed on both demand and supply sides.

On the external demand front, some of the exceptionally favorable conditions that the BRICS nations enjoyed over long stretches during the post-2000 period are not likely to return soon. They will face a potentially less supportive external environment than in the past. Waning potential output growth in advanced economies will lead to weaker demand growth for the BRICS nations. Additional complications include the risk of protectionism in some advanced economies, a less favorable view of trade integration and the tightening of US monetary policy. According to the World Economic Outlook (WEO, April 2017), while some of these effects may be offset by the rising demand among emerging market and

---

[3] According to World Bank (2016), middle-income nations are those whose GNI per capita range from USD 1,026 to USD 12,475.

developing economies, growth in external demand, on average, is expected to be weaker during 2017–2022 than in the past.

On the supply side, low-cost (especially cheap labor) advantage is disappearing. According to Olivier Scalabre (2016), manufacturing cost in Brazil was already as expensive as in France in 2015; by 2018, manufacturing cost in China will be at par with the US. In this case, whether the BRICS nations can gain enough new momentum derived from innovation is still a big challenge.

## What Can BRICS Cooperative Mechanism Do in This New Era?

With potentially persistent structural shifts occurring in the global economy, the BRICS nations may face a less supportive external environment going forward. However, steady catch-up growth has not been automatic in the past. As shown in Figure 4, the BRICS nations have exhibited episodes of accelerations and reversals over time in terms of per capita income growth. These economies still need to lay solid foundations for growth and get the most out of a weaker growth impulse from external conditions by coordinating their policies and strengthening cooperation in many areas such as protecting trade integration and containing vulnerabilities arising from high current account deficits and external borrowing, as well as large public debt. BRICS, as an independent international organization encouraging commercial, political and cultural cooperation between the BRICS nations, provides a very effective platform for coordination and cooperation.

BRICS cooperative mechanism has already made substantial progress since its inception, especially in financial cooperation. Aiming at financing infrastructure projects and promoting sustainable development in BRICS member states and other emerging economies, the New Development Bank (NDB), a multilateral development bank operated by the BRICS states, with initial authorized capital of $100 billion, started business on 21 July 2015. Almost at the same time, the Treaty for the Establishment of a BRICS Contingent Reserve Arrangement (CRA), as a framework for providing protection against global liquidity pressures, signed at Fortaleza in July 2014, entered into force on 30 July 2015. The overall volume of the CRA is $100 billion with China contributing $41 billion, Brazil, India and Russia $18 billion each and South Africa $5 billion.

Now, in order to better accommodate this new era by grasping the immense chances arising from the new era and addressing common challenges posed by the new era, BRICS requires bolder decisions and bigger stride in making this mechanism more vibrant and effective. Here are some possible recommendations for the BRICS nations to work together and coordinate their development strategies under BRICS mechanism in the following areas:

First, BRICS should play a more important role in managing the process of re-globalization, especially in global governance. Since its birth in 2006, BRICS has become one of the most important locomotives for the world's economic development and an indispensable force behind global economic governance reforms and international financial stability. Closer inter-BRICS cooperation and better coordination in multilateral platforms is the key to cope with the challenges and complexities of the global economic and political landscape. Such vehicles as the NDB, the CRA, the Asian Infrastructure Investment Bank and the Belt and Road Initiative should be on full play for the five economies to coordinate their development strategies. Besides, as a bloc that represents the interests of the developing world, BRICS is also counted on to drive the wheels of South–South Cooperation, improve global governance and establish a fair, just and inclusive international order.

Second, in order to mitigate the negative impacts of the new era, BRICS should further foster and utilize their market by negotiating a Brazil, Russia, India and China's Free Trade Agreement (BRICSFTA) which aim to lay down market (trade and investment) rules, standards and norms to the interests of BRICS and other developing economies. For example, while having robots run things in factories will be cheaper, it's important not to just let those companies (mostly from advanced economies) get richer and richer as a result. Maybe it's time to negotiate a BRICSFTA in which robot tax might be included as a new policy issue.

Third, in order to embrace the fourth industrial revolution and fully utilize the internal BRICS market, BRICS needs to bridge both hard and soft connectivity deficiencies through cooperation. Infrastructure connectivity should be the cooperation priority. According to visionary strategist, connectivity is the most revolutionary force of the 21st century as tax concessions in the past globalization only contributed 5 percentage points to world's economic growth while connectivity in the new round of globalization may lead to 10–15 percentage points to world's economic growth.

Fourth, BRICS should strengthen cooperation in both fossil and renewable energy sector. Based on the new energy revolution and current demand and supply structure, BRICS has great potential for cooperation in energy trade and finance, security, efficiency technology and renewable energy technology.

Last but not the least, BRICS needs to be future-oriented, especially in terms of stressing cooperation in education and training programs. AI and increased automation are already having a significant impact on employment and could lead to a crisis of workforce development, contributing to a growing global inequality gap. By one frightening estimate, 65% of children entering primary school today will have jobs in categories that don't yet exist. Therefore, we urgently need to educate and train our people, especially prepare our young people for the workforce of tomorrow, investing in areas such as STEM (science, technology, engineering and mathematics) education and in creating apprenticeships as paths to career readiness. In this regards, BRICS mechanism can also do a lot to promote cooperation in education and training programs among members.

# References

Frey, C. B. and Osborne, M. The Future of Employment, http://www.oxfordmartin.ox.ac.uk/publications/ view/1314.

Kharas, H. (2010) The Emerging Middle Class in Developing Countries. OECD Development Centre, Working papers.

Olivier, S. (2016) The Next Manufacturing Revolution is Here, TED Talk Show, May 2016. http://www.ted.com/talks/olivier_scalabre_the_next_manufacturing_revolution_is_here.

# Chapter 6

# Difficulties and Path of BRICS Countries' Structural Reform

Huang Maoxing

*School of Economics, Fujian Normal University, Fujian, China*

## Introduction

As latecomers in global governance, the BRICS countries cannot change the status and scope of international governance and cannot receive a truly equal status in international systems such as the World Bank or the International Monetary Fund. Only through strengthening of their own structural reforms can they equally participate in international affairs achieve equal rights, equal opportunities and equal rules.

## Difficulties and Challenges Faced by BRICS Countries in Structural Reform

### Risk of global economic uncertainty increases

First, the wave of "deglobalization" is becoming stronger. Deglobalization has brought new inequalities to different countries and ranks and aroused an "anti-globalization" campaign in the West focused around anti-free trade and anti-financial liberalization. Brexit and Trump's announcement of US exiting the Transpacific Trade Partnership can all be seen as against globalization. At the same time, newcomer countries like China push toward globalization, for example, the Belt and Road strategy pushing for global integration. The power struggle between globalization and deglobalization forces filled the global economy with uncertainties. Second, there's an increasing trend of uncertainty in developed economies' policies. US president Trump has not released a clear economic policy since he took office. His policy changes in trade and immigration might cancel out the benefits of fiscal stimulation. The policy prospects of Britain aren't clear after it parted ways with the European Nation. Furthermore, the tightening of global fiscal conditions might trigger more intense waves in the financial market. Third, trade protectionism tendencies are getting more serious. Since the financial crisis in 2008, the developed countries have increased the implementation of trade protectionism policies, regional trade negotiations keep impacting WTO's multilateral trade mechanism, some countries only exercise free trade in particular ranges and are excluding others, speeding global trade protectionism. Fourth, geopolitics risks are making the security situation tenser. Risks in geopolitics concern global security and cooperation. Eurasia Group, a global top-notch political risk consulting firm, sent out a report in January 2017 saying 2017 is the most unstable year for risks in geopolitics since the World War II ended.

## *BRICS still faces hard task of domestic structural reform*

First, China faces systematic obstacles in supply structural reforms. It faces issues such as sluggishness in the transformation of economic development method, lack of vitality in economic motivation and also no breakthrough in the marketization reforms in key processes and areas such as State-company reform, public finance, pricing economy, land system, social security, etc. Second, Russia needs transformation in economic structure and authoritarian politics. Russia is overly reliant on resource-based economy. Right now, price of international resources continues to fall, giving it a huge blow. On the contrary, the political and economic ruling within Russia has a strong authoritarian spin to it. For example, when Russia stroke down on oligopolistic economy, it actually made way for the executive branch's over-interference and monopoly, which is disadvantageous for the formation of a free market competition. Third, India has long-term "bipolar" structural issues. First of all, in India there is a large gap between the rich and the poor. According to statistics, the per capita GDP of India's richest state Kerala is four times that of India's most backward state Bihar. Furthermore, there are large differences in India's industry development. The service industries (most of which are software) take up more than 50% of India's GDP, but manufacturing is lagging behind. Lastly, India's development of high-tech information industry coexists with its backward infrastructure. The center of India's software industry Bangalore, which is nicknamed "the Indian Silicon Valley", is equipped with bad road conditions and often meets blackouts and power-cuts. Fourth, Brazil's bad governance and unstable politics have made it tiresome for reform. During the ruling of former president Lula, high-speed economic growth has accumulated a lot of wealth for Brazil. But then, a huge sum of expenditure has expanded Brazil's debt scale. Uncertainty of future economic development is also enhanced by political issues, such as the tension between the Brazilian government and parliament and the corruption case of Brazil's state-controlled oil company. Fifth, South Africa is overly reliant on outside sources, which reduces its autonomy. South African economy is highly reliant on large merchandise, especially minerals. But since the beginning of this century, South African mining industry began to bog down due to rising costs and reduction in mining reserves. Besides, political conflict between the South African president and the opposition fraction might destroy regional stability.

## Delay of the Effects Due to the Nature of the Long Term of Structural Reform

The system and mechanism issues accumulated in the long-term development of the BRICS, rigidity of interest groups and the development mode determined that its structural reform must be a long-term one. The BRICS countries have an overall weak economic prowess and weak economic foundation and lack complete systematic support to resist economic fluctuations. If the reforms are too large and quick, it might shake the foundation for economic development and may not be beneficial for further

## Goal and Direction of BRICS Structural Reform

### *Transformation from policy follower to system innovator*

For a long term, global governance was controlled by developed countries led by the US, and developing countries joined the international system passively, accepting international rules made by developed countries, and the making of domestic macro policies were affected by changes in international environment and adjusted according to developed countries' macro policies. Being followers made BRICS and other developing countries lack autonomy in the making of macro policies. But as the abilities of these newcomer countries increase, they are in urgent need to participate in more international affairs and fight for more, say, in global governance. Therefore, BRICS countries should transform from passive policy followers to system innovators in structural reforms, implement innovative driving strategies, and integrate domestic system and mechanism to international standards through experimentation and innovation. They should demonstrate the success of reform through steady domestic economic growth and actively participate in building international rules. They should form a system more suitable for pushing global economic growth through actively seeking and trial and error, so as to influence reform and innovation of international rule through their own culture and concepts, and push forward global governance in the role of system innovator and regulation provider.

### *Transformation from emphasis on demand to emphasis on supply*

A common problem faced by BRICS countries is that for a long time, they've focused on demand to push for economic growth and accumulated conflicts in the supply side, such as low product quality, an extensive production method, low ratio of factor productivity, environmental pollution and destruction, low ability of technology innovation, etc.

Even though China first brought up supply structural reform, this strategy can also be adapted to BRICS and other developing countries, which can deepen reform of the administrative system and accumulate economic growth motivation through perfecting a mechanism and system where the market plays a decisive role in resource allocation. For example, Russia should establish a new industry department in order to break off the restriction of a resource-based economy, support development of private economy and shape a benign domestic environment for competition. Brazil should push for industrialization and promote manufacturing factor's development. India should have a balanced and coordinated development strategy and strive to reduce bipolar differences. South Africa should place its emphasis on the domestic market and lower reliance on the mining industry, lower unemployment rate through industry upgrades, etc. Only through increasing measures at the supply area can it better join with demand and provide a sturdy foundation for economy's continuous rise.

## *Transformation from adjusting surface issues to challenging root issues concerning profits*

Structural reform isn't adjustment to surface issues, but hopes to solve deeper issues. At present, the issues BRICS countries have shown, such as lack of increasing power, reduction in exports, business failure and industries with high debts, can be connected to the shrinking of international market and increase in cost from the surface, but at the root, these are deep-level structural issues in economic development. Therefore, the countries need to see the root causes of BRICS economic development's dilemma and turn mindsets from raising questions to finding causes, from adjusting sectional policies toward looking at the whole picture. This will require the countries to challenge monopolistic groups, resource occupants, corrupted groups and other beneficiaries. Reform might cause economic fluctuations and even setbacks and might be thwarted by beneficiaries, so this requires the countries to have steady determination and courage for reform and to form a stable economic and political environment.

## Transformation from relying on outside power to stabilizing domestic foundations

Most of the BRICS countries implemented export-oriented strategies when they were trying to catch up and be advanced. They increased foreign exchange earnings by product export, opened up domestic market to draw in foreign technology and became reliant on foreign market and on developed countries' technology. After the financial crisis, BRICS and other developing countries found themselves in trouble because of the rapid decrease in international market's demand and adjustment in developed countries' policies. They are faced with some of the following issues: setbacks in economic development caused by export decrease, export industries facing bankruptcy and closure, resource-oriented countries such as Russia and South Africa are in a slump because prices of international bulk commodities kept falling, lots of industries went back to their respective countries because of developed countries' "reindustrialization" strategy, countries like Brazil and South Africa are facing the possibility of a debt crisis because of the US dollar's rise in value, etc. Therefore, structural reform in BRICS countries should be based on autonomy and independence, placing emphasis on domestic elements and market, increasing ratio of factor productivity, establishing a complete production system, perfecting market environment and basic infrastructure, making sturdy the foundation for economic development and helping structural reform to be steadier and more concrete.

## Transformation from exclusive competition to tolerant cooperation

BRICS countries have mutual benefits in a series of important international issues, such as reforming international financial system and climate change carbon emission reduction negations, but there are also differences. They cooperate under the G20 framework but have exclusive competitions for their respective benefits, which undermines the BRICS composition of forces. There are stark differences in the BRICS countries' economic prowess and status. For example, China's economic scale is far ahead, and differences in prowess and status generate different takes on the common identity. In trade, China mostly exports manufactured goods with high added value, such as electronics, machine and equipment, and imports raw products with low added value, such as agricultural products. The difference in trade structure has prompted India and Brazil to implement trade protectionism policies against China. The BRICS countries also have fierce competition on right pricing of bulk commodities such as iron ore and oil. In structural reform, BRICS countries should set aside their differences, cooperate on the basis of the entity's benefits — such as increase cooperation in macroeconomic policies — call for developed countries to take responsible macroeconomic policies and oppose trade protectionism. They should also actively implement outcomes of the G20 Summit; actively make progress in key fields such as structural reform, infrastructure investment or international tax cooperation, to increase BRICS' say in G20. They should actively explore new mechanism and areas BRICS can cooperate in, increase cooperation levels and develop tolerantly.

## Ways BRICS Countries' Structural Reform Can Increase Vitality of Global Economy

### Complete cooperation mechanism for BRICS, build new global economic development engine

First, they should have a cooperation consensus and increase cooperation efficiency. BRICS countries can implement the BRICS Summit consensus through effective negotiations, communications and coordination — such as through BRICS summits, researching and exploring consensus in areas like economic and trade cooperation on a state level, policy environment and financial risks. Second, they should deepen cooperation areas and build growing points for economic cooperation. BRICS countries should expand and deepen cooperation areas on the basis of continuing economic cooperation; on the one hand they should enhance cooperation within BRICS, and on the other hand they can enhance cooperation of BRICS with other countries, especially second-tier newcomer market nations. Third, they should innovate cooperation mode and enhance real effects of economic cooperation. BRICS countries should continue deepening cooperation in productivity and innovation, focusing on the new motion and new wills of BRICS countries, keep renewing cooperation modes and enhance real effects of economic cooperation.

## *Actively participate in global industrial division and actively join world economic developmental system*

First, they should push BRICS countries to cooperate in productivity and promote status of international industries' division. The countries should gradually break away from the former inferior status of international industry division and pricing structure through enhancing productivity and innovation, speeding up industry structural transformation and upgrade of BRICS countries' industry structures. Besides, BRICS countries should enhance cooperation in strategic and new rising industries, play comparative advantages and coordinate development strategies. Second, they should participate in making new regulations for global economy; actively join in the world economy's development system. BRICS countries need to, on the one hand, enhance trade cooperation within and develop unity and, on the other hand, they should increase multilateral cooperation with other countries or international organizations and coordinate cooperation abilities. In the future, BRICS can also consider expanding and absorbing more newcomer economies, to increase their own representation and influence and to lead the making of a new round of rules for global economic trade.

## *Oppose trade protectionism, promote construction of multilateral trade mechanisms*

First, the countries should oppose trade protectionism and construct an open world economy. BRICS should firmly oppose any form of trade protectionism and propose liberalization of international investment and trade, speeding up the construction of an open world economy in which there can be mutual benefits and win–win situations. Second, the countries should enhance a multilateral trade mechanism and push again for Doha Round of World Trade Talks. BRICS countries should actively participate in multilateral trade and bilateral trade, especially cooperate with WTO member states on investment and trade, maintain and push for multilateral trade mechanism such as the WTO and increase openness and tolerance of BRICS international investment and trade.

## *Enhance policy coordination among the countries, promote macroeconomic control*

First, the countries should enhance international coordination of macroeconomic policies and push for the countries to go through economic structural adjustments within. BRICS can construct an all-aspect, wide-range cooperation partnership and lead a new round of global innovation and economic structural reform through multilayered and multiarea international policy coordination, especially macroeconomic policies such as monetary policy, financial policy, exchange rate policy and financial regulation policy and the coordination of financial policy. Second, they should push for strategic connection in economic development and cultivate a win–win and mutually beneficial common community. BRICS should deepen partnership and implement BRICS Economic Partnership Strategy; push for cooperation among BRICS countries in key regions such as trade investment, manufacturing, energy, agriculture, technology innovation, finances, interconnection, information and communication technology; and keep increasing cooperation level and layers.

## *Deepen Cooperation in International Financial Regulation, Prevent Risk of Cross-border Transmission in the Financial Market*

First, they should increase global capital mobile monitoring, preventing cross-border transmission of risks in the financial market. BRICS countries should face financial risks in the new international scope and situation, insist on continuing to monitor and evaluate capital flow of foreign investment organizations and cross-border projects under the framework of BRICS cooperation framework. They should establish an effective alert mechanism on global finance risks and recognize, prevent and solve the cross-border transmission of global financial risks. Second, they should have a cautious supervision both in macro and micro levels, prevent systematic risks in the financial system. On the one hand, they should establish diverse cooperation in financial supervision and enhance cooperation with macro financial prudential supervision in international organizations such as the International Monetary Fund, World Bank or the WTO, constructing a macro credential supervision framework on the higher level; on the other hand, they should establish systems that release information on international financial risks, financial information search and protection of financial privacy, push for reform and innovation in micro credential supervision, ensuring the rights of financial consumers.

# Chapter 7

# Dynamics from BRICS Countries — A Perspective on BRICS Development Strategies: Prospects and Issues

Vinod Anand

*Vivekananda International Foundation, New Delhi, India*

## Looking Back

In 2017 BRICS conducted its summit in October under the Chairmanship of India. PM Modi had outlined "Building Responsive, Inclusive and Collective Solutions" as the core theme for BRICS chairmanship. Enhancing greater people-to-people participation in BRICS events was also given priority. In fact, a five-pronged approach comprising "Institution Building, Implementation, Integration, Innovation, and Continuity with Consolidation" was suggested. Thus, "Development with Continuity" was said to be the fundamental basis for BRICS cooperation that was emphasized during the last summit. For BRICS summit of 2017, the theme "Stronger Partnership for Brighter Future" and the five key priority areas of "deepening cooperation for common development, strengthening global governance, carrying out people to people exchanges, making institutional improvements and building broader partnerships" rhyme very well with the thrusts of previous summits.

The overall goal during India's stewardship of BRICS had been to give it shape and substance both in terms of making it a responsible

## 68 Vinod Anand

multilateral institution, first, as an important factor in geopolitics and, second, in the emerging economic discourse.

## Terrorism and Global Governance

PM Modi's preferences and direction of his efforts can be easily discerned from his speeches at the last summit as well as the summit held at Ufa in 2015. Countering global and regional terrorism through a unified approach has been one of his major themes which is also linked to global governance in many ways although, it is a different matter at the international level, there is still no agreement on the definition of terrorism. Thus, under India's stewardship, an attempt was made to shift the emphasis from the narrow aspects of economy to the larger aspects of global issues where combating terrorism has acquired increasing urgency. As terrorism has become globalized, the response to it also has to be at a global level.

A common approach on terrorism by the BRICS countries could contribute positively to the emerging international security architecture. In its joint statement of October 2016, BRICS had strongly condemned terror attacks against its member countries, including that in India. The statement also strongly condemned terrorism in all its forms and manifestations and stressed that there can be no justification whatsoever for any acts of terrorism, whether based upon ideological, religious, political, racial, ethnic or any other reasons. It also emphasized the need to strengthen cooperation in combating international terrorism both at the bilateral level and international fora.

BRICS Foreign Ministers meeting held in June 2017 leading up to the forthcoming summit in Xiamen, China had again reiterated their commitment to fight against terrorism and form a broad coalition under the aegis of UN which could provide a coordination role. India has been seeking cooperation of BRICS partners to support the adoption of a comprehensive convention on terrorism at the UN and not to differentiate between "good" and "bad" terrorists. While declarations on the need for joining forces to counter terrorism are routinely made either from the BRICS platform or elsewhere, it is quite evident that there are not only differences between the BRICS members on approaches to terrorism but also there is no agreement on the definition of a terrorist at the international level.

## Goa Summit

Of course, looking at the year-long list of events organized by India in connection with BRICS that ranged from renewable energy to scientific research, from measures to adopt for combating corruption to the establishment of a film festival, the agenda was far more diversified and comprehensive. As it is quite evident, all the five members of BRICS share common perspectives on many of the global issues and have been working to change the western-dominated narrative, be it economic or strategic issues.

Building on the theme of continuity and consolidation, the last BRICS Summit in Goa had kept the Ufa declaration in view which aimed at working out a strategy for economic partnership, and consequently, India had worked on a program to develop trade, investment and economic cooperation in a number of fields, including manufacturing, minerals processing, energy and agriculture. This was in line with a 10-point program for consensus between member countries, to impart momentum to the process of closer cooperation between BRICS nations. The 10 steps for enhancing cooperation include a BRICS trade fair, a railway research center, cooperation among supreme audit institutions, a digital initiative, an agricultural research center, a forum of state/local governments among the BRICS nations, cooperation among cities in the field of urbanization, a sports council and an annual sports meet, first major project of New Development Bank to be in the field of clean energy and a film festival. These initiatives were given a practical shape for implementation.

India also showcased its initiatives like "Make in India" project and sought investments from BRICS countries in the field of infrastructure development. India also held a Trade Fair and an Investor Forum to promote programs such as "Make in India", "Smart City Mission", "Digital India" and "Start-up India" all part of PM Modi's initiatives where BRICS members could cooperate in many ways.

## BRICS and Sustainable Development

BRICS has also aligned itself with the 2030 Agenda for Sustainable Development of the UN. The Sustainable Development Goals (SDGs) indeed have very ambitious targets and results to be achieved by the international community; the BRICS community would have to really work very hard to achieve them. The SDGs would provide guidance for development strategies and priorities of BRICS members. According to one assessment, the BRICS countries have achieved a degree of success in advancing SDG 7 (on clean and energy) and SDG 9 (on infrastructure development) through the NDB's rollout of renewable energy infrastructure projects. Sustainable use of water resources is another area where progress can be made through mutual cooperation. India has been successful in its efforts of water conservation in the State of Rajasthan where the age-old traditions of water conservation and practices of sustainable use of water resources had virtually made it a drought-free State. Therefore, effective implementation of Sustainable Development Agenda 2030 and ensuring adequate funding for the same should continue to be the objective of BRICS group.

Sustainable development becomes more relevant and important at a time when the US has revised its stance on climate change. BRICS can lead the new discourse and stick to their commitments given during Paris Climate Change conference and work together for bolstering the green economy. The European leaders have been critical of the US move on climate change and they could be coopted for providing green technologies. Thus, success of sustainable agenda is heavily dependent upon its successful implementation by BRICS countries.

The BRICS has also been cooperating with a number of UN initiatives, programs and organizations like UNESCO, WHO and the United Nations Industrial Development Organization (UNIDO) to advance shared objectives and coordinate policies for development in a variety of diverse fields. During BRICS summits, the host nations have also been reaching out to regional multilateral groupings to advance shared agendas, like India invited the Bay of Bengal Initiative for Multi-Sectoral Technical and Economic Cooperation (BIMSTEC). The overall aim was to boost ties between the BRICS countries and BIMSTEC as part of the regional outreach efforts to fortify South–South cooperation. Other members have also organized similar outreaches during their turn for hosting the summits.

## BRICS: State of Economies

It is quite evident that among the BRICS economies both India and China are growing at a good pace despite the fact that Chinese economy has been decelerating in the recent years. While India needs investments for its infrastructure development China has the capacities and desire to cooperate with India for a win–win outcome. Many Chinese companies have been looking at India to deploy their surplus capacities and funds in India. Some have already come in with big investments in reality sector (Wanda group), electronic sector and infrastructure development (construction of roads as also survey for railway line). India wants to export its IT services, pharmaceuticals and other services and products for which ways need to be found for mutually beneficial cooperation. Both sides need to work on reducing the impediments and improve ease of doing business with each other.

All BRICS members have their unique strength and characteristics despite the fact that other than China and India their economies have not been doing well. Apparently, Russian economy seems to have returned to growth path in recent months. Similarly, Brazilian economy is reported to have recovered from recession of the previous years and its GDP growth is forecasted to be 0.5% in 2017 compared to −3.3% in 2016. South Africa is also expected to post a GDP growth of 1.4% in 2017 versus 0.5% in 2016 and projected to rise further to 1.8% in 2018 (see Figure 1).

Russia continues to be an important strategic partner of India in many ways and has been cooperating with India in both civil nuclear energy and hydro carbon sectors besides the defense sector. Russia has been supportive of India's membership in UN Security Council and other multilateral platforms. Brazil is an important country not only because of its size and population but also as a launch pad for rest of the Latin Americas. During 2017, on the sidelines of the BRICS summit, India and Brazil had finalized the text of a bilateral investment agreement and inked pacts to deepen cooperation in the fields of cattle genomics and agriculture. There is a great scope for cooperation in the areas of ship building, pharmaceuticals, defense production, ethanol production and oil and gas. Similarly, the India–South Africa equation remains very important both on bilateral basis and as partner in BRICS and IBSA (India, Brazil and South Africa). South Africa is

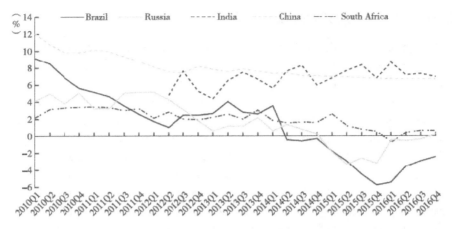

Figure 1. GDP growth rate of BRICS.
*Source*: S&P Global Ratings Projections, The BRICS Post, 20 March 2017.

also important as a launch for the other countries in the African Continent. Strengthening of relationship in multiple areas with BRICS partners was India's agenda for the last summit and also for the forthcoming summit.

## BRICS Institutions

Developing BRICS as an institution has been one of the important goals of the member countries.

Thus, New Development Bank is seen as an achievement of the BRICS, and with India in the lead, it has sought to advance sustainable development projects through lending. Ways to strengthen the NDB both bilaterally and multilaterally would continue to be an important part of the BRICS' deliberations. NDB has already approved loans of over 800 million USD for renewable green energy projects in India, China, Brazil and South Africa.

India, of course, has an insatiable requirement for infrastructure investment funds. In April 2017, India has proposed projects worth 2 billion USD for loans. Evidently, this offers an enormous opportunity to an institution like the NDB, whose core mandate is sustainable infrastructure development. In 2017, NDB issued the first set of green bonds in RMB (for about 447 million USD). In addition, the BRICS Contingent Reserve

*Dynamics from BRICS Countries — A Perspective on BRICS Development Strategies* **73**

Arrangements (CRA) was operationalized thus strengthening the global financial safety net.

On the contrary, emergence of BRICS as an alternative forum to the West-dominated worldview of established economies is proceeding on a very gradual and incremental path. Some feel that the nature of differing political systems of BRICS members also contributes to differing approaches being adopted at the global level.

At times, adopting a common view on global macroeconomics, development aid and international resource transfers and global governance, etc. also present a challenge.

Further, some research reports indicate that there is a negative impact of the trade policies of individual BRICS members on each other. Commercial ties between them are still characterized by a lack of harmony and discriminatory trade distortions. Trade imbalance between China and India, non-tariff barriers or other kinds of discriminatory practices prevent a balanced and harmonious economic relationship occurring between both sides. There are also concerns regarding less than required trade and commercial relationship between India and rest of the BRICS members.

India's goal is also to work for greater cooperation among BRICS in services and in ways to deal with non-tariff measures restricting goods trade between BRICS member countries. As you would be aware, India has much strength in this sector as compared to the manufacturing sector.

Many other BRICS institutions like Brics Agriculture Research Centre, Brics Railway Research Network and Brics Sports Council, to name a few, are in the offing to derive benefits from mutual cooperation and synergies. Possibility of establishing a BRICS Rating Agency based on market-oriented principles, in order to further strengthen the global governance architecture is also being explored.

Space is another area where BRICS has moved ahead in cooperating with each other. BRICS space agencies have agreed in early February 2017 on a protocol to share and exchange data, including images of natural resources from remote-sensing satellites for mutual benefit. While only Brazil, Russia, India and China have remote-sensing satellites in the sun-synchronous orbit, they will share data with South Africa also as it does not have similar space assets. Such a step would exploit the existing capacities optimally. BRICS space agencies have plans to exchange data for tele-education, tele-medicine and for a variety of other applications which would benefit people of the member nations.

## Status of BRICS Platform: India–China Equation and FTAs

While development of BRICS mechanism which definitely has a clout given the size of its economies, populations and resources is proceeding in the right direction, it is yet to acquire much heft both geopolitically and economically. Strategic divergences between the members at times prevent a coordinated approach to be adopted by members for evolving common positions on international issues. Insofar as India and China are concerned both can work closely in a number of areas, yet heightened strategic dissonance between the two would obviously have a negative impact on the effectiveness and functioning of the BRICS as an important forum.

President Xi in fact had said that "China is willing to work with India to maintain their hard-won sound relations and further advance their cooperation."

In 2017, there was also a proposal by China for a Free Trade Agreement (FTA) between the five major emerging economies which could not find much favor with the other members of the grouping. Evidently, China's aim was to expand trade between BRICS members but fears of Chinese imports hurting their local manufactures are paramount. Other countries were also not keen to start negotiations on a separate "BRICS Investment (protection & promotion) Treaty". India in any case is participating in RCEP (Regional Comprehensive Economic Partnership) which would be a regional FTA that includes India and China. It is another matter that even RCEP may not turn out to be of much benefit to India. There is also a possibility of India and Eurasian Economic Union signing an FTA in July 2017 as both sides have accepted a report prepared by the Joint Feasibility Study Group.

A BRICS Roadmap for Trade, Economic and Investment Cooperation until 2020 has been evolved which involves a number of projects and mechanisms to realize the same. The emphasis is on enhanced cooperation in e-commerce, "single window", IPR cooperation, trade promotion and micro, small and medium enterprises (MSMEs).

In fact, during 2017 five companies, i.e. one each from BRICS, came together to form a joint venture to exploit a Siberian Gold mine located in Chita region. The pre-production investment was said to be in the range of 400–500 million USD. It is expected to produce 12 million tons of gold ore annually. This project can provide a model for future cooperation within BRICS and even for joint ventures in countries outside the BRICS.

In November 2017, BRICS' Communication Ministers had prepared an action plan to institutionalize cooperation in Information and Communication Technologies arena through identifiable goals and objectives for developing knowledge societies in the group. In 2017, it is hoped that this BRICS initiative will be taken forward for implementation as part of sustainable development goals.

BRICS in general and India in particular have been looking to cooperate in e-governance, financial inclusion and targeted delivery of benefits, e-commerce, open government, digital content and services and bridging the digital divide. Joint efforts are aimed at capacity building for effective participation in e-commerce trade to ensure shared benefits. In fact, Chinese firm Alibaba has a very strong presence in Indian e-commerce market and is a strong competitor to Amazon. The graph depicted in Figure 2 gives the projections for India's projected growth in the area of e-commerce.

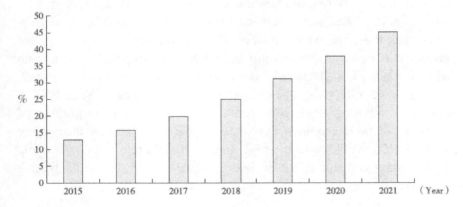

Figure 2.　India's projected e-commerce growth.
*Source*: *The Hindustan Times*.

India is also promoting "Blue Economy" which lays emphasis on bringing sustainable utilization of the fisheries' wealth from marine and other aquatic resources. The use of information technology (IT) and space technology for improving the capacities of the fishing community and strengthening the monitoring, control and surveillance system are the areas where there could be mutual cooperation between the BRICS countries as they are all nations endowed with marine and aquatic wealth. However, such resources are extremely vulnerable to environmental degradation, overfishing, climate change and pollution. Thus, in conformity with UN Sustainable Development Goal number 14, BRICS should evolve suitable mechanisms/frameworks to promote the sustainable use and preservation of marine and coastal ecosystems.

## Concluding Observations

While development of BRICS mechanism, which definitely has a clout given the size of its economies, populations and resources, is proceeding in the right direction it is yet to acquire much heft both geopolitically and economically. Strategic divergences between the members at times prevent a unified approach to be adopted by members for evolving common positions on international issues. Similarly, economic issues also need to be dealt with in a manner that there is a win–win situation for all the stakeholders. While the US under the new administration is moving toward more protectionist tendencies and as it looks inward, the BRICS group has the opportunity to emerge as an important voice in global governance, its associated reforms and developmental policies. As a basic framework, the UN SDGs provide an important guideline based on which mutual cooperation should be pursued in the coming years. While BRICS partners have broadened their mutual cooperation in large number of areas, it still has to acquire depth in most of the areas. Thus, in the coming years BRICS would have to strive hard to remain relevant and become an important and significant institution which can present an alternative narrative.

# Chapter 8

# Brazil's Participation in BRICS Cooperation Mechanism: Strategic Consideration and Analysis of Results

Zhou Zhiwei

*Brazil Research Center and the Latin American Institute,
Freie Universität Berlin, Berlin, Germany*

*International Relations Research Center, Chinese Academy of Social
Sciences, Beijing, P. R. China*

## Introduction

Since the beginning of the new century, the group rising of newcomer states has become the phenomenon that receives the most outside attention in international systems. It not only directly reflects new changes in power comparisons in international structure but also provides logic for adjustments and reforms in international systems. BRICS is a multilateral platform that was formed and rapidly developed during this process and achieved "soft balance" to the present US-led global order. "Soft power" is a feasible strategy for second-rate great powers to deal with US' monopolar predominance. It's not a direct challenge to the US' military hegemony but can use non-military methods to procrastinate, block and even sabotage superpower's unilateral policies (Pape, 2005, p. 10). This non-military method includes the strategy of mechanism arrangements, which is to have a number of countries bonding in diplomatic unity or alliance in order to restrict the power of a super nation. "BRICS", "India–Brazil–South Africa forum" and G21 all have such characteristics, in order to help weaker countries to win more leeway when facing powerful nations. So, they are also called "buffer" mechanisms (Gries, 2005).

In fact, from formation to specification of cooperation, BRICS coincided with Brazil's diplomatic strategy that prioritizes "South–South Cooperation" in timeline. It not only reflects Brazil's policy log that enhances BRICS cooperation but also reflects its diplomatic consideration on BRICS cooperation. This report hopes to analyze Brazil's strategic consideration from the angle of Brazil's state identity and core goal in foreign policy and evaluate Brazil's participation in BRICS cooperation in the past 10 years based on this.

## Positioning Brazil's National Identity and its Foreign Policies and Goals

Brazil's positioning of its national identity is not only based on its acknowledgement of its comprehensive national strength but also based on its judgment of the status of world scope and trend. Based on these two factors, Brazil's important foreign relations records in the past decade clearly show its core evaluation of the international situation and national identity First, the international power structure shows a "hegemonic structure", composed of three layers: an international system center made up with a few economic giant powers, political giants and military giants, a periphery made up with large quantity of medium, small and micro countries. Between these two categories, there are a limited number of peripheral large countries, that's what Brazil belongs to, it's "a country that's underdeveloped, populous, with a wide range of land, moderate climate, with economic potential, has an industrial system and strong domestic market" (Guimaraes, 2011). There are a few countries with similar identities as Brazil, such as Argentina, South Africa, India, Iran, South Korea, Indonesia, etc. Second, the international system is a compound full of conflicts, competitions and cooperation. The interaction between powers and interest groups decides the form of international system. But the system has shifted from a monopolar pattern to a process becoming more diversified by day (Guimaraes, 2001). In this global system, an important challenge Brazil faces is to overcome its own "external vulnerability". This type of vulnerability is shown as frequent project deficit on the economic level, lack of technical ability on the technology level, lack of hard power on the military level, adherence to American cultural hegemon on the ideology level and lack of participation in international mainstream decision-making mechanisms on the political level (Guimaraes, 2011, p. 190). Based on this judgment, Brazil faces realistic tasks in its foreign policy. The first one is a breakthrough of its "peripheral" identity in international power structure and participate in international policymaking mechanisms as much as possible, to show and increase its voice and influence in international affairs. The second one is to seek a diverse and effective participatory path of global governance, to realize the goal of breaking through the restriction of its national identity. Internally, the elite class in Brazil believes the country shouldn't be restricted to the position of an "ordinary country" or a "peripheral large country." Even though Brazil's economic prowess can't match to global leaders, it has advantages other "peripheral countries" can't compete with, such as population and land scale, resources and economic structure. This shows that Brazil has preconditions to go beyond "peripheral" and launch wider global participation. A senior Brazilian diplomat, Celso Amorim had declared on multiple occasions that Brazil plays an important role on the international stage and has multiple advantages in land size, politics and democracy, and economic prowess. At the same time, it is a developing country and is faced with serious economic and social fragility. But, Brazil is not a small country and it can't and shouldn't have a foreign policy of a small country's. Based on this, it can be seen from some angles at least that in the past 20 years, Brazil has positioned itself as a "developing country that can play an important role", and the important role is that of a regional leader as well as a world-changing one.

As early as 2001, before the BRICS concept was brought forth, famous Brazilian think tank on foreign policy CEBRI had prepared a questionnaire with 149 members of the Brazil Foreign Policy Committee on topics of "Brazil's international agenda", including Brazil's national identity, global power and situation and Brazil's priorities in foreign policy, etc.

## 80  Zhou Zhiwei

This questionnaire reflects accurately the perception of Brazil's elite class in foreign affairs of priority issues in Brazil's foreign policy, as well as painting a picture of Brazil's goals in foreign strategies to the understanding of the author, in this stage the goals of Brazil's foreign strategy are shown in the following three areas: first, to realize the political and economic unity of South America. Since the 1980s, the integration of South America has always been a prior topic in Brazil's foreign policy, and the core of its regional strategy has always been to "build a South American economic and political group" and to construct South America as "a pole in the multipolar structure in the future". In fact, realizing the peaceful existence with South American neighboring countries and pushing for regional development is an important aspect of Brazil performing its international duties (Amorim, 2007). Second, create a beneficial international environment for domestic economic development through a wide-range of international participation. In the above research, out of the top six topics ranked "extremely important", four were economic ones. They are "trade promotion, reducing trade deficit" (73%), "development of Mercosur" (64%), "WTO negotiations" (55%) and "unification of South American energy and transportation infrastructure" (53%). Furthermore, "free trade negotiations with Europe and the US" and "International finance system reform" were deemed as "extremely important" by 43% and 39% of interviewees, respectively (de Souza, 2001). In fact, since the 1990s, development has always been the core of Brazil's foreign policy and is an important basis of judging the rationality of its foreign policy (Cervo, 2002). Third, increased international society's recognition of Brazil's "big country status", increases Brazil's participation in global affairs and increases Brazil's influence in international decision-making process. Even though Brazil's foreign polices throughout historical stages differed and had adjusted its national positioning many times, seeking international society's recognition of its "big country status" has always been the core of Brazil's foreign strategy.

## Brazil's Strategic Consideration toward BRICS Cooperation

After entering the new age, as emerging countries rapidly rise as a group and the speedup of world's bipolarization under its push, during the labor government's reign (2003–2016), Brazil's foreign policy has shown a more diversified and independent way of thinking on the foundation of "participatory autonomy". It especially stresses to deepen Brazil's participation in global affairs through South–South cooperation and promote Brazil's negotiation abilities in relations with developed countries, in order to change its passiveness in an asymmetric international system. No matter whether it was a "participatory autonomy" in the Cardozo government or a "diversified autonomy" during the labor government rule, it shows that Brazil has a proactive attitude. Comparatively speaking, "diversified autonomy" stresses more in the diverse choice of participation ways, and South–South cooperation is its main method.

BRICS cooperation is the core reflection of Brazil's strengthening of South–South cooperation strategy and an option Brazil has exerted force on in its external strategy in the past 10 years. Under the policy consideration of prioritizing South–South cooperation, Brazil has placed the cooperation with similar emerging countries as top priority. Brazil's foreign policy strategist Guimaraes has once stressed that both single polarization and bipolarization of the world system are in discordance with Brazil's national interest, even contrary to Brazil's national interest. For developing countries like Brazil, who have weak economic, political and military powers, they can only benefit through more balanced and diverse situation of international powers. However, deepening political and economic cooperation with "peripheral powers" who might have similar strategic interests and realizing a multipolar international scale is one of the main challenges of Brazil's international strategy (Guimarses, 2001, pp. 28–30). Therefore, having contacts with countries like India and China, who have the goal of pushing for the form and stabilization of a multipolar world order, should be a realistic and prior goal in Brazil's foreign policy (Guimarses, 2011, p. 218).

As stated above, after the BRICS concept was brought forth, it received high emphasis from the Brazilian government. The Lula government immediately ensured a diplomatic priority strategy targeting large developing countries, and as the international situation changes and the importance of BRICS increases, BRICS cooperation is becoming a more and more important makeup of Brazil's international strategy (Amorim, 2008). Specifically speaking, Brazil's strategic consideration of the BRICS cooperation mechanism can be shown from these two aspects.

First, BRICS has provided an important external passageway for Brazil to achieve development. Looking back at Brazil's foreign relations in the last century, development has become a main topic in its foreign relations and constantly occupies center stage in its foreign policies. The reason is Brazil's perception of outside threats is focused in economic areas. This point is also proven from the "Brazil's international agenda" investigation mentioned above. In many international topics, "promote trade and reduce trade deficit" is widely seen as the most important one because of the characteristics of Brazil's economy and the development needed to change its economic fragility. Seen from this level, diplomacy is a policy instrument to support the planning of economy and social development (Amorim, 2004). Since the beginning of the new century, as a new round of crisis arises with the expansion of world economy and a new round of trade, as well as Brazil's domestic economic adjustments and political party's rotation, Brazil's development-oriented foreign policy and social agenda become more prominent (Zhang, 2014). As to BRICS cooperation, Brazil's considerations on the development dimension focus on two areas.

First, emerging economies such as the BRICS (or developing countries) are playing more and more of a leading role to global economy. The emergence of new large countries is an important phenomenon in the post-Cold War era, and this trend has become clearer after the global economic crisis that erupted in 2008 (Amorim, 2010). The rise of emerging economies is not only shown by the launch of concepts such as BRICS but also reflected in this group's changing economic size and contribution to the growth of global economy. For example, from 2000 to 2008, China, India, Russia and Brazil have contributed more than 30% to the growth of world economy, while only 10 years ago the number was only 16% (Wei, 2011). Therefore, from medium and long-term trends, emerging economies can gradually become the "growth pole" of a global economy. Looking back at Brazil's foreign affairs, it's obvious that the shift of global economy's center gravity can be reflected to its foreign policy. The most obvious example is Brazil's shift in foreign policy from Europe to North America at the beginning of the 20th century.

Therefore, strengthening cooperation with emerging states might provide an external passageway for Brazil to realize its economic and social development goals.

Second, it's an important choice to lower economic dependence on developed countries. An important guidance rule of Brazil's foreign policy is to create a benign external environment for Brazil's economy, fight for outside sources and obtain a better negotiation condition with developed countries. A benign external environment means reducing Brazil economy's external vulnerability and dependence, increase Brazil economy development's autonomy, keep domestic economic structure balanced as well as building a diverse outward trade and change the situation where trade and investment are reliant on European and American traditional market, build a fair and logical international trade and financing system. As newcomer states emerge in groups, Brazil has the possibility to look for "substitutes" or "supplements" of market and investment from developed countries, such as Europe or America. In this aspect, Brazil's former minister Antonio Patriota compares Brazil and BRICS' coordination to the diplomatic shift at the beginning of the 20th century when Brazil aligned with the US. At that time, global economic emphasis and power core have transferred from Europe to the US, making an allegiance between Brazil and the US. As the international scale develops, Brazil and BRICS' cooperation is a similar policy adjustment in the same category.

Furthermore, BRICS has provided an important multilateral cooperation platform for Brazil's international participation, in order to promote its national autonomy and international influence. Multilateralism is an important principle and tradition of Brazilian foreign policy. Since joining the Hague Conference in 1907 till now, Brazil has actively participated in the establishment of important international multilateral mechanisms (such as League of Nations and UN). Brazil's elite class believes a multilateral policy is Brazil's "calling card", and Brazil can exhibit to the world its views and demands on international affairs through the platform of international multilateral mechanisms (Souto, 2005). Since entering the new millennium, as the world's "flat" trend develops, Brazil has played active roles in creating new international multilateral cooperation mechanisms, such as G20 under the WTO, the India–Brazil–South Africa Dialogue Forum, BASIC, etc. Its policy not only focuses on pushing for reform of international system but serves its own "big country dream". This type of strategy can protect national sovereignty, the flexibility and independence of Brazil's foreign policy in the utmost way (Flemes, 2010). BRICS is an important practice of the multilateral foreign relations tradition and participation in multilateral cooperation mechanism, which Brazil has always observed. The goal is "not to overthrow the international system, but to push for systematic reform and benefit developing countries," and the "result of collective voice is something member state's individual actions cannot compare to" (de Sá Pimental, 2013). At the same time, as the implementation of strengthening through unity, BRICS is also an important way for Brazil to upgrade its international influence. First, the participation in BRICS can help Brazil expand dimensions of international strategy and increase Brazil's, say in, prominent global affairs and help Brazil receive more attention in international society.

Second, by cooperating with BRICS, it can increase developing countries' recognition of Brazil's international status and sculpt Brazil as a "spokesperson" for developing countries in international multilateral organizations. Again, BRICS is a path that can be chosen by Brazil to realize its international strategic goals. "To have a place in international powerplay is a core goal of Brazil's global strategy" (Lohbauer, 2004). Brazil's former president, Luiz Inácio Lula da Silva even proposed that "Brazil will try to make a UN Security Council that's fitting to reality". From this, we can see that Brazil wants to enter a "power center" of international policymaking system through the way of UN reform. Brazil's comprehensive strength is rather weak among the BRICS, China and Russia are permanent members on the UN Security Council while India and South Africa bear the mission of becoming members, like Brazil. Therefore, if Brazil enhances cooperation with BRICS, it can be in accord with India and South Africa on the issue and can maintain good public relations with China and Russia on the issue. As a result of this, Brazil hopes to keep enhancing the system of the BRICS and gradually form a united economic and political strategy, so that the international society not only can sense a united political determination of BRICS but also turn BRICS into a string of power in global governance. Based on the above analysis, Ruebens Barbosa, Brazil's senior diplomat believes BRICS is more important to Brazil than other member states (de Sá Pimental, 2013).

## Analysis of the Result of Brazil Participating in BRICS Cooperation

As a BRICS member state, Brazil's participation in BRICS cooperation showed its unique characteristics. The evaluation of the effects of Brazil participating in BRICS cooperation is based both in a previous analysis of Brazil's strategic consideration in participation of BRICS cooperation as well as a characteristic analysis of Brazil's push for BRICS cooperation.

First, a good effect in trade is the most obvious result of cooperation between Brazil and BRICS (de Sá Pimental, 2013). The most successful part, or the most obvious part of BRICS, is its economic cooperation. After entering the new century, under the guidance of policies such as South–South cooperation and economic and trade cooperation, the pace of cooperation between Brazil and developing countries pushed rapidly forward. For example, trade scale between Brazil and developing countries increased 570.8% from 2002 to 2013, higher than the trade share between Brazil and developed countries during the same era (215.8%). The trend is especially obvious in the trade relationship between Brazil and BRICS. Brazil's export and import increases from BRICS are exceeding other markets, showing that BRICS is taking a more and more important role in Brazil's foreign trade. According to Brazil's official statistics, from 2002 to 2013, Brazil's trade scale with BRICS increased from 7.64 to 101.02 billion USD in 2013 (about 38.2% of total scale between Brazil and developing countries back in the day). If we start counting from the first BRIC leadership summit in 2009, from 2009 to 2013, Brazil's trade with BRICS increases by 27% annually, higher than the 20.1% annual increase between Brazil and the developing countries. Starting from 2013, Brazil's trade has an overall downward trend. But comparatively speaking, BRICS is still the market group whose trade with Brazil decreased the least. From 2013 to 2016, Brazil's trade with developed countries decreased by a total of 31.7%, trade with developing countries decreased by 33.6%, but trade with BRICS shrank only by 30.5% (Table 1). Furthermore, judging from balance of trade, from 2009 to 2016, Brazil has a trade surplus in its trade with BRICS and is in trade deficit with developing countries at the same time (with the exception of 2016, with 4.14 billion USD trade surplus). Therefore, from a trade perspective, BRICS can not only become

## 86 *Zhou Zhiwei*

Table 1. Changes in Brazil's export share to targeted markets.

| Year | Developed countries | Developing countries | Other BRICS nations |
|------|--------------------|--------------------|--------------------|
| 2009 | −31.3% | −13.8% | 18.8% |
| 2010 | 29.3% | 33.8% | 39.2% |
| 2011 | 28.3% | 25.5% | 34.4% |
| 2012 | −4.6% | −5.9% | −3.2% |
| 2013 | −3.0% | 2.4% | 4.4% |
| 2014 | −5.3% | −8.3% | −6.5% |
| 2015 | −17.8% | −12.3% | −14.7% |
| 2016 | −1.9% | −3.3% | −2.4% |

*Source*: Brazil's Ministry of Industry, Foreign Trade and Services (http://www.mdic.gov.br/).

a "stabilizer" for Brazil's foreign trade but also is a core market for Brazil's trade to earn foreign exchange, playing a key role in balancing its frequent projects. However, Brazil's trade with BRICS mostly concentrates around bilateral trade with China, only having limited trade with other members. In 2016, China's trade with Brazil took up 83.3% of Brazil's total trade with BRICS, China's import from Brazil was 83.7% of Brazil's total export to BRICS countries and Brazil's import from China took up 82.8% of total import from BRICS. Objectively speaking, the deepening of trade between China and Brazil doesn't depend entirely on BRICS mechanism, but on the complementary demand–supply relationship between the two countries. However, BRICS cooperation has provided an advantageous outside environment and corresponding systematic support for deepening of trade between China and Brazil, which especially can be seen with the policy BRICS kept implementing which allows bill settlement in home currency. Just like in trade, BRICS' investment in Brazil is shown collectively from the strong entrance of Chinese investment into Brazil market. This report will not discuss specific situation of China–Brazil investment relationship, but it's worth noting that BRICS' New Development Bank has provided an important financing channel for Brazil. In April 2017, NDB and Brazilian Development Bank (BNDES) signed the first loan contract specifically targeting Brazil, supporting Brazil's renewable energy resources, with a total of 300 million dollars and for a period of 12 years. Besides, NDB also said it will support Brazil's urban construction and participate in its basic infrastructure projects. It can be expected that NDB will be a supplement to Brazil's lack of investment abilities.

Second, BRICS cooperation has opened up a channel for Brazil to participate in global politics and security affairs. Through channels such as leadership summit, minister meetings and conferences of high-level representatives of security affairs, BRICS' consultations and discussions on politics and security have strengthened, extending from terrorism only during the first leadership summit in 2009 to specific topics like UN reform, the situation in Libya, Arab–Israeli conflict, the situation in Syria, Iran's nuclear issue, Afghanistan, humanitarian crisis in South Sudan, the Ukraine crisis, cross-border organized crime, Internet security, pirate issue, drug, situation in Somali and extraterrestrial arms race. Even though BRICS cooperation has mostly focused on trade and economic cooperation and system construction and reform of global financial system between member states in the past 10 years, it has naturally shown rising influence in international politics and security affairs, especially in solving region conflicts. It has become a "soft balance" power that can go against US' unilateral military action to some degree. Brazil has been comparatively cautious in the participation of global politics and security affairs, which is connected to Brazil's own geopolitical environment and positioning of its profits overseas. Therefore, Brazil does not wish to give BRICS more political and security definition. But as BRICS' dialogue channels increase and the area for topics of negotiation widens, Brazil becomes more in accordance with other member states in topics like global politics and security. Even though there are obvious differences, its position clearly draws closer to other member states, a change from a formerly opposing stance to some of the BRICS members.

Third, BRICS cooperation has provided Brazil with "political dividend" and prominently increased its international influence. Brazil's international influence is greatly connected to the expansion and strengthening of BRICS cooperation. Brazil's political circles and academia have even declared that BRICS' appearance is an important example of global system revolution in the past 30 years. For Brazil, it is a perfect case of "global marketing", judging from practical matters, Brazil benefited most from BRICS cooperation (de Sá Pimental, 2013, pp. 347–357). Besides the "economic dividend" mentioned above, the "political dividend" Brazil received from BRICS cooperation can be shown in the following aspects: first, BRICS has become an important platform for Brazil to push forward its goal of becoming a permanent member of the UN Security Council. Concerning this issue, the Brazilian academia had heated debate, the core of which was focused on China's attitude (Zhou, 2014). Right now, Brazil's position in this issue is gradually becoming more national. Even though BRICS is not certain on the number of UN Security Council expansion, the countries have reached a consensus on reform, which is to the benefit of Brazil (de Sá Pimental, 2013, p. 50). In fact, all around reform in UN has always been a key subject at BRICS leadership summits, especially emphasizing on "Brazil, India and South Africa's status in international affairs, supporting their wish to play a bigger role in UN". Therefore, besides the union formed on the issue of becoming permanent members (Japan, Germany, Brazil, India), BRICS has become another platform for Brazil's strategy of becoming a permanent member. Second, BRICS cooperation has promoted Brazil's status in global economic governance. In global economic topics, Brazil's influence is mainly restricted in trade areas. The country actively participated in drafting not only the General Agreement on Tariffs and Trade but also the multilateral negotiations of WTO. But in the core policymaking mechanisms of global finance affairs (especially in the World Bank and IMF), Brazil has played only a peripheral role. After the formation of BRICS, the negotiation efficiency of the five countries has rapidly surpassed G11, which represents developing countries and has quickly come to a decision of registering capital to IMF, which later on pushed through the organization's 2010 quota reform plans (de Sá Pimental, 2013, pp. 467–469). After this round of reform, Brazil's share went up from the 14th to the 10th place, with an increase second only to China (Table 2). Third, being a BRICS country not only promoted Brazil's international status but also intensified international society's recognition of its identity. The development of G20 is strongly correlated to the formation of BRICS. These two important mechanisms gave Brazil's international identity a more accurate positioning. On the one hand, being part of G20 is recognition of Brazil's identity as an emerging economy; on the other hand, being in BRICS shows Brazil's importance as a representative of the emerging economies.

Table 2. Status of IMF share reform (%).

| | Before reform | | | 2008 reform | | | | 2010 reform | | | |
|---|---|---|---|---|---|---|---|---|---|---|---|
| | Share | Right to vote | Ranking | Share | Increase rate | Right to vote | Ranking | Share | Increase rate | Right to vote | Ranking |
| South Africa | 0.859 | 0.854 | 25 | 0.784 | −0.075 | 0.770 | 27 | 0.640 | −0.144 | 0.634 | 34 |
| Brazil | 1.395 | 1.375 | 18 | 1.783 | 0.388 | 1.714 | 14 | 2.316 | 0.533 | 2.218 | 10 |
| China | 3.718 | 3.650 | 6 | 3.996 | 0.278 | 3.806 | 6 | 6.394 | 2.398 | 6.071 | 3 |
| India | 1.911 | 1.886 | 13 | 2.442 | 0.531 | 2.337 | 11 | 2.751 | 0.309 | 2.629 | 8 |
| Russia | 2.732 | 2.690 | 10 | 2.494 | −0.238 | 2.386 | 10 | 2.706 | 0.212 | 2.587 | 9 |
| BRICS | 10.615 | 10.455 | | 11.499 | 0.884 | 11.013 | | 14.807 | 3.308 | 14.139 | |
| Other developing countries | — | — | — | 0.0 | 1.768 | 2.7 | — | 2.8 | 2.7 | 2.6 | — |

*Source*: IMF.

Through BRICS cooperation and "active and confident" diplomatic arrangements, Brazil's importance in global affairs has increased. On the issue of joining the Permanent Members of the United Nations Security Council, Brazil received the support of most developing countries as well as three Big Five members — UK, France and Russia. International society's recognition of Brazil becoming a member has reached a historical high (Zhou, 2012). Besides, in the election of international multilateral organization leader, Brazil received the director-general position of two important organizations: United Nation Food and Agriculture Organization and the World Trade Organization, which is recognition of Brazil's active global participation and rising international influence.

## Conclusion

The BRICS' formation and development have become a political reality, even though it started out as a concept implanted by Goldman & Sachs. But its evolution was based on member states' will to deepen cooperation. Brazil holds an active and participatory attitude toward BRICS cooperation, which originates from its position and is closely related to Brazil's diplomatic arrangement since the new century that prioritizes "South–South Cooperation", as well as the group rising of newcomer states and the transformation of international systems. Brazil's policy goals in BRICS cooperation is based on its consideration of economic development and international participation, which is in high unison with Brazil's foreign policy goals. In this logic, BRICS cooperation is not only an important part of Brazil's international strategy but also the best path for executing international strategies. From the result of participation, it can be seen that Brazil has realized its strategic goals through BRICS cooperation, enhanced trade connections with important newcomer states, achieving "political dividend", and also increased its own international influence and received some recognition in the international society. Because of that, BRICS cooperation can be seen as a multilateral diplomatic practice with high a "cost–benefit ratio" for Brazil.

In 2016, Brazil's government went through an important shift. After Michel Temer came into power, Brazil's foreign policy direction came in the spotlight of the outside world. In fact, on 18 April 2016, the day after the lower house of the Brazil National Congress passed the impeachment of former president Dilma Rousseff with majority votes, Aloysio Nunes, the then president of the Brazil Senate Foreign Relations Committee, went on a state visit to the US. During the visit, he said while being interviewed by BBC that the labor party's foreign policy is based on the judgment that "US is a decaying large country and imperialist country", holding an attitude of proximity toward new groups, and this needs to be changed, the US needs to include Brazil as a partner in free trade negotiations (Fellet, 2016). Judging from this attitude, the adjustment of foreign policy of Temer's government focuses on "balancing between north and south", which differs from the "prioritizing South–South cooperation" policy in the previous Labor Party ruling era. The policy of "improving relations to the US" also became an important incremental option of Temer government's foreign policy. Influenced by the adjustment of policy, South–South cooperation might gradually derail the mainstream of Brazil's foreign policy, and according to the analysis of this chapter's second section, there is a possibility of policy reconstruction in Brazil toward the BRICS cooperation. However, after Trump won the American election, its policy of isolationism and Temer government's demands toward the US are clearly mismatched. So, there is necessity for Brazil to "readjust" its foreign policies. Under such circumstances, the strategic support of BRICS cooperation seems key to Brazil's foreign policy, especially considering how important China is in Brazil's dealing with its economic dilemma. Therefore, it's unlikely that Brazil might turn back on the Labor Government's policies on BRICS cooperation. Furthermore, looking at Brazil's domestic situation, Temer's governance didn't bring Brazil out of a political and economic crisis. Factors such as complicated domestic political struggle, continuous economic setbacks and low public support not only determined the marginal position of foreign relations in government work but also couldn't provide a political environment for reconstructing foreign policy. Because Brazil has already received obvious dividend through BRICS cooperation, and the fact that multilateralism has always been an important tradition in Brazilian foreign relations, Brazil is still continuing the coordination between global governance and newcomer nations. Comparatively speaking, in the unstable situation of Brazil politics, it will be more cautious on policy proposals that promote political

## 92 *Zhou Zhiwei*

and security cooperation among the BRICS and prioritize development and cooperation on trade and investment in BRICS cooperation.

# References

Amorim, C. (2004) "Conceitos e estratégias da diplomacia do Governo Lula", Diplomacia, Estratégia de Política, Out/ Dez 2004, p. 41.

Amorim, C. (2007) Brazil's Multilateral Diplomacy. Remarks at the Second National Conference on Foreign Policy and International Politics, Brazilian Embassy, Washington, 27 November 2007.

Amorim, C. (2008) "Palestra na Reuniao Especial do Fórum Nacional do Instituto Nacional de Altos Estudos (INAE): 'Como ser o melhor dos BRICs'", MRE, 3 de Setembro de 2008.

Amorim, C. (2010) Brazilian foreign policy under president Lula (2003–2010): An overview. *Revista Brasileira de Política Internacional* **53** (Special Edition), p. 215.

Cervo, A. L. (2002) Relacoes internacionais do Brasil: um balanco da era Cardoso. *Revista Brasileira de Política Internacional* **45** (1), p. 7.

de Sá Pimental, J. V. (2013) *Debatendo o BRICS*, Brasília: FUNAG, 2013, pp. 50–53.

de Sá Pimental, J. V. (2013) *O Brasil, os BRICS e a agenda internacional*, Brasília: FUNAG, 2013, 2a edicao, p. 352.

de Sá Pimental, J. V. (2013) *Debatendo o BRICS e a agenda internacional*, Brasília: FUNAG, 2013, 2a edicao, p. 17.

de Souza, A. (2001) *A Agenda Internacional do Brasil: Um Estudo sobre a Comunidade Brasileira de Política Esterna* (Centro Brasileiro de Relações Internacionais) p. 42.

Fellet, J. (2016) Temer pediu ajuda para rebater 'discurso de golpe' no exterior, diz tucano em miss'ao nos EUA, BBC Brasil, 19 de abril (http://www.bbc.com/portuguese/noticias/2016/04/160419_entrevista_aloysio_nunes_jf_ab) (accessed on 27 May 2017).

Flemes, D. (2010) O Brasil na iniciativa BRIC: Soft balancing numa ordem global em mudança? *Revista Brasileira de Política Internacional* **53** (1), p. 148.

Gries, P. H. (2005) China eyes the Hegemon. *Orbis* **49** (3), 401–412.

Guimarses, S. P. (2001) Insercao Internacional do Brasil. *Economia e Sociedade,* **2001** (17), 3–6.

Guimaraes, S. P. (2011) *Brazil's Challenge*, Chen Duqing trans (Contemporary World Press) pp. 179–186.

Pape, R. A. (2005) Soft balancing against the United States. *International Security* **30** (1), 7–45.

Souto, C. V. (2005) *Multilateralismo na Política Externa Brasileira: Um novo Papel no século XXI. Anais Suplementares do XXIII Simpósio Nacional de História*, Universidade de Londrina, 2005, p. 4.

Wei, Z. (2011) Group rise of emerging powers and global governance reform. *International Politics* **2011** (2), 87–98.

Zhang, F. (2014) The development of Brazil's diplomacy. *Latin America's Studies* **2014** (6), 22–29.

Zhou, Z. (2012) *The Rise of Brazil and the World Pattern* (Social Sciences Academic Press), p. 188.

Zhou, Z. (2014) Partnership and competition in Sino-Brazilian relations: A Brazilian perspective. *Journal of Latin America Studies* **2014** (2), 17–23.

# Chapter 9

# Brazil in the BRICS After Davos 2017: Coordinating Development Strategies in a New Epoch

Ana Flávia Barros Platiau

*International Relations Institute, University of Brasilia, Brasilia, Brazil*

Jorge Gomes do Cravo Barros

*Independent Consultant, Brasilia, Brazil*

## Introduction

This chapter departs from the fact that each BRICS member has different development strategies for the group and they have to be coordinated. It focuses on the coordination challenges from two viewpoints: The first one is the empowerment of China since the United States refused to assure leadership in the current global order, increased with the election of Donald Trump. The second one is the Brazilian perspectives for the BRICS. Although the BRICS has evolved significantly since 2006, the main challenge for the group now is to tackle the asymmetry among its members in order to forge a group strategy aiming at responding to key global changes.

## The BRICS in a New Epoch

The BRICS faces a new epoch,[1] after the 2017 World Economic Forum at Davos, since President Donald Trump decided to abandon the leadership of the liberal western order. Accordingly, President Xi Jinping took the opportunity to reaffirm the central role of China as a key promoter of free trade, climate stability and global governance. When we consider recent outcomes from meetings such as the 2017 Davos, the G7 summit in Italy, the 2015 Paris Climate Regime (CoP 21), it is clear that they do need a leader. Likewise, the NAFTA, the Transpacific Trade Partnership (TPP), the Transatlantic Trade and Investments Partnership (TTIP), the support for the UN system and the EU, and last but not least, the North American Asian policy clearly show that multilateral institutions and certainties are more fragile now than they were in 2016.

In this rapidly changing context, although the BRICS changed considerably since 2006, there is still a long list of challenges the group has to adapt to. It is still a loose coalition of countries promoting different diplomatic strategies and seeking for more recognition and voice in the global arenas. But it is only an informal group for consultations and *ad hoc* diplomatic consensus, whose main goal is to assure a "more multipolar world", that is, to reduce the G7's sphere of influence. This means the BRICS no longer aims at only promoting the reform of multilateral institutions, but it has become one of the platforms from which China has to promote its interests globally, although not yet connected to other initiatives like the "new silk road" (OBOR).[2] It is also of paramount importance to mention what the BRICS is not. It neither holds a community of destiny nor holds shared views (Barros-Platiau and Mazzega, 2017; Kalout and Degaut, 2017). It is not a strategic alliance against the West from Russian

---

[1] It could be also argued that the tipping point was the US failure to persuade allies not to join the Asian Infrastructure Investment Bank, for example, see: http://www.johnrosseconomics.com/foreign-policy.html. Accessed on 12 June 2017.

[2] One Belt, One Road, launched by President Xi Jinping at the OBOR Summit in Beijing in May 2017. Shepherd, C. "China's Xi says Belt and Road summit reaches consensus, achieves positive outcomes." Available at: http://www.reuters.com/article/us-china-silkroad-idUSKCN18B11S. Accessed on 12 June 2017. There are also other initiatives that could be tighter to the BRICS agenda, like the maritime initiative or other initiatives related to trade.

initiative and also not an economic bloc that could be comparable to the European Union in the future.

Roughly, since its formal launch in Russia, it may be said that BRICS had three main results, all of them directly related to Beijing. First of all, South Africa became the fifth member, due to Chinese interests of expanding the group to an African key country. Second, the empowerment of China is a long process. In 2008, China's GDP corresponded to less than 50% of the BRICS total GDP. Nowadays, it is close to 70%. Therefore, it can be said that the BRICS is more Chinese-oriented because Beijing has become the only paymaster in the group. At the same time, the BRICS evolved to a more consolidated group, whereas the IBSA[3] vanished away. Third, the New Development Bank (NDB) established in 2014 may be considered a decisive step in the consolidation of BRICS, or at least it brings up new concrete opportunities for that in the near future.

Aiming at discussing the coordination of BRICS development strategies, this chapter will focus on China as the "game changer" (Part 1) and on the Brazilian perspectives for coordination of development strategies. In the Brazilian view, the BRICS is a win–win alternative, since it is an opportunity to enhance cooperation with Russia and Asia, even though there is still a long road ahead (Part 2).

## Part 1 — The Chinese "Leadership of Thought"?

John Ross (2017) wrote that the Chinese development model outperformed the Western ones and therefore, China had the "leadership of thought" as the defender of global rules. Although it is still too early to predict the failure of the "Make America Great Again" (MAGA) strategy and that China is the new hegemon, an increasing number of observers agree that China's diplomatic and trade initiatives have global impacts, including the probable military conflicts (Allison, 2017; French, 2017).

---

[3] India, Brazil and South Africa Forum, created in 2003 after a Brazilian initiative. Its last summit was held in Pretoria, 2011. http://www.itamaraty.gov.br/pt-BR/politica-externa/mecanismos-inter-regionais/3673-forum-dedialogo-india-brasil-e-africa-do-sul-ibas. Accessed on 12 June 2017.

The Chinese empowerment has two main roots: The first one is obviously the Chinese economic success in the last 30 years, although its economic growth was around 6.5% in 2017. Along with these results, Chinese insertion in global order may be considered the most important for recent history. Not only did China join the most central multilateral organizations from the trade sector to Antarctica but also Beijing ratified the key multilateral treaties under the United Nations' auspices and others, notably the World Trade Organization treaty in 2001.[4]

In terms of long-standing development based on infrastructure, the Chinese One Belt One Road Strategy (OBOR) and the maritime strategy are considered as important as the Marshall Plan was for the European reconstruction after the Second World War. Obviously, their context and scopes are very different, but they are "big plans" that bring significant changes to the global routine. While Beijing published a 50 billion US dollars budget plan, some observers mentioned investments could be five times higher, around 250 billion dollars. In this sense, OBOR is so ambitious that it has enhanced diplomatic sensitivities of other BRICS members, notably Russia and India — Russia, because its sphere of influence is already attracted to the Chinese influence; India, because Chinese investments in Pakistan and neighboring countries will encircle India, not to mention their competing interests in Africa.

Brazil and South Africa were left out of OBOR for the time being, since Beijing's plan is to foster connectivity in five different aspects: political, economic, trade, infrastructure and people. But this does not mean investments are lacking in Brazil or in Africa. In the Brazilian case, since 2009 China is the first trade partner and currently one of the most motivated investor in strategic sectors such as infrastructure, logistics, energy, oil and banking (Ramos-Becard, 2017). Furthermore, the biggest infrastructure project currently under discussion is the bioceanic railway, across Brazil and Peru. For Africa, Chinese investments have been

---

[4] However, the EU and the USA did not grant China the market economy status yet, so Beijing took them to the WTO dispute mechanism. Hornby, L.; Donnan, S.; Toplensky, R. "Beijing's ire over WTO status mars unity with EU on climate". *Financial Times*, 12 June 2017. Available at: https://www.ft.com/content/bdd7da32-4e53-11e7-bfb8997009366969. Accessed on 17 June 2017.

growing rapidly and correspond to almost 15% of all foreign investments (Pilling, 2017). For instance, Egypt, Algeria and Nigeria are the top destinations for Chinese investments from 2003 to 2017, summing up to 35 billion USD (Pilling, 2017). Ethiopia and Kenya have inaugurated expensive Chinese-built railways recently. Also in the trade agenda, the fact that President Donald Trump withdrew from the TPP opens up a new opportunity for China. In this vein, China has shown a remarkable "adaptative diplomacy", that is, an excellent diplomatic skill to respond quickly to opportunities created by big changes in the international chessboard. It remains to be seen if Beijing will be accepted in a pact it did not contribute to negotiate, but all the possibilities are on the table now, even a possible comeback from the USA in case President Trump loses his mandate soon. In the meantime, the ASEAN and the Regional Comprehensive Economic Partnership (RCEP) are trying to adapt to the new scenario.

Another big issue is climate change. Since 1992, multilateral negotiations were polarized in terms of common but differentiated responsibilities. After a fragile accord in 2009, countries achieved the 2015 Paris Agreement, from which President Trump also pulled the United States out, another "vacuum of leadership" China took benefit from in a matter of hours, since China signed a joint declaration with the Europeans to "save" the climate regime from the North American negative impacts (Jansson, 2017).

In terms of services, technology and innovation, it is key to avoid the theoretical distinction between hard and soft power.[5] Also, cooperation among BRICS countries bilaterally is much bigger and older than in the group level. Therefore, this could lead to a more focused group agenda in the short term. China and Brazil cooperate on satellites since 1988.[6] China and Russia work commercial flights aircrafts and China works with India for high-speed railway to mention only three cases. India is considered the "world office" and is expanding its services toward the East, at an annual

---

[5]Available at: http://www.chinausfocus.com/foreign-policy/latin-america-is-the-latest-focus-of-chinas-major power-diplomacy. Accessed on 17 June 2017.
[6]Available at: http://www.cbers.inpe.br/sobre_satelite/historico.php. Accessed on 12 June 2017.

national economic growth of around 7%. Many western brands are facing competition with young Chinese ones, like Weixin and Tencent, and also Taobao, Alibaba, Didi Chuxing and 99, to mention a few.

Moreover, in the human and cultural exchanges agenda, China expanded its networks of Confucius Institutes and centers around the world. They are already comparable to other "cultural" initiatives from the US, France, Germany and Spain. In Brazil, there are currently nine Confucius Institutes. Although they are less in number in relation to other European cultural centers, they are based on the campuses of the top universities. In the academic set, China has imposed the Shanghai Jiatong Universities Ranking as the most respectful globally, and the country has also proved the fastest improvement in university quality, to such an extent that China is no longer comparable to the other BRICS members' universities.

Furthermore, last century the USA launched the "American Dream" in order to create convergent expectations around the world of the benefits the *pax americana* could assure. Likewise, President Xi Jinping created the "Chinese Dream" with the same aims of convincing the world about the peaceful rise of China, inextricably linked to the OBOR.

In short, China is taking the global lead in many aspects, as shown in Table 1. Until last year, there was a vast consensus on the US–China talks as the new axis of global entente. Many observers even mentioned a "would-be G2". This meant the materialization of the power shift to Asia since Europe lost a lot of power due to the severe institutional crisis since 2008. But after President Trump's decisions to quit multilateral arrangements and trade partnerships, there is a growing "vacuum of

Table 1.   Chinese partners.

| Leadership | Agenda |
| --- | --- |
| China–EU | Energy, climate and environmental issues |
| China–Russia | Security |
| China–India | Services |
| Chinese-led coalition | OBOR and maritime strategy |
| BRICS | G20, trade and parallel order |

*Brazil in the BRICS After Davos 2017* **101**

leadership". In fact, the traditional Euro–Atlantic axis seems to be too fragile now and hence a new one could emerge. It could be a Chinese-led coalition, a China–EU axis, a China–Russia or a China–India one. The axis depends on the agenda. Whatever the axis, China is part of it. As a consequence, President Xi Jinping launched the Chinese "leadership of thought".

President Xi states that the Western liberal order failed since the 2008 crisis and President Trump is the result of that. So are populism and the BREXIT. The industrialized nations are no longer able to provide the public goods they promised to deliver with the multilateral institutions they dominate: world peace and security, food security, climate stability (Prantl, 2014). Not to mention prosperity, justice, equality and dignity for all. The context has changed to such a point that the West needs the East to improve living standards for all. This implies negotiating new trade rules and delegating new roles for rising powers like China and India.

The second root of Chinese empowerment is the progressive construction of what Oliver Stuenkel[7] (2015, 2016, 2017) has called a "parallel order" when he mentions how new institutions are being created in parallel to existing ones. However, it may be argued that it is not a parallel order because parallel lines never touch, and this is not the case. Rather, the new institutions are still embedded in the old order, but they are competing with existing ones.[8] This is the point in which Beijing does need the BRICS. Indeed, the Western liberal order has been showing evident signs of weakness in terms of its capacity of delivering public goods (Prantl, 2014). The security agenda is the most emblematic case, in which peace and security in Syria and neighboring countries are the public goods the Euro–Atlantic leaders failed to deliver. The same may be said about climate stability and the global development agenda if we consider the 2015 Paris Agreement and the sustainable development goals (SDGs) are only diplomatic promises still deprived of a strong political leadership.

---

[7]"O Brasil, o BRICS e a Agenda Internacional" ("Brazil, the BRICS and the International Agenda"). Fourth Roundtable on BRICS, 18 May 2017. Ministry of Foreign Affairs (Itamaraty) and FUNAG, Brasilia, Brazil. Available at: https://www.youtube.com/watch?v=esUCnPZhiQk&t=14563s. Accessed on 17 June 2017.

[8]I am grateful to Dr. Jochen Prantl from the Australian National University for this comment.

Furthermore, the economic, trade and financial global governance failed to open up to emerging economies and it is currently paying the high price of Washington's disengagement after President Obama's end of term and the BREXIT in 2016.

In this context of sluggish reforms of western multilateral institutions, it is impressive to assess how "the power shift to Asia" has materialized in institutions comparable to the ones already existing in the United Nations system and outside. Thus, their main characteristic is that they are small, intercontinental and progressively led by Beijing. This implies that numerous countries have been left behind, notably the least developed ones. However, in terms of legitimacy, this issue must be taken from the fact that together the BRICS countries include almost half of the human population, bearing the highest percentage of those living close to the poverty line. In other words, there are more poor people in BRICS than outside the group. In diplomatic terms, this is already a huge challenge to the UN system, since no one can claim the institutions representing half of the world's population in four continents are not legitimate.

BRICS, compared to the G7 in terms of global governance, aims to shape the 21st century development pathways and other public goods. The NDB and the Asian Infrastructure Investment Bank (AIIB) are unarguably competing directly with the World Bank (WB) and the International Monetary Fund (IMF). They are also not confronting with these long set institutions, but rather claiming their right to promote a Southern-oriented agenda.

Although security and geopolitics are much more complex, it can be argued that the Shanghai Cooperation Organization (SCO) is evolving to something with comparable vocation to the North Atlantic Treaty Organization (NATO). Concerning the security and foreign policy agenda, President Xi Jinping promoted significant institutional changes (Cabestan, 2017). The fact that India recently joined the SCO is key because the United States and Japan are also New Delhi's strategic partners. Cybersecurity, nuclear proliferation, peace talks, Asian geopolitics, sea disputes, terrorism and conflicts management will probably receive a different treatment in the near future.

In sum, the BRICS agenda is likely to be more and more influenced by Beijing's aspirations. Therefore, the other members will have to cope

## Part 2 — Coordinating BRICS Development Strategies from a Brazilian Perspective

with the growing power asymmetry inside the group and its impacts. Beijing's task to coordinate strategies inside the BRICS in Xiamen in 2017 is therefore much harder than it was in 2011.

For the 21st Century, Brazil has two main ambitions: promoting the reform of the UN system and boosting the South–South cooperation agenda. It has at least four main axes of foreign policy: regional integration, trade expansion, UN Security Council reform and the BRICS. But none of them were really successful and Brazil did not manage well to shape its own "grand strategy" (Barros-Platiau and Barros, 2016; Kalout and Degaut, 2017).

Before discussing diplomatic strategies, the main question is what does BRICS mean for Brazil? When it was proposed to Brazil, under President Lula and Foreign Affairs Minister Celso Amorim, the BRIC corresponded to the Brazilian paradigm of a more "active and autonomous diplomacy" (Amorim, 2015). This meant Brazil intended to seek for multilateralism that would accommodate a new multipolarity in the name of rising powers. When President Dilma Rousseff succeeded Lula in 2010, she did not carry on the same diplomatic ambitions. On the contrary, her mandate is considered the turning point where Brazil disengaged from all its diplomatic ambitions (Cervo and Lessa, 2014). In May 2016, President Dilma Rousseff was impeached and her Vice-President Michel Temer replaced her. However, the Brazilian foreign policy did not regain momentum since Brasilia had to focus on domestic crisis and economic breakdowns, not to mention unprecedented corruption probes involving the three presidents mentioned above.

In this vein, the IBSA died, the BRICS was left aside and the public authorities are split about Mercosul. Some propose Brazil should leave the regional bloc and try to join a more results-oriented trade partnership, following Chile's profile. Others say the Mercosul will not be a free trade area, but it could enhance market facilitation mechanisms in the short term. But the more conservative authorities still believe the Mercosul has a promising future and that the agreement with the European Union became a reality by the end of 2017. As a result, the BRICS is the only strong group Brazil is part of.

As paradoxal as it may seem, Brazil is very cautious about the BRICS agenda. The BRICS will remain just a mechanism for dialogue, not a political coordination group. Therefore, Ambassador Marcos Caramuru de Paiva stated in May 2017 that the BRICS agenda should be restrained and focus on points they already share a view.[9] This seems to be the mainstream opinion in the Brazilian government for now, in the sense that the diplomatic strategy would be to share views, then set the priorities and finally agree on the necessary instruments to achieve the common goals.

The challenges and opportunities for Brazil will therefore remain limited concerning the BRICS (Degaut, 2015). In other words, Brazil needs less the BRICS than the NDB and bilateral partnerships to intensify foreign investment flows. The diplomatic agenda is much less preoccupied with strategic issues, except for nuclear disarmament as mentioned before, than with economic and trade *enjeux*. In other words, Brazil does not have a "grand strategy" nor what Goh and Prantl (2017) call a "strategic diplomacy" for the BRICS (Kalout and Degaut, 2017).

Considered as a hostage of its economic and political fragilities, Brazil may have a very precautious development strategy for the BRICS, described in three points: First of all, no expansion of the group would be welcome, even less for countries that are clearly opposed to the Western order, like Indonesia, Iran, Turkey or Egypt. In fact, different from all the other BRICS members, Brazil considers itself a western country and an unhesitating promoter of the UN multilateral order and law. Second, in relation to the BRICS agenda, Brazil would agree more with broad development issues and financing focused on the South than with geopolitical issues, be it Syria, Ukraine, North Korea or cybersecurity. In terms of agenda expansion, Brazil prefers agribusiness and energy to other issues.

---

[9] He is the Brazilian Ambassador to China. "O Brasil, o BRICS e a Agenda Internacional" ("Brazil, the BRICS and the International Agenda"). Fourth Roundtable on BRICS, 18 May 2017. Ministry of Foreign Affairs (Itamaraty) and FUNAG, Brasilia, Brazil. Available at: https://www.youtube.com/watch?v=esUCnPZhiQk&t=14563s. Accessed on 17 June 2017.

Finally, Brasilia, like Pretoria, does not seem to be ready for a deeper institutionalization of the BRICS. Matters such as the creation of a secretariat, more rules and loyalty are not part of the Brazilian development view for the BRICS.

In other words, for Brazil the BRICS is a priority as long as it assures foreign direct investment in the short term. This means Brazil is also looking forward to improving its relations with the Europeans and the Japanese, and even the USA and Canada, expanding diplomatic talks to the so-called "traditional partners". Brasilia is also planning to join the OECD in the near future. In this context of global and national uncertainties, Brazil cannot afford to take risks in the name of a more democratic global governance or more geopolitical prestige. So, the foreign policy has only one aim, that is, demonstrating that the political and institutional crisis is over and that Brazil is a perfect country to invest in.[10]

This explains, to a large extent, the Brazilian diplomatic low profile in other issues related to the UN reform and the current security agenda. The two main exceptions are the Brazilian support for the French initiative "responsibility not to *veto*" and to the "total ban on nuclear weapons" UN campaign. In fact, given the end of the commodities super cycle, the Brazilian diplomatic discourse no longer diverges substantially from its ongoing national reality and constraints. This also means that if President Michel Temer achieves to stay in office until the end of his mandate in December 2018, little may be changed in relation to the BRICS. Finally, the Brazilian economy is deeply dependent on the Chinese one.

What would be the BRICS main challenge? Undoubtedly, its coordination and expansion. So far, the group has had a hard time discussing time and again case-by-case issues, without managing to have neither a shared view nor a clear basic strategy. However, the group was not designed to be a coordination structure. It was only designed to be a consultation mechanism and, as far as possible, a consensus-building mechanism. As a result, confidence-building and sharing views are two necessary efforts for the group to evolve more rapidly. In this sense, coordination is

---

[10]Temer, M. O Brasil na Rússia e na Noruega. *O Estado de S.o Paulo Newspaper*, June 17, 2017. Available at: http://opiniao.estadao.com.br/noticias/geral,o-brasil-na-russia-e-na-noruega,70001843448. Accessed on 18 June 2017.

## 106 Ana Flávia Barros Platiau & Jorge Gomes do Cravo Barros

more a diplomatic ideal for those in favor of a strong BRICS than a reality in terms of diplomatic pragmatism. The BRICS has certainly reinforced processes in terms of agenda-setting, ministerial meetings and consultations, agendas ranging from trade defense measures harmonization to universities networks, and some opening was promoted since the adoption of the Durban outreach mechanism. Certainly, the 2017 summit in Xiamen will focus on pragmatic cooperation and South–South dialogue,[11]but Brazil is expecting a focus on shared views, means and tools to achieve the BRICS goals.

## Conclusions

There seem to be two opposed views about what the BRICS represents now. Some analysts defend the BRICS should play a central role for all five members. The reason for this is two-fold. First of all, China and India showed vigorous growth of around 6.5% and 7%, respectively. The BRICS was created in terms of diplomatic interest in gaining voice to promote international organization reforms, starting with the IMF, while now the BRICS has a new agenda of institutions building. The South African membership may be considered the beginning of this new turn, but the most important is undoubtedly the creation of the NDB and its initial focus on energy projects.

On the contrary, more realistic analysts prefer to pin down the limits the BRICS faces currently. First of all, BRICS is not a priority for all its members. For China, the BRICS is an interesting tool to have diplomatic voice in coordination with other big countries around the globe. For Russia, it is an opportunity to belong to a group free from the western jug. For India and Brazil, they are empowered with a low cost of commitment. For South Africa, it is the opportunity to participate in the international

---

[11]Ambassador Li Jinzhang. "O Brasil, o BRICS e a Agenda Internacional" ("Brazil, the BRICS and the International Agenda"). Fourth Roundtable on BRICS, 18 May 2017. Ministry of Foreign Affairs (Itamaraty) and FUNAG, Brasilia, Brazil. Available at: https://www.youtube.com/watch?v=esUCnPZhiQk&t=14563s. Also: http://riodejaneiro.china-consulate.org/pot/bxyw/t1462789.htm. Accessed on 17 June 2017.

system as an African leadership. But the BRICS evolved and so did the global order, accommodating China's role as the "game changer".

However, for Brazil the BRICS represents both an opportunity and a big challenge in terms of asymmetry, identity and commitment. Brazil's perception is that the BRICS must not become an anti-western coalition nor prevent it from joining the OECD or reinforcing the Mercosul. China and India are eager to maintain their growth rates and to impose more competition against traditional powers in Eurasia, Africa and Latin America. Russia and the others smaller BRICS members are interested in reinforcing intra-BRICS flows of investments and trade. Finally, security is the most complex agenda, since Brazil does not have threats at its borders, but China, India and Russia are themselves threats to each other.

In terms of development strategies for the BRICS, Brasilia is not in favor of an expansion in the coming years to countries like Iran, Indonesia, Turkey and others, while some Chinese and Russian observers believe a Muslim country could bring more legitimacy to the BRICS. Brasilia is not officially promoting the development of the agenda to other issues for which they still need to build shared views and prefers to focus on investment and trade, or on topics they have already started to work on. Finally, Brasilia needs more time before investing in the BRICS formalization. These three issues were key for the 2017 summit coordination agenda.

# References

Allison, G. (2017) *Destined for War: Can America and China Escape Thucydides' Trap?* (Houghton Mifflin Harcourt Books), 364 p. ISBN 9780544935273.

Amorim, C. (2015) *Teerã, Ramalá e Doha: memórias da política externa ativa e altiva* (Editora Benvirá, Brazil).

Barros-Platiau, A. F. and Barros, J. C. (2016) Is Brazil still in the BRICS and IBSA? A multidimensional assessment. The dragon and the elephant meet the jaguars: China and India in Latin America International seminar, October 6 and 7. IRI Instituto de Rela..es Internacionai. BRICS Policy Center, PUC Rio University, Brazil, 2016.

Barros-Platiau, A. F. and Mazzega, P. (2017) *Strange bedfellows? la circulation artificielle des valeurs et des principes d'action intra-BRICS dans la gouvernance climatique globale* (2009–2016). Submitted.

108 *Ana Flávia Barros Platiau & Jorge Gomes do Cravo Barros*

Cabestan, J. P. (2017) China's Institutional Changes in the Foreign and Security Policy Realm Under Xi Jinping: Power Concentration vs. Fragmentation Without Institutionalization. East Asia Forum, DOI 10.1007/s12140-017-9271-4.

Cervo, A. and Lessa, A. (2014) *O declínio: inserção internacional do Brasil (2011–2014)*. *Revista Brasileira de Política Internacional* **57** (2), 133–151.

Degaut, M. (2015) Do the BRICS still matter? Center for Strategic and International Studies (CIS). Washington, DC. Available at: https://www.csis.org/analysis/do-brics-still matter. Accessed on 17 June 2017. SOKO.indd 89 2017/8/18 14:51:04

French, H. (2017) *Everything Under the Heavens: How the Past Helps Shape China's Push for Global Powe*r (Alfred A. Knopf), 330 p. ASIN: B01HA4JUKE.

Goh, E. and Prantl, J. (2017) Why strategic diplomacy matters for Southeast Asia. *East Asia Forum Quarterly* April–June, 36–39.

Jansson, A. (2017) Analysis of Europe: MAGA is MEGA. Available at: https://www.linkedin.com/pulse/analysiseurope-maga-mega-alexander-jansson. Accessed on 12 June 2017.

Kalout, H. and Degaut, M. (2017) *Brasil: um país em busca de uma grande estratégia. Relatório de conjuntura n.01. Secretaria de Assuntos Estratégicos da Presidência da República* (Strategic Affairs Secretariat to the President). Brasilia, Brazil.

Prantl, J. (2014) Taming hegemony: Informal institutions and the challenge to western liberal order. *Chinese Journal of International Politics* **7** (4), 449–482. DOI: https://doi. org/10.1093/cjip/pou036.

Pilling, D. (2017) Chinese investments in Africa: Beijing's testing ground. *Financial Times*, 14 June 2017.

Ramos-Becard, D. (2017) *China y Brasil: .modelo de relaciones Sur-Sur?* In Pastrana, E. and Gehring, H. *La proyección de China en América Latina y el Caribe* (Editorial Pontificia Universidad Javeriana, Bogotá), Fundación Konrad Adenauer, ISBN: 978-958-781-087-5.

Ross, J. (2017) *Semanas que valem por décadas. A lideran.a do pensamento global passa dos Estados Unidos para a China em Davos. China Hoje, Edi..o Brasileira de China Today.* **2** (12), 16–19.

Stuenkel, O. (2015) *The BRICS and the Future of Global Order* (Lexington Books), ISBN 13: 978-1498512749.

Stuenkel, O. (2016) *Post-Western World: How Emerging Powers are Remaking Global Order* (Polity).

# Chapter 10

# Balance of Power and International Trade: The Perception of the Brazilian Public Opinion about China and BRICS

Amancio Jorge de Oliveira and Janina Onuki

*Institute of International Relations, University of São Paulo (USP), Brazil*

## Introduction

The risk of "dependence" has been a very systematic and recurring problem, as appointed by the diplomacy and the Brazilian international relations community as justification for the refusal of any trade agreement with the US. Refractoriness is greater when it comes to a bilateral agreement between Brazil and the US and will diminish as the potential for agreement becomes, frankly, more multilateral. By order of magnitude, difficulties decrease according to a ranking ranging from bilateral, like the four plus one (Mercosur and the US), to hemispheric and multilateral as is the case of the WTO agreement.

Based on this argument, Brazil has, in all instances, not just regions seeking to establish containment coalitions whose ultimate goal is to increase bargaining power with the great powers, particularly with the United States, but its position, and that of other non-hegemonies, as a strategy of soft balancing, or measures aimed to appear as a counterweight to US hegemony. China and BRICS are part of the soft balancing in Brazilian perceptions, as we try to demonstrate in this chapter.

It is possible, but not entirely reasonable, to limit the notion of dependence merely to an economic dimension. In fact, in line with concerns about dependency, issues arise regarding the risk of deindustrialization and displacement of the workforce. There are, however, in discourse and practice, indications that, in this type of argument, there are components related to the size of relative power in the international system.

The objective of this work is to precisely explore the extent to which the idea of balance of power is linked to people's preferences with regard to international trade. In general, it is aimed at understanding to what extent notions such as hegemony and concentration of power affect people's perception in relation to international trade.

More recurrently, preferences in international trade are derived from generated interests based on the relative position of factor endowments in international trade. The argument is valid for governments or for work, according to the idea of endogenous formation of trade preference.

If the argument of endogenous factors is valid, there is no reason for there to be trade preferences in relation to specific countries *per se*, but the types of countries with regard to the economic complementarily and comparative advantages of international trade. If country A or B has the domestic economic structure, there is no reason to have a preference for A or B.

This leads us to consider that there are other factors that determine the position of countries in trade beyond economic factors. Among these factors is the idea of balance of power.

The link between international trade and power, however, is little explored in the literature. Generally, this link is brought up to explain decisions at the government level. In this sense, theoretical rational is based on the assumption that countries are less sensitive to the issue of relative gains when dealing with multilateral environments (Grieco, 1988). By inverse reasoning, countries are more sensitive to bilateral agreements when marked by asymmetric contexts, as in the case of Brazil and the US.

This chapter is based on a premise similar to that put forward by this literature, and takes as the explanatory element for trade preference the issue of relative gains. It seeks, however, to contribute in diminishing two gaps in the literature of this analytical approach.

First is the fact that the literature on relative gains is eminently theoretical. There has been no empirical work done to examine how the notion, expressed or implied, of relative gains determines or at least influences preference regarding trade.

The second point has to do with the fact that the notion of relative gains is considered specifically for the executive level. It is reasonable that it be this way, given that the decision maker of last resort, with the technical resources to measure the expected utility of decision-making, is the executive. There is no discussion aimed at understanding the extent to which public opinion is influenced by similar questions in the formation of their preferences in the area of international trade.

## Objectives and Methods

The aim of this chapter is to examine the relationship between perception of world power and preferences in international trade. More specifically, its purpose is to examine how the perception of Brazilian public opinion about China as a US challenger for world power affects, or is related to, attitudes in the liberalist and protectionist continuum.

The hypothesis is that this empirical study tends to support the argument about what provides propensity for asymmetric agreements and multilateralism. Based on this theoretical argument, our specific hypothesis is that people, refractory to liberalism (protectionists), tend to view with favor the emergence of China as an actor capable of reducing the relative power of the US in the world.

As a liberalism indicator, the dependent variable of the model was the question about tariff barriers. The question inquired whether the respondent agreed or not that Brazil should reduce tariff barriers for foreign products. A set of variables about the perception of China's emergence as a world power was taken as the independent variables.

The data used in this chapter are from the survey research — The Americas and the World. It is an ongoing research project that aims to study public opinion and political culture in the Americas on key issues in foreign policy and international relations. The project consists of a biennial survey administered in different countries in Latin America to gather basic information with respect to the opinions, attitudes, beliefs, interests, aspirations and values of their citizens in a global context. The survey is carried out every 2 years with representative samples of the national population in various countries throughout the region.[1]

The Brazilian survey research was based on face-to-face interviews with 2,000 people in Brazil. The sample is a representative at the national level, and was distributed throughout the major regions of the country. The questionnaire contained, in addition to demographic questions, 54 substantive questions.

## Relative Gains and International Trade

The notion of relative gains is essential, in the realist understanding of international processes, for explaining why states may resist cooperating even in a situation of mutual gains. Apart from the concern about absolute gains in bargaining processes, states are concerned, according to this analytical viewpoint, with the idea of balance of power, and hence why the prerequisite for cooperation is the maintenance or expansion of relative power gains.

The argument of relative gains seeks to counteract the assumption that international institutions induce, or serve as incentives for international cooperation. If both countries are oriented to a relative gains game type, the only possibility of cooperation will be with integrative bargaining in which the proportionality of gains between the participants is maintained.

Duncan Snidal (1991a) introduced a qualifying element in the relationship between relative gains and propensity to cooperate. In his view, the players are no longer sensitive to relative gains when it comes to a bilateral dynamic. Its increase in this model resides with the idea that the increase in the number of actors in the process dramatically reduces the impact of relative gains as a negative inducing factor to cooperation.

---

[1] The complete information and disaggregated data on the questions included in the surveys and the five data bases for these countries, in SPSS format, may be consulted free of charge at http://mexicoyelmundo.cide.edu.

Commentators of Snidal (Grieco, 1993; Morrow, 1997; Powell, 1991; Suzuki, 2004) drew attention to the fact that Snidal's analysis loses perspective of at least two central elements. The first has to do with the different uses countries make of surplus gains from cooperation, even when balanced. A country can efficiently transform economic surpluses into surplus power. The second point has to do with the fact that the negotiations even though instructed by relative gains can be unlocked based on side-payments.

It is precisely this qualifying effect, suggested by Snidal (1991a) which incites the debate on the role of emerging powers in the international system and how this emergence impacts perception of international trade with Brazil. The emergence of China as a new power represents, in practice, an element of counterweight to US hegemony in the Brazilian's view.

Opinions in this regard are polarized. One portion of the public welcomes the fact that China has the conditions to fulfill the role of counterweight. Others think that China introduces to the system more elements of risk than earnings. For the magnate, a China Power introduces an economic and political alternative, which allows for the reduction of dependence on the US economy.

What interests us here is to know how one's view regarding China's emergence as a world power impacts one's view of international trade. In theory, as previously mentioned, there is no reason to believe that the dimensions of commerce and power are highly correlated. In fact, an opinion about trade should be determined by matters of economic costs and benefits. Let's look at the results of this relationship between trade and power.

# Results

Parallel to the examination of the specific weight of China's counterweight to the US on the global scale, we observed the weight of the ideology between the left and the right regarding trade preference. To this end, we used two explanatory variables: political parties and political ideological spectrum on a scale ranging from 1 to 10, 1 being the leftmost and 10 rightmost.

In the case of political parties, the respondents were asked which party they considered themselves usual supporters of, regardless of the

**114**  *Amancio Jorge de Oliveira & Janina Onuki*

party they had voted for in the last elections. Only the most relevant parties of Brazil were listed (PT, PSDB, PT, PV).

The variable on the political spectrum was used in three different formats: The first was the original format, i.e. broken down into a scale of 10 levels. The second format was joined at two levels: at levels 1–5 of the left group and 6–10 in right group. The cut separated two groups of approximately 50% each. The third was by dividing respondents into those from the center and those respondents representative of the extremes of the spectrum.

None of these political variables, be it the political parties or the political spectrum, appear to be associated with individuals' preferences in terms of international trade. At least in the Brazilian case, the thesis that argues that left-wing voters are more likely to be protectionist, as well as the right are more liberal, does not hold.

The picture changes entirely when the independent variables change from being political variables and become variables related to the theme of world power. To capture this dimension, two independent variables were considered: The first was people's perception about the possibility of China becoming a world power. The second, the possibility that China will grow until it becomes as big as the US.

As seen in Table 1, there is a positive correlation between agreeing with economic openness of the Brazilian economy and considering the emergence of China as a threat. In the same way, there is a positive association between disagreeing with greater openness of the Brazilian economy and considering China's emergence as a world power a non-threatening event. As such, there is a positive relationship between liberalism and anti-China power attitudes and a positive relationship between protectionism and pro-China power attitudes. The association between variables is positive with a $p$-value of 0.000.

The intersection shown in Table 2 is even more explicit about the idea of China presenting itself as a counterweight to the US on the global plain. The question asked for the perception about the possibility of China's growing to be the same size as the US. Again here, the relationship between protectionism and an optimistic position regarding China's global ascension is highlighted. The association is less intense than the

*Balance of Power and International Trade* **115**

Table 1. China as world power.

| | | Grave threat | Important threat, but not grave | Little important threat | Not a threat | Total |
|---|---|---|---|---|---|---|
| | Strongly agree | 184 | 112 | 85 | 62 | 443 |
| | | 32.6% | 22.3% | 23.1% | 23.8% | 26.1% |
| | | 36.7 | −19.4 | −11.1 | −6.2 | |
| | Agree | 233 | 245 | 166 | 87 | 731 |
| | | 41.3% | 48.7% | 45.1% | 33.3% | 43.1% |
| | | −10.1 | 28.2 | 7.4 | −25.5 | |
| Openness | Disagree | 82 | 84 | 59 | 43 | 268 |
| | | 14.5% | 16.7% | 16.0% | 16.5% | 15.8% |
| | | −7.1 | 4.5 | .8 | 1.8 | |
| | Strongly disagree | 65 | 62 | 58 | 69 | 254 |
| | | 11.5% | 12.3% | 15.8% | 26.4% | 15.0% |
| | | −19.5 | −13.3 | 2.9 | 29.9 | |
| Total | | 564 | 503 | 368 | 261 | 1696 |
| | | 100.0% | 100.0% | 100.0% | 100.0% | 100.0% |

*Notes*: Chi-square = 54.848, $p = 0.000$.

emergence of China as a world power, but it is still significant ($p$-value = 0.05).

With reference to Table 2, the questions addressed are as follows: "would you agree or not if Brazil reduces its barriers for entry of foreign products?"; "in your opinion, if China's economy grows to be as big as the US, do you think that this would be a positive or negative factor for the world?"

As seen in Tables 1 and 2, both variables show a clear association between trade preference and the perception of global power dispersion. The chi-square is less than 5% in both cases.

The tables show, moreover, that there is an association between trade preferences and the type of perception about China's rising power. The group of people who disagree with trade openness (protectionist) tends to take a positive view of China's emergence as a new world power.

#### 116 *Amancio Jorge de Oliveira & Janina Onuki*

Table 2. China's growth.

| | | Negative | Positive | Equally positive or negative | Total |
|---|---|---|---|---|---|
| Openness | Strongly agree | 141 | 250 | 43 | 434 |
| | | 29.2% | 25.2% | 20.7% | 25.8% |
| | | 16.4 | −5.8 | −10.6 | |
| | Agree | 213 | 424 | 93 | 730 |
| | | 44.1% | 42.7% | 44.7% | 43.4% |
| | | 3.5 | −6.3 | 2.8 | |
| | Disagree | 64 | 163 | 45 | 272 |
| | | 13.3% | 16.4% | 21.6% | 16.2% |
| | | −14.1 | 2.7 | 11.4 | |
| | Strongly disagree | 65 | 125 | 27 | 247 |
| | | 13.5% | 15.6% | 13.0% | 14.7% |
| | | −5.9 | 9.4 | −3.5 | |
| Total | | 483 | 992 | 208 | 1683 |
| | | 100.0% | 100.0% | 100.0% | 100.0% |

*Notes*: Chi-square = 12,586; $p$ = 0,05.

The opposing group, composed of people who agree with more open trade (liberals), tend to see China's emergence as a world power as more of a risk rather than a benefit.

## Perceptions About BRICS

Beyond isolated emerging powers, as the case of China mentioned in the previous section, international alliances and coalitions are often indicated as tools for balancing power against US. Several international coalitions have been potentially playing this role in the Brazilian foreign policy perspective.

Taking this information into consideration, the new wave of survey conducted by Institute of International Relations in 2014 included one question specifically to measure perceptions of public opinion about the BRICS

*Balance of Power and International Trade* **117**

Table 3. Confidence in BRICS as a counterweight against traditional potential power.

| Political orientation | Balance | Embarrassing | Total (100%) |
| --- | --- | --- | --- |
| | 262 | 272 | |
| Left | 49.1% | 50.9% | 534 |
| | −1.0 | 1.1 | |
| | 173 | 130 | |
| Center | 57.1% | 42.9% | 303 |
| | 1.2 | −1.2 | |
| | 214 | 192 | |
| Right | 52.7% | 47.3% | 406 |
| | .1 | −.1 | |
| Total (100%) | 649 | 594 | 1243 |
| | 52.2% | 47.8% | |

*Notes*: Chi-square = 5.058, $p$ = 0.08.

as counterweight of traditional powers. The respondents were asked to choose one of the two following options: (1) "the BRICS are an embarrassing alliance with authoritarian countries or who have high social exclusion" or (2) "the BRICS are a force capable of balancing world power against the traditional powers". No intermediate options were included.

As it is seen Table 3, perceptions were relatively well-balanced. About 52% of respondents, which forms 1243 in total, expressed confidence in BRICS as a counterweight against traditional potential power. On the other hand, about 48% of respondents expressed pessimism about the alliance. The same table shows that the difference between left and right respondents is very small. The respondents from right spectrum were seamlessly more optimistic about BRICS than equivalent in the left spectrum.

The results about BRICS show that, indeed, perceptions about international affairs in Brazil are polarized. This polarization is present in different issues of international affairs and the BRICS should not be different. At the same time, the results show something counterintuitive. The South–South coalition as a soft balancing tool of great powers is often considered as a project of left wing governments, like the Work Party (PT) in Brazil. So, it

## Discussion

An important point of discussion concerns the precise meaning attributed by respondents to the idea of the emergence of China as a world power. One possibility is that China's rise may be interpreted, in line with our theoretical discussion, as a means of dispersion of global power.

From the viewpoint of Brazilian diplomatic discourse, this idea of power dispersion and attitudes contrary to US hegemony appear recurrently. Dispersion, in this line of argument, would serve two main purposes: On the one hand, the possibility of diversification of economic dependence. On the other, the possibility of the emergence of new actors with power in the international system so that said countries can follow the line of diplomacy of the bargain, i.e. using one power to extract advantage from the other and vice versa.

In this sense, those who have a more refractory position toward liberalism see the emergence of China as positive. If the reasoning is correct, the same empirical evidence must be established in case the issue concerns the emergence of any other country as a dispersing agent of world power. This idea is empirically verifiable.

Yet, there is another possibility about the positive relationship between protectionism and positive outlook on China. It is the idea that people with protectionist bias in Brazil support China's emergence because they see in the Asian country a model of political economy to be followed. In other words, the association would have much more to do with the preference for domestic factors than for international factors.

The argument is, in fact, plausible. Historically, the national-developmentalist favored greater state intervention in the economy. In this sense, the Chinese model would be a model to be used as a reference by the Brazilian government.

The counterargument to this interpretation is that the economic interventionist viewpoint is strongly correlated with the spectrum of the political left, the opposite being true. When we controlled, however, trade preferences by the ideological spectrum, as seen above, the result was that we did not identify any association. The result does not corroborate the first thesis.

## Conclusion

The research sought to bring outside elements to the field of endowment factors to understand the preference of the median voter in terms of trade policy. The findings tend to corroborate the thesis that there is a positive association between liberalism and relative gains. The group of protectionists comprised people who have a critical attitude toward the US and are favorable toward China. The emergence of China and BRICS introduces a factor of dispersion to the world power system.

With regard to the BRICS, it is important to emphasize the fact that there is a strong support among elite segments. There is no significant variation in perceptions across the most important political parties and voters about the relevance of BRICS. It is a good indication that regardless of coalition in power, Brazil will keep BRICS as a strategic part of its foreign policy.

## References

Grieco, J. (1988) Anarchy and the limits of international cooperation. *International Organization* **42**, 485–507.

Morrow, J. (1997) When do "relative gains" impede trade? *The Journal of Conflict Resolution* **41** (1), 12–37.

Powell, R. (1991) Absolute and relative gains in international relations theory. *American Political Science Review* **85**, 1303–1320.

Snidal, D. (1991a) Relative gains and the pattern of international cooperation. *American Political Science Review* **85**, 701–726.

Snidal, D. (1991b) International cooperation among relative gains maximizers. *International Studies Quarterly* **35**, 387–402.

# Chapter 11

# Coordinating BRICS Strategies: A Russian Point of View and Suggestions

Georgy Toloraya

*Russian National Committee on BRICS Research, Russia*

*Center for Russian Strategy in Asia, Institute of Economics, Russian Academy of Science, Moscow, Russia*

*MGIMO University, Moscow, Russia*

## The Need for Coordination of Policies

The BRICS has become one of the important features of the emerging polycentric world. It is thus mostly a political project, not a purely economic global project. The more economic difficulties its members experience, the more — contrary to popular opinion — those members need to coordinate their policies so that the synergy of their combined efforts could help solve problems that would be difficult to tackle single-handedly. Thus, coordination of national strategies is essential.

The first decade of BRICS' history produced no clear understanding of the ultimate goal of the group and why it mattered in international relations. It has not yet become a successful "union of reformers". However, it has not degraded into yet another occasion for high-level meetings and photo opportunities and is considered an important format for emerging countries to coordinate their approaches.

## 122 *Georgy Toloraya*

Several questions arise: Can BRICS members' national goals have a common denominator? BRICS states have many differences. How to combine the goals?

- Will BRICS become a replica of a cold war era "anti-Western alliance" or a "non-aligned movement"?
- Can BRICS play the role of "Union of reformers"?
- Can BRICS develop a common strategy?

BRICS is the constant object of criticism in developed countries. The modalities of BRICS activities are discussed mostly with much negativism and skepticism in the West. The deterioration of the economic situation in some member countries and the political problems, especially in Brazil, are the causes for criticism. At the same time, BRICS is still recognized as a new element of global governance reflecting the need for a contemporary transformation period in international relations. The reason for this dichotomy is the lack of full understanding of BRICS' role and prospects.

What cannot be expected from BRICS in the next decade?

- There will not be a complete unity of views, no dominance and imposition of views within BRICS.
- The BRICS will not institutionalize to EU level or bureaucratic structure.
- The BRICS will not be an anti-Western club.
- The BRICS is not going to become a military bloc like NATO.
- The BRICS will not get rid of the critics and skeptics.
- The BRICS adversaries will not leave their attempts to pull the five apart.

What realistically can be expected from BRICS and what is its common strategy aimed at?

- The BRICS countries are to increase their role as sovereign centers of power.
- Five countries will play an increasing role in the world order of the 21st century.

- The BRICS economies will continue to grow faster than the G7.
- BRICS will strive to reform the foundations of the world political and economic independence in policy and the primacy of international law, maintaining the UN's role as guarantor of international security, the Security Council reform, cooperation in the economy and society, and modernization within BRICS and the Global South.
- BRICS will not achieve adequate representation in the IMF and the World Bank.
- The BRICS will be most effective when acting in a unified manner within the framework of the "Group of Twenty" and other international institutions.
- BRICS' nature will be the catalyst for a new international architecture.[1]

## BRICS and the Global Governance

There are two approaches to BRICS' strategy and its goals in global governance: The first is to quantitatively strengthen the positions of the BRICS countries based on their previously acquired place in the existing global economic and financial system, and the second is to create parallel structures in international governance.

The BRICS, in general, is against ignoring or decreasing the role of the existing institutions of global management, such as the UN, the IMF and the WTO. The critical issues include:

- Reform of the UN, which in recent years has increasingly been criticized for failing to confront global challenges quickly and effectively. The Ufa Summit in 2015 noted the need to make the organization more representative and responsive to security threats. It recognized the need to expand the permanent membership of the UN Security Council (UNSC), which was especially important for India and Brazil. Finalization of the current reform of IMF and further revision of quotas for the benefit of the developing countries;

---

[1] See for more details: BRICS *Realizing the BRICS Long-term Goals: Roadmap and Pathways* (Observer Research Foundation, Delhi), 2017, pp. 69–70.

- Election of developing countries as representatives to the leadership of International Financial Institutions;
- Cooperation within the WTO, study of the possible harmful effects of conflicting/competing projects of trans-regional integration;
- Raising profile of the BRICS-created financial institutions, their integration into the global governance system;
- Modernization of global Internet governance.

However, it is true that the current five permanent members are reluctant to cede any authority to the newcomers, which has become a source of tension inside BRICS. Russia and China, advocating the centrality of the UN, face a dilemma. Without reform, the UN would slide further down into irrelevance, as its decision-making and implementing processes are outdated and do not reflect the current balance of power. But any reform of the UNSC, even by bringing in BRICS partners such as India and Brazil, would undermine China and Russia's positions as permanent UNSC members. Moreover, China is especially wary of increasing the status of India, its long-term rival, although Russia holds a more nuanced position. For example, Russian experts suggest compromise, such as bringing in India and Brazil as permanent members with a moratorium on *veto* power for 10 years.

The efforts of the BRICS to ensure a more prominent place in the existing governance system cannot be underestimated. For example, the role of BRICS and its coordinated strategies is especially noticeable in G20.

However, one should not be overoptimistic. Without changing the basic *modus operandi* of the international governance system and its bodies, there is a danger that western countries will use their experience, personnel and soft power to remain the center of agenda setting and, in the long run, push through decisions that benefit them. There are limits to increasing the role of the BRICS in decision-making within these institutions.

Another option is to impose new rules of the game or corresponding "mirror" structures that parallel existing ones or are separate from others. However, the BRICS countries so far have neither the desire nor the will even to formulate such new rules, let alone the opportunities to implement such radical changes. But if the BRICS abstains from fulfilling this mission, it would be threatened with stagnation and the inertia in effecting any transformation. Since BRICS is no longer the global economic locomotive it used to be, the creation of such institutions are of critical importance for the fate of BRICS.

Recently, there has been more experimenting with an alternative governance system. The adherence to universalism does not preclude the creation of the BRICS structures. The first of such institutions were the New Development Bank (NDB) and the Contingent Reserve Arrangement (CRA), as decided by the leaders at the BRICS summit in Fortaleza in 2014. The NDB began operating after the Ufa Summit in 2015. According to Russian president Vladimir Putin, creating a new development bank and pool of foreign exchange reserves would enable the BRICS countries to coordinate macroeconomic policies much more successfully.[2]

It is important that the NDB works in areas where the western financial institutions do not want to work and considers BRICS countries' needs rather than only profitability. However, the NDB's initial activities were criticized for a lack of strategy and insufficient transparency.

## Whither BRICS Institutionalization?

The degree of importance of BRICS in the process of global changes is far from being determined, but it is nonetheless a phenomenon that is here to stay. However, it needs more effective intra-BRICS coordination mechanism to be able to carry out that task. That makes the issue of institutionalization one of the most important among the controversial issues concerning BRICS' future. So far, the countries have shied away from creating any supra-national bodies as sovereignty is the basis for their foreign policy and they do not want to give even a fraction of its independent decision-making to a group. There are several scenarios of BRICS institutional and capacity building.

The *optimistic scenarios* could see BRICS as a solid political and economic grouping with a coordination mechanism, exerting considerable

---

[2] *Russia Today* (2014), https://russian.rt.com/.

influence on international peace and security system, as well as meeting global challenges from common and coordinated points of view.

The *pessimistic scenario is* that of "degrading" to just a photo-op or venue for sectoral meetings or even dissolution.

A *realistic scenario* should be somewhere in between with bigger emphasis remaining on economic and social issues as least contradictory ones for joint BRICS position. The realistic scenario could move closer to the optimistic one in case consensus is reached on clear-cut institutions created in the area of peace and security — similar to NDB and CRA mechanisms for technological, economic and financial cooperation.

There are indeed disagreements on some issues among the BRICS countries and sometimes their interests do not coincide. It is necessary to ensure coordination on a systematic basis, to coordinate plans for implementing agreements and monitoring that implementation on a global scale, including interactions with other countries. Some kind of structure that would allow agreements to be registered (and ensure that all countries understand them uniformly) and monitor their implementation seems necessary.

A majority of researchers and statesmen consider it necessary to institutionalize the BRICS and turn it into a full-fledged international organization. Institution building may progress as long as BRICS will move on two interconnected tracks: strengthening the solidarity of countries in the global governance system and intensifying their efforts to change (or improve) and deepen cooperation within the association in various areas of cooperation. It seems that the BRICS countries are already in the stage of transition to institutionalization, which can be beneficial for the development of relations between the BRICS countries, and vice versa, the absence of which can further differentiate and disunite the union.

Informal nature of agreements between leaders on the one hand, and the need to coordinate their actions without creating a permanent secretariat and bureaucratic procedures on the other, presume the most appropriate, in this case, format of focus groups on a particular topic in the peak of a crisis.

However, there is a need for a coordination mechanism that could systematically control the implementation of decisions and follow up on their execution. The current mechanisms of summits and interministerial consultations are unable to fulfill those functions on a daily basis. The virtual secretariat that now exists only serves as information exchange.

There are stages from low-level to high-level institutionalization.

*First*, may limit it to permanently working BRICS Technical Secretariat. Second, can see the formation of BRICS Joint Organs:

- Permanently functioning supporting mechanisms between domestic agencies, offices, enterprises and epistemic community;
- A Multilateral Intergovernmental Commission on Economic, Scientific and Technical Cooperation headed by deputy prime-ministers;
- A permanent technical Secretariat;
- Subcommities/Working groups;
- A Study Institution for joint analysis of the international economic situation to work out a "BRICS consensus".

Especially, creation of a multilateral intergovernmental commission on economic, scientific and technical cooperation headed by deputy prime ministers is a choice. It should direct corresponding subcommissions and working groups meeting regularly. It would bring together all the many interministerial tracks, which today are often uncoordinated. It is also possible to create the basis of a permanent technical secretariat for the BRICS, although members remain wary of too much formalization and bureaucratization.

The parallel track of BRICS development, addressing the issue of BRICS' possible enlargement and its relations with other emerging countries in the global context, may also include:

- Creation of a status of permanent observers and partners for dialogue (BRICS+);
- Organizing a network of sectoral consultative bodies including both BRICS and interested observer/dialogue partner;
- Establishing a mechanism to collectively elaborate and promote unified BRICS position within the international institutions;

## 128 *Georgy Toloraya*

- Elaborating joint suggestions for the UN for improving mechanisms of prevention and resolution of conflicts;
- Working out joint responses to challenges in the "global commons";
- Creation of Interregional Coordination Council of Regional Security Organizations with BRICS countries membership.

## A New Development Paradigm?

Another reason for the BRICS's existence, although much less publicly known than the task of increasing the role of emerging countries in global affairs, is to find a new development paradigm. The group's basic unifying goal is to suggest new ways for the socioeconomic development of countries facing rising challenges. Its mission is to develop a new, more egalitarian model than the liberal market-based model. In all probability, it should remain market based with a coordination mechanism based on the "invisible hand", although with bigger roles for the state and central regulator to solve not only profitability issues but also major challenges confronting the society. This model should also take into account the environmental imperatives, preventing excessive consumerism and waste of resources.

Such a model could be based on new technologies — for example, 3D printing could mean a shift to totally new modes of mass production, distribution and marketing. The information and communication technology (ICT) of tomorrow would also become a basis for that new economy.

In recent years, the applicability of sustainable development to the needs of economic growth in rising countries has become increasingly important. However, BRICS countries are also not all on the same page with regard to environmental concerns and related global initiatives.

The disastrous environmental situation in countries such as China and India highlights the special importance of these efforts. Promoting a green economy often means curbing economic growth, which the rising countries consider unfair. So, if the BRICS is to succeed in formulating a new development model, in the long run it will have much more impact on what shape the global economy would take and how it will be governed. The strategic goals may include:

- Eradication of poverty;
- Softening income disparities;
- BRICS as leaders of educational space;
- Promotion of national languages of BRICS countries;
- Humanitarian and cultural exchanges;
- Healthy lives and "wellness", high quality of healthcare systems and others.

How can such a model, even if formulated, be agreed on — should it be within the existing format of universal international institutions such as the World Trade Organization (WTO), or should it come to being through regional and closed structures, such as free trade agreements, through trial and error?

The experts of the five countries in the framework of BRICS Think Tank Council (BTTC), created in 2013 at the Durban summit, worked out some recommendations which include:

- The BRICS should work with other economies that are part of the G20 to align policies and positions for an optimal outcome.
- BRICS central banks should tailor their regulatory frameworks and coordinate closely to engage in the global regulatory agenda-setting process.
- The BRICS should promote the inclusion of the currencies of emerging market economies and developing countries that meet the current criteria for IMF's special drawing rights in its currency basket.
- The BRICS should set an independent rating agency to prevent a build-up of unsustainable corporate debt levels, maintain a check on banking assets, mitigate the negative effects of the largely unregulated shadow banking sector and monitor the performance of the global economy.
- The BRICS should conduct the value-laden conditionality discourse through collective resolve and close collaboration complementing the international safety net with initiatives such as the CRA.
- The BRICS should develop a long-term strategy provision for concessional lending to respond to the development needs of least-developed countries (LDCs).

- The BRICS should further its cross-region monetary cooperation and enhance the CRA's effectiveness, supplementing global financial safety nets.
- The BRICS should coordinate interests on climate adaptation at the UN Framework Convention on Climate Change. The technology mechanism established at the 16th Conference of the Parties meeting in Cancun should be leveraged to enhance action on technology development and transfer, and a commensurate share of the resources of the Green Climate Fund should be channeled toward adaptation activities.
- The BRICS should coordinate its position within the WTO to withstand pressure from developed countries on the basis of existing and projected achievements and domestic viability. Duty-free, quota-free market access is a crucial measure to help LDCs leverage the opportunities offered by the multilateral trading regime.
- The BRICS should commit to having a stronger and rules-based multilateral trading system at the heart of world trade governance and to bring more transparency to regional agreements at the WTO.[3]

## BRICS in Russian Foreign Strategy

During the St Petersburg Economic Forum on 29 May 2017, President Putin disclosed that the BRICS idea "was actually born in St Petersburg" in 2005 at the meeting of Russia, China and India leaders.[4] BRICS acquired great significance in Russia's foreign policy strategy. Because of the confrontation with the West and imposed sanctions, Russia began to rely on Asia and the BRICS to a greater extent.[5] For the BRICS, Russia can become a bridge leading to the West and the East, and to the North and the South. Participation in the BRICS could enable it not to feel opposed to the existing world system, but, on the contrary, to present new opportunities.

[3]7th BRICS Academic Forum. Moscow, NCR/BRICS 2015, pp. 511–515.
[4]https://ria.ru/world/20161013/1479108386.html.
[5]TASS 2015 http://tass.ru/.

The concept of Russian Foreign policy in 2013 emphasized the BRICS as "one of the most important geopolitical events since the beginning of the new century" that had rapidly become "a significant factor in global policy".[6] The BRICS reflects polycentric international relations, as a new model for global relations that transcends old East–West/North–South polarities.

The "Concept of the Russian Federation's Presidency in the BRICS in 2015–2016" indicated that strengthening the forum was one of Russia's foreign policy priorities.[7] One of its objectives was the gradual transformation of the BRICS from a dialogue forum into a full-fledged mechanism for strategic and current interaction on key political and economic problems. Russia wanted to bolster its position in the BRICS and contribute to improving and strengthening the prestige of this organization in the international arena, as well as to help reform the international monetary system, contribute to the creation of the BRICS's own financial mechanisms and develop new activities for the group. Better coordination of the world's financial structures in the context of the G20 and IMF reform were priorities. The creation of national payment systems and rating mechanism within the BRICS format was also of interest. Cooperation with the BRICS countries was important for the development of Russian provinces, especially for Siberia and the Far Eastern region.[8]

The concept especially stresses that the efforts of the BRICS countries are aimed at giving the international monetary system a more just, stable and efficient character with a view of creating conditions to overcome the global crisis, and to develop the economy and financial systems of the group's member states. Russia is also interested in promoting a dialogue and, if possible, coordinating positions on strategic stability, international and regional security, the non-proliferation of weapons of mass destruction, settlement of regional conflicts, and the maintenance of regional stability. The concept notes that work to strengthen the UN's central role

---

[6]Toloraya G. How is the Sixth BRICS Summit Rated in Russia? 20.08.2014 // LEAP URL: http://www.leap2020.net/euro-brics/2014/08/20/how-is-the-sixth-brics-summit-rated-in-russia/?lang=en.

[7]http://en.brics2015.ru/russia_and_brics/20150301/19483.html.

[8]http://en.brics2015.ru/russia_and_brics/20150301/19483.html.

**132** *Georgy Toloraya*

in ensuring global stability and preserving and consolidating the UNSC's role will continue.

Although Russia's strategic goal in the BRICS is the creation of a full-scale mechanism for strategic cooperation for increasing BRICS' clout in global governance, not all members share this point of view equally. There are some concerns among the countries in the "southern wing". During the Indian presidency in 2016, Russia paid increasing attention to the implementation of Economic partnership strategy adopted in 2015 as well as to increase the role of BRICS in international affairs. President Putin in an interview with Indian press agency called BRICS "one of the key elements of the forming multipolar world".[9] Russia was extremely satisfied with the outcome of the Goa Summit which supported it on Syria issue and discussed vital political and global security issues as well as gave boost to economic cooperation.

In June 2017, in a program speech at the St Petersburg Economic Forum, Putin underlined the importance of BRICS for coordinated development.[10]

Chinese Presidency in BRICS in 2017 includes the following themes that would contribute to the further consolidation of BRICS:

1. Deepen BRICS Cooperation for Common Development
   a. Strengthen Economic Partnership
   b. Promote International Cooperation on Development
2. Strengthen global governance to jointly meet challenges
   a. Maintain International Peace and Stability, Foster an Open World Economy, Improve International Financial and Monetary Systems
   b. Strengthen Coordination and Cooperation in Multilateral Mechanisms
3. Carry out people-to-people exchanges to support BRICS cooperation
   a. Engage in Cultural Exchanges and Mutual Learning, Promote Development of Sports

---

[9] https://www.1tv.ru/news/2016-10-13/311903-v_putin_briks_odin_iz_klyuchevyh_elementov_formiruyuschegosya_mnogopolyarnogo_mira.

[10] https://riafan.ru/801977-putin-o-celyah-briks-my-hotim-chtoby-vse-razvivalis.

4. Make institutional improvements and build broader partnerships
    a. Improve Cooperation Mechanisms to Provide Guarantee for Cooperation in Various Fields
    b. Build Broader Partnerships

These goals fit well in Russia's understanding of BRICS' role and prospects, so the cooperation between the two countries at the BRICS venue is sure to deepen.

# References

Pommeranz, W. (2013) Why Russia needs the BRICS? // Fareed Zakaria Global Public Square. 3.09.2013. URL: http://globalpublicsquare.blogs.cnn.com/2013/09/03/why-russia-needs-the-brics/.

Toloraya, G. and Chukov, R. (2017) BRICS in G20: Opportunities for participation coordination.

## Chapter 12

# South Africa Beware the BRIC Bearing BRICS, as the Soothsayer Hath Warned Caesar "Beware the Ides of March!"*

Matlotleng Matlou

*Excelsior Afrika Consulting, South Africa*

## Introduction

International relations have numerous theories providing varied lenses to understand the world. The dominant schools of thought have been liberalism and realism, but have been challenged as inadequate in portraying global variety and complexity, by critical theorists. The debate is between nature-based and socially created drivers of behavior by individuals, organizations or states. Or is there an alternative, that nature influences social construction and vice versa? From time immemorial, human nature or self-interest has always been an underlying motive of the behavior of individuals, organizations and nations. Morgenthau (1978, pp. 4–15) quotes Thucydides averring that "identity of interests is the surest bonds whether between states or individuals" and Washington and Weber, respectively, concurring thus "with far the greatest part of mankind, interest is the governing principle ... almost every man is more or less under

---

*In Shakespeare's Julius Caesar.

**136** *Matlotleng Matlou*

its influence"; and "interests (material and ideal), not ideas dominate directly the actions of men".

Goldberg (2016) refers to Prime Minister Palmerston's speech on 1 March 1848 in the English parliament saying England had "no eternal allies and … no perpetual enemies, our interests are eternal and perpetual and those interests it is our duty to follow". Kissinger (1979) reiterated this by saying, "America has no permanent friends or enemies, only interests". Friends serve our interests and if not we dispose them; just as we befriend our enemies if it benefits us. Is this really always the case; is power the motive for all actions? Surely individuals, organizations and states do more than compete for power, they are not always in completion with others. Cooperation can create mutual benefit, greater transnational ties, improved levels of integration and seeking of peaceful means to deal with issues rather than war; a cobweb model of international relations that involves each segment of society rather than only states.[1] Thus, there are situations like during the period of thermonuclear tension between the USSR and USA that a conflict would result in mutually assured destruction; cooperation was more mutually beneficial; it was a win–win outcome. Indeed, the contentions among the different international relations theories are governed by their varied frames constructed around certain hypotheses and knowledge bases, analyzing complex, multifaceted events and pursuing their own explanations. Consequently, they draw different conclusions; neither is necessarily "wrong" or "right". Nevertheless, this chapter argues that camaraderie or commonality are subservient to national interest in relations between inter-state and inter-BRICS relations are largely no different, especially *vis-à-vis* South Africa and other members.

## Formation of BRIC and the Metamorphosis to BRICS

The Group of Seven, G7 developed from the G5 in 1973, as a platform where Western Finance Ministers jointly review their separate objectives and common compatibility: an attempt to coordinate policies more

---

[1] John Burton, *World Society* (Cambridge University Press, Cambridge), 1972.

actively than in modern times. However, over the last decade the G7 has appeared more of a knowledge management hub and largely abstained from any dynamic sway over global proceedings and markets. O'Neill (2001, p. 1) postulated that in 2001 and 2002, real GDP growth in large emerging nations would surpass that of the G7. Brazil, India, Russia and China (BRIC), spread across Asia, Europe and Latin America, large emerging economies formed a counterweight to the G8 (richest western countries) which has historically dominated the global political and economic governance structures. In global terms, they comprised 30% land, 43% population, 21% gross domestic product (GDP), 17.3% merchandise trade, 12.7% commercial services[2] and 45% agricultural production. In line with these attributes, world policymaking forums should have been reorganized to incorporate BRIC representatives for balanced representation and more effectiveness. Of course, Russia participated in the short-lived G8 Summits which fizzled out over political differences on global issues and subsequent imposition of sanctions on it. Meanwhile, with the formation of the G20, some could argue there is no need to expand the G7. Alternatively, would the BRIC actually want to be in a G9 "club?" The existing G20 meetings are perhaps an extended club version of this proposal, but it is not the G7! In 2006, the initial meeting of BRIC leaders occurred at the G8 Outreach Summit in St Petersburg; while their foreign ministers continued informal discussions especially on the sidelines of the UN General Assembly meetings. The first summit of this informal grouping was in 2009 in Russia and has rotated to other members annually.

However, the glaring omission of Africa sitting squarely in the middle of BRIC members as indicated in Table 1 presented a crisis of legitimacy, suggesting irrelevance of Africa and being only useful as a supplier of raw materials and market for foreign goods. BRIC did not want to deal with global issues and without more balanced representation of the global South. There were various choices and possibly the country chosen had to be close to BRIC members, be of strategic value bilaterally and for the group, have African and international clout. Some of the big hitters were Algeria, Angola, Egypt, Ethiopia, Kenya, Nigeria, Senegal and

---

[2]WTO statistics gateway. FAO Statistics.

South Africa. The latter eventually was invited first as an observer and then full member, possibly because it was Africa's largest economy then, was a member of G20, had strategic partnerships with all the BRIC members, was a regional hegemon, was major producer of natural resources and was an influential African nation. Working to its advantage were soft power attributes like modern infrastructure, sophisticated corporate sector, innovative culture, world-renowned finance system, relatively stable macro and micro financial markets, strong regulatory frameworks and gateway for BRICS investment and other engagements with the rest of the 1 billion plus Africans. Thus, in 2010 when South Africa was invited as an observer to the Summit in Brazil it made it all the more easier since it has strategic partnerships with all the BRIC members. Later, in September 2010 the BRIC foreign ministers recommended the formalization of South Africa's membership and it was duly invited to fully participate in the 2011 Summit in China, where the name BRICS was adopted. India hosted the 2012 Summit and South Africa the 2013, where it spearheaded the participation of a group of African leaders in a Dialogue Forum with the BRICS leaders under the heading "Unlocking Africa's Potential: BRICS and Africa Cooperation on Infrastructure". While some observers praised South Africa for its inclusive spirit and its nurturing of the same with its BRIC partners, others saw this as a further entrenchment of BRICS hegemony over African countries.

## South Africa Learns the Hard Way at Size Matters

The BRICS members are a complex amalgam of countries from the largest to the relatively smallest globally — China one-party state; Russia highly centralized; and Brazil, India and South Africa democracies dominated by significant corruption and/or ethnic strife, as shown in Tables 1 and 2 on political structures, population, income inequality, gross domestic product based on purchasing power parity, trade volumes and commodities and key socioeconomic sectors requiring investment portray. They can learn a lot from each other. The tables depict the small size of South Africa in relation to all other members and makes it relatively weak in engaging these partners. However, this also presents vast opportunities to possibly turn the tables, as Hong Kong, Mauritius, Singapore and United Arab Emirates

*South Africa Beware the BRIC Bearing BRICS* **139**

Table 1. Linkages of BRICS ($ billions).

| Exports from Brazil | Russia | India | China | South Africa | Advanced economies | Europe |
|---|---|---|---|---|---|---|
| 1990 | — | 0.2 | 0.4 | 0.2 | 22.9 | 8 |
| 2000 | 0.4 | 0.38 | 1.1 | 0.3 | 34.6 | 13 |
| 2009 | 25 | 3.4 | 24 | 1.1 | 65.1 | 28.5 |

| Exports from Russia | Brazil | | India | South Africa | Advanced countries | Europe |
|---|---|---|---|---|---|---|
| 1990 | — | — | — | — | — | — |
| 2000 | 0.6 | 1.1 | 5.2 | .03 | 60 | 34.492.4 |
| 2009 | 1.4 | 4.8 | 16.1 | 0.2 | 138.1 | |

| Exports from India | Brazil | Russia | China | South Africa | Advanced countries | Europe |
|---|---|---|---|---|---|---|
| 1990 | 0.0 | — | 0.0 | 0.0 | 11.1 | 3.0 |
| 2000 | 0.3 | 0.9 | 0.8 | 0.3 | 27.4 | 7.6 |
| 2009 | 2.2 | 0.9 | 10.2 | 1.9 | 79.0 | |

| Exports from China | Brazil | Russia | India | South Africa | Advanced countries | Europe |
|---|---|---|---|---|---|---|
| 1990 | 0.1 | — | 0.2 | 0.0 | 52 | 5.1 |
| 2000 | 1.2 | 2.2 | 1.6 | 1.0 | 208.3 | 30.6 |
| 2009 | 15.9 | 17.5 | 29.7 | 7.4 | 858.5 | 174.4 |

| Exports from South Africa | Brazil | Russia | India | China | Advanced countries | Europe |
|---|---|---|---|---|---|---|
| 1990 | — | — | — | — | — | — |
| 2000 | 0.2 | 0.03 | 0.4 | 0.3 | 15.7 | 6.2 |
| 2009 | 0.4 | 0.2 | 2.0 | 5.6 | 30.9 | 10.7 |

*Source*: IMF, Dictionary of Trade Statistics.

highlight how to operate in the VUCA World. Your people are and must be your greatest asset; invest in them, coupled with good governance and strategic leadership and you reap the returns. South African elite must fashion means to convert weaknesses into strength rather than wallow in self-pity.

Table 2. Key sectors where additional development funds are required.

| Brazil | Russia | India | China | South Africa |
|---|---|---|---|---|
| • Infrastructure: Ports, Airports, High-speed rail<br>• Oil and gas<br>• Electricity | • Transport<br>• Manufacturing<br>• Mining<br>• Electricity<br>• Gas<br>• Water supply | • MSMEs<br>• Infrastructure: Roads, Bridges, Railways, Ports, Airports<br>• Electricity<br>• Telecom | • Healthcare<br>• Biotech<br>• Pharmaceuticals<br>• Renewable energy<br>• High-end equipment manufacturing | • Infrastructure<br>• Mining<br>• Clean tech<br>• Manufacturing<br>• Tourism |

*Source*: Saran *et al.* (2015, p. 42).

These countries have some of the largest land areas globally, varied landscapes with challenging environments requiring complex governing systems to meet the needs of their people and to ensure they achieve their development goals.

The population of BRICS members ranges from a few million to over a billion, with China and India having the world's largest number of people, figures they are endeavoring to manage to control over population.

The income and wealth differentials in the BRICS countries are relatively unequal, especially, Brazil and South Africa which are some of the most unequal countries globally. The large populations in the other countries mean that the proportion of deprived people remains high. Collectively, BRICS members must work diligently in meeting the Sustainable Development Goals (SDGs) and achieving high human development in order to engender social cohesion and nation building.

Of the BRICS members, South Africa's economy has stagnated over the past few years and is now in recession, meaning it is regressing in comparison to other countries and dropping on the ranking scales. The growth in China and India has been phenomenal, while Russia and Brazil have made significant progress as their ranks indicate.

The Sanya, Delhi, Durban and Fortaleza Summits approved constructing an Economic Partnership (referred hereinafter as the BRICS Strategy), to enhance "stability, growth and development" to supplement and reinforce subsisting bilateral and multilateral linkages between Member States. It prioritizes trade and investment; manufacturing and minerals processing; energy; agricultural cooperation; science, technology and innovation; financial cooperation; connectivity (institutional, physical and people to people); and ICT cooperation. However, the engagement between the countries, especially with South Africa, is unbalanced with some areas like manufacturing, minerals processing, agricultural cooperation and physical connectivity hardly receiving attention. Furthermore, there are too many areas for cooperation and insufficient resources for administrative and institution building, with no permanent secretariat. Each country drives the agenda of the annual summit that it hosts and Sherpas (personal representatives of heads of state) review the BRICS strategy every 5 years or earlier if apropos and report annually to their principals. This tends to create ineffectiveness, if the responsible country does not prioritize the BRICS issues.

China and India have become venues of production of goods globally which is supported by their first- and third-economy ranks globally. They are followed by Russia and Brazil at the sixth and seventh ranks, respectively. South Africa is at a distant 33rd rank which is 5.3 times smaller than the Russian economy, suggesting it needs to invest more in converting natural resources into value-added products in order to increase skilled employment and enjoy the multiplier effect in the creation of ancillary industries. It must also deal with its high unemployment, poverty and inequality which create huge wastage and fuel social conflicts.

Unsurprisingly, geo-economics propels BRIC relations with South Africa as a target for their goods and services because of an emergent youth bulge, burgeoning middle class and rising urbanization engendering demand for physical and services infrastructure and abundant skilled personnel. Terms of trade are unfavorable to South Africa in value, quantity and quality with all BRIC members as Table 1 indicates. It largely trades in raw materials, losing the knowledge, skills, institutional development and extra revenue from value-add, and received, with its comparative advantage stymied at the raw material stage. Furthermore, all other BRICS members are relatively strong in South Africa's sphere of immediate interest in Africa and not vice versa as Table 9 signifies, further weakening her in the BRICS grouping. The BRIC engagement with South Africa is a microcosm of its relationship with Africa. It is seen as a springboard for trade, investment and additional opportunities into other African countries, especially through its membership in regional economic

## 142 *Matlotleng Matlou*

communities and trade agreements with the European Union and United States which other BRICS members can ride on to enter these markets.

BRICS established two $100 billion funds — one for the New Development Bank to fund infrastructure projects and the other as a reserve fund to secure their currency markets against new global crises and dependency on economic and financial rules imposed on the world by the wealthiest nations. The global and African headquarters of the New Development Bank will be China and South Africa, respectively. Each member contributes $10 billion with an eventual capital base of $100 billion. Total annual loan ceiling is $34 billion. The BRICS Bank will assist with funding key sectors, the ones in Table 2 being a pointer of present requirements and others being added as apropos. BRICS members also plan creating their own rating agencies to challenge the hegemony of western ones and investors who take decisions based on the so-called market sentiment largely to their benefit.

South Africa is particularly concerned about the contradictory goals of mutual benefit and non-interference where BRICS members are major arms sellers to Africa and fuel conflicts or their support bolsters autocratic regimes, leading to a vicious cycle of forced migration and underdevelopment since the impacts spillover into neighbors and across Africa, which must now seek to solve these challenges. Surely, partners are more considerate.

BRICS cooperation does not negate the dictum that nations have no permanent friends or allies, they only have permanent interests. For example, cheap and subsidized goods from Brazil, China and India have strangulated South African industries like manufacturing (shoes and textiles), medicines and poultry, further exacerbating its growing unemployment situation. The relationship of the four to South Africa supports the realist position of national interests being supreme. There is nothing sinister about this, as long as countries do not seek to deceive by suggesting more gravitas to Global South solidarity and the fight against western domination than they deserve.

Partnerships create shared strength and common positions toward issues and in relation to other countries or alliances. However, since countries are members of more than one collective, they spread their options which can be contradictory as shown, especially with China. It is the indispensable partner with the greatest resources and linkages with the other countries, while the reverse ties are weaker. It could utilize its power benevolently to assist the others or it may become a bully as time goes on. Furthermore, it has other partnerships and these often seem more important than BRICS, while the bilateral ties between other members themselves are also not that strong. Thus, BRICS has to determine how to reinforce linkages across and ensure that one partner or a few are not overdominant to the disadvantage of others.

## How are Other Cooperation Initiatives Impacting BRICS and Vice Versa?

As the earlier discussion on strategic partnerships indicated, they are formed to achieve specific goals and they must be evaluated to test their effectiveness. Thus, countries have to question whether joining a particular or numerous groups can be justified, the challenges of managing these numerous obligations and relationships, etc. On the contrary, not joining some initiatives could lead to major losses. South Africa in particular has to ensure that the plethora of initiatives that it spearheaded with other countries and BRIC members do not fall victim to the BRICS hammer. For example, the Brazilian, Indian and South African (IBSA) Forum was formed following its leaders being invited to the 2003 G8 summit in Evian, France as observers and they were irritated by the minimal role ascribed to developing nations in the global arena. Consequently, they resolved to form their own inter-governmental group to campaign for reform of the global governance regime — permanent seats on the UN Security Council, more representation on the IMF and World Bank boards, greater concerns for development issues of developing countries, etc. Since then various governmental, civil society and business meetings of the three members occurred. However, over time the organization fossilified, especially after the exit of presidents Lula and Mbeki and prime minster Singh from power. Their successors placed their fortunes into BRICS, indicating the challenges of not sufficiently institutionalizing initiatives. The three may also not have had sufficient resources to bankroll initiatives as China does in BRICS.

India, Brazil and South Africa — IBSA — commenced with much promise in 2003. However, after years there were few concrete

144 *Matlotleng Matlou*

achievements and it is dying from lack of support from members, especially since the formation of BRICS and now One Belt One Road which all give more prominence. It is ironic that when South Africa joined BRIC, Foreign Minister Nkoana-Mashabane promised that it would complement IBSA, but the opposite has happened. Why can't the three countries continue their initiatives implemented under the BRICs umbrella?

The initiatives that will probably continue to stand tall and gather strength are the continent and country ones like the Forum for China–Africa Cooperation (FOCAC) established at the October 2000 Ministerial Conference of the Forum on China–Africa Cooperation (FOCAC) in Beijing under the auspices of Africa and China in order to further strengthen friendly cooperation and common development between Africa and China and to tackle the challenges of socioeconomic globalization, based on corresponding consultation, improving understanding and growing unanimity. Since then political and socioeconomic relations between Africa and China have solidified. Another example is the India Africa Forum established in 2008 as India sought to catch up with other competitors who had established similar bodies to consolidate their politico–cultural and socioeconomic relations with Africa.

The tremendous wealth of China and its global power ambitions means it leads numerous bilateral and multilateral plus regional and global cooperation initiatives. A few of these will be highlighted in relation to their impact on BRICS. Poor treatment by US and its allies dominating the World Bank and IMF, where China is insignificant even as the world's second largest economy prompted the establishment of the Asia Infrastructure Investment Bank (AIIB) in January 2016, with major western nations except Japan, joining despite US pressure not to do so. With headquarters in Beijing, the president is Chinese and only Chinese and Indian governors presently act as the largest shareholders representing only their countries and have compatriots as alternates,[3] virtually replicating the western ills. Feng and Mitchell (2001) state that Brazil and South

---

[3] China $29,780.4 billion; votes 300,746; percent of total 27.5186. India $8,367.3; votes 86,615; percent of total 8.9978. Russia $6,536; votes 68,304 and percent of total 6.2499, making them the 1st to 3rd largest voters.

Africa, of the 57 inaugural members, have been given an extra year to join the AIIB, after missing the 31 December 2016 deadline. But economic challenges faced by the two and possibly having been overstretched in providing their initial contributions to the New Development Bank might have caused constraints in finalizing their membership and what percentage of voting power they will command.

The AIIB will largely fund the ambitious Belt and Road Initiative or One Belt, One Road (OBOR) conceptualized by China covering 57 countries and representing 75% and 55% of global population and economic output, respectively. Regional members — Asia, Middle East and Pacific — have 79% and 77% of the share capital and voting, respectively, confirming that most of its work will be in this region. Bafflingly, the "road" is a sea route coupling China's southern coast to east Africa and Mediterranean; the "belt" comprises varied land-based corridors linking China, Central Asia, Middle East and Europe. The publicized OBOR objective is initiative "open for cooperation ... open to all countries, and international and regional organizations for engagement ..." However, critics see it as seeking to cement Beijing's economic leadership through multinational infrastructure development to fuel growth in its underdeveloped peripheral regions, curtail its chronic excess capacity, gain geopolitical leverage over neighbors, create markets for its goods and to invest vast foreign reserves (+$3 trillion).

Presently, Chinese investment is over $50 billion in 56 economic and trade cooperation zones, creating approximately 180,000 jobs in about 20 Belt and Road states. During the May 2017 OBOR Summit, China supposedly pledged about $900 billion investment in OBOR states over the next few years. Trade between the other states and China is over $3 trillion; of this, $2 trillion could be exports to China in 5 years' time. Brazil, India and South Africa are not OBOR members. India declined participation in the OBOR Summit stating that "Connectivity projects must be pursued in a manner that respects sovereignty and territorial integrity," rejecting Chinese invitation to participate in the recent Belt and Road Initiative summit, based on concerns about $52 billion China–Pakistan Economic Corridor traversing disputed Kashmir and resultant Pakistani economic growth; though some question if this a strategic move. Furthermore, India warned of Chinese hegemony, providing the example of Sri Lanka being expected to give China Hambantota harbor for failing to repay $8 billion loan.

The plethora of cooperation initiatives (IBSA, FOCAC, India–Africa Forum, Africa Latin America Association, BRICS, etc.) require significant resources from members to prepare and participate in various engagements, pay dues, implement and evaluate programs, balance sometimes conflicting objectives, manage expectations and rivalries between fellow members, on the one hand, and outside parties, on the other hand. Unlike China, its BRICS partners are resource constrained and this limits the extent to which they are able to meet just their BRICS obligations considering that they are members of various other partnerships. China has the capacity to engage in an ever-increasing number of international bodies, but there is a limit to how effective and efficient it can be. Thus, it could suffer from attention deficit and neglect some of its obligations.

## Sustainable Development Goals — Whither the BRICS?

On 25 September 2015, the United Nations adopted 17 SDGs with 169 targets as its vision to transmute our unbalanced world by 2030 assuming that indeed nations are committed. History tells us the difference between commitments and reality, suggesting the unlikeliness of meeting these targets. The goals are interlinked and failure in one has impacts on the others. Goal 16 on Peace, Justice and Strong Institutions aims to institute rule of law, diminish every kind of violence and obtain enduring answers to conflict and insecurity is particularly pertinent in the positive impact its realization will have on forced migration. BRICS must commit to ensuring that individually and collectively they cooperate to fulfill the SDGs agenda. Each country has experience in tackling socioeconomic development challenges which must be shared. Let us hope that the domestic and foreign policy of all the BRICS members, their elite and people can espouse and practice the South African Ubuntu concept of Motho ke Motho ka batho (a person is a person thought other persons) to engender a fairer, peaceful and highly developed world when all humans can reach their full potential.

## BRIC and Transnational Organized Crime in South Africa

The UN General Assembly approved the Convention on Transnational Organized Crime and supplementary Protocols to Prevent, Suppress and Punish Trafficking in Persons, Especially Women and Children (TiP); against the Smuggling of Migrants by Land, Sea and Air (SoM); and against Illicit Manufacturing of and Trafficking in Firearms, Their Parts and Components and Ammunition (TiF) on 15 November 2000, opening it for signature by all States and regional organizations, provided that at least one Member State of such organization has signed the Convention, from 12 to 15 December 2000 at the Palazzi di Giustizia in Palermo, Italy, and thereafter, at United Nations Headquarters in New York until 12 December 2002. It entered into force on 29 September 2003, and presently has 147 signatories and 187 ratifiers; TiP on 25 December 2003 has 117 signatories and 170 ratifiers; SoM on 28 January 2004, has 112 signatories and 143 ratifies; and TiF on 3 July 2005 and has 52 signatories and 114 ratifies. The UN Convention against Corruption (UNCAC) was adopted by the UNGA on 31 October 2003 and availed for signature in Merida, Yucatan, Mexico, from 9 to 11 December 2003 and thereafter, at UN headquarters in New York, 140 nations signed it. It came into force on 14 December 2005, and by December 2016, there were 181 rectifiers and 16 non-ratifications. It seeks to curb this cancer undermining democracy, rule of law and sustainable development.

Between 2003 and 2011, all the BRICS countries ratified the Transnational Organized Crime Convention and TiP Protocol; while China has not ratified the SoM and with Russia the TiF. Furthermore, it is laudable their BRICS members have ratified the UN Convention against Corruption, but more important is their implementation of its articles, especially in their inter-relationships. Examples of South Africa which seems to have become a weak spot for other members to target will now be elucidated on. BRICS can supposedly assist in supporting international security cooperation, particularly in the fields such as conflict resolution, non-proliferation of weapons of mass destruction, combating international terrorism, drug trafficking, piracy, money laundering, illegal small arms trading and migration, etc. However, as South Africa opened up to the

148  *Matlotleng Matlou*

international community from 1990 onward before majority rule in 1994, transnational organized crime syndicates commenced targeting her. Those from the BRIC members would not be left behind. Some of their activities have been abalone and rhino poaching (China), drugs syndicates (Brazil and Russia), human trafficking, smuggling of migrants, illegal document fraud (China, India and Russia), trading in counterfeit goods and illegal arms, prostitution and money laundering (Brazil, China, India and Russia) among others. Public and private officials often collude through receiving financial and other benefits from these illegal activities.

The Chinese obsession with men seeking to regain youthful energy is fueling the illegal transnational trade in fauna and flora from across the world. Recently, it was lion bones and now donkeys in South Africa. This industry, worth billions of dollars worldwide are bludgeoned to death before being skinned to produce gelatin, known in Chinese as ejiao, then combined with hot beverages, nuts and seeds; donkey meat is supposed to be more nourishing than beef and is served in burgers and stews. Donkey numbers in China fell from 11 to 6 million between the 1990s and 2013. Raborife (2017) reports that 1,000 donkey and seven tiger skins were found on a farm plot in Gauteng Province, driven by increased demand from China which is leading to cruelty to and stealing of animals, coupled with a growing illegal trade of some endangered species. Pijoos (2017) reports that the Asset Forfeiture Unit (AFU) of the South African National Prosecuting Authority (NPA) has obtained a preservation order for donkey hides with an estimated value of R4,381,500. Following Niger, Senegal, Mali, Burkina Faso and Gambia, Botswana is reported to have banned the export of donkeys.

The Gupta family originally from Saharanpur, India arrived in South Africa in 1993 and is alleged to have assiduously courted politicians (they are close friends to the president and his family) and corrupted some of them in order to win favors including being granted early citizenship; confidential information; business deals, etc. — capturing the state as they are accused of by the previous Public Protector. Almost daily the media is awash with allegations of their wrongdoing, presently estimated in billions of Rands; destruction of state institutions; engendering poor trust of government; fostering divisions in the ruling party and resentment, unfairly toward Indians. The judiciary is seized with numerous cases brought against those implicated. The Gupta scandal has united various sectors of society and emboldened them to campaign for the resignation of the president and the recovery of the vast resources lost to corruption, already having led to the resignation of the chief executive and chairperson of the board of ESKOM, the national electricity company.

The Southern African Faith Communities Environment Institute and Earthlife Africa filed litigation in respect to a 2014 inter-governmental agreement between South Africa and Russia, for the construction of eight nuclear reactors costing between R500 million and 1 trillion, which obliged the South African government to work exclusively with ROSATOM in violation of national legislation for a public tendering process and included giving it a favorable tax regime. There have also been public concerns about possible corruption and affordability. In April 2017, a South African court cancelled the agreement and planned procurement process, instructing that the matter must revert to parliament for its consideration and direction as constitutionally required.

South Africa is urged to raise the debilitating effects of transnational organized crime that other BRICS members are rendering on it and insist that these issues are collectively tackled, including providing information to successfully prosecute the perpetuators.

**The Fifth Estate: Think Tank and their Knowledge and Development roles**: Think tanks do not merely contemplate over the past, present and future, but through multifaceted teams of specialists work to realize policy and legislative change; plus concrete solutions to issues to effectively assist society tackle today's VUCA world. Thus, they must ensure their research is of maximum value, opportune and widely available, especially for those with limited access to financial, human, information and technological resources. The amount of data and speedy analysis required today call for nimbleness, which can be achieved through cooperation since no single think tank can have the reach and knowledge (language, culture, locality, etc.) to deal with the breadth of issues at hand. However, think tanks require alertness to dangers of being embedded into states' agendas and being insufficiently objective, while endorsing many unsavory policies and practices creating chaos across the globe.

McGann (2017) has been producing a global think tanks index for 10 years, which seeks to be as comprehensive as possible. Recognizing

## 150  *Matlotleng Matlou*

that there are huge gaps, this report ranks BRICS members among the 25 countries with the largest number of think tanks globally, the USA with 1835, is 1st; China 2nd; India 3rd; Russia 8th; Brazil 12th and South Africa 13th with 435, 280, 122, 89 and 86, respectively.

Ranking individual think tanks globally excluding the ones of USA, has Fundacao Getulio Vargas as 12th; China Institutes of Contemporary International Relations as 14th; Carnegie Moscow Center as 23rd; Institute for Defence Studies and Analyses as 30th; and African Centre for the Constructive Resolution of Disputes as 32rd. Inexplicably, when the USA is included, Brazil becomes 9th, Russia 24th, China 33rd, South Africa 50th and India 54th. At the regional level, for the BRICS in chronological order Fundacao Getulio Vargas is 1st in Central and Latin America; Carnegie Moscow Center is 2nd in Central and Eastern Europe; Indian Institute for Defense Studies and Analyses, and China Institutes of Contemporary International Relations are 7th and 5th in the China, India, Japan and South Korea group; and the African Centre for the Constructive Resolution of Disputes is 5th in Africa South of the Sahara. There are further rankings according to the areas of specialization and other criteria. Indeed, the BRICS think tanks feature prominently at the top echelons. However, there are some significant gaps and members must work on strengthening the capacity in these fields.

McGann (2017, pp. 8–9) provides the following reasons for increases in think tanks: information and technological revolutions; ending governments' control on information; growing intricacies and technical nature of policy; larger governments; lack of trust in governments; globalization and multiplicity of actors; ICT revolution; requirement appropriate and accurate information and analysis — right form, in right hands, at right time. Alternatively, reasons for decreases are resent toward think tanks by authority (civil, public and private) figures; constrained resources; donor short-termism and project-specific funding; weak institutional capacity; increased competition from advocacy organizations, for-profit consulting firms, law firms; poor adaptation to change political and regulatory environment growing hostile to think tanks and NGOs in many countries; 24/7 electronic media and attrition. In addition, he states that there are four more threats to think tanks — issues, actors, competition and conflicts. Think tanks in developing countries are particularly susceptible to depending on donors, especially foreigners who consequently influence their agendas and survival, often being subjective. However, it can work the other way, especially in oppressive states where their harm can be exposed. McGann suggests four "more" — mission, markets, manpower and money — to tackle the challenges that think tanks face in navigating the global odyssey we are embarking upon.

The BRICS Think Tank Council formed in 2013 is the brains trust of the organization tasked with undertaking research, disseminating information and knowledge, exchanging ideas and providing advice to states on various policy issues. The Academic Forum is scheduled to meet annually. The BRICS members are highly positioned in terms of numbers, quality and areas of research covered, even as they face similar challenges like other countries. There are also peculiarities like the strong state-affiliated and-supported think tanks in China particularly. This limits the extent to which they can criticize the state and be objective. Russia is to some extent similar, while in the other three countries the think tanks operate more freely. An advantage of the Chinese state support is that more resources are availed to think tanks, recognizing that the more the work they undertake, the more the knowledge the Chinese can have of the other members of the group and global issues in general. Furthermore, the Chinese invest in languages and therefore understand the languages of the other members while the opposite is not true. Nevertheless, China can learn a lot from the other countries that have longer histories of think tanks operating, even those supported by governments. There is greater scope for more intensive cooperation between the BRICS think tanks, including capacity building, strengthening institutions and sharpening focus on the issues being dealt with.

## Questions for South Africa to Ponder Pertaining to Her National Interests

If, as realists suggest, politicians need to always be guided by the national interests and necessity for the state to survive, are the South African leaders following this theoretical dictates? Have they sufficiently questioned the concepts of common and shared prosperity prevalent in the BRICS' Summits declarations? Is there a belief that the members are equal not a mirage? Have they considered that connectivity is actually a vehicle for extraction of natural resources, which then return as expensive finished goods with no multiplier effects for the country? Why are they now silent on the deindustrialization, unemployment and social challenges caused by the cheap imports, increasing numbers of Chinese and Indians (many coming is as asylum seekers) taking part in the retail trade in South Africa? When will they seek equal treatment for South Africans who may want to participate in the retail sectors in these countries? How can the largely one-sided bilateral relationship with and little relative autonomy with China be minimized? How can South Africa counter penetrate BRIC members? Lastly, how can South Africa's weakening socio-economic influence and soft power regionally and globally be halted in order for it to play a more strategic role in BRICS? All these and other questions require deep reflection and development and implementation of appropriate strategies to ensure that South African national interests are defined and protected? McKaiser (2017) among others believes that the majority governing party since 1994, the ANC, is incapable of cogently answering the questions raised above and leading South Africa on a sustainable development path, being so riddled with incompetence, corruption and self-aggrandizement.

## Conclusion

There is a naive view by many Africans that only the West exploited them in the past and present; and countries from the global South engage with them with altruistic intentions. Indeed, many are unaware that Arabs from their entry in Africa since the mid-7th century began enslaving Africans. The hospitality of Africans was taken advantage of then and continues today with many other foreigners engaging with Africa. This weakness largely emanates from weak political and socioeconomic leadership and governance. Mills and Qobo (2016, p. 98) conclude that the "contemporary era of global diplomacy has witnessed growing and intense political and economic competition ... between developed and developing countries, but also among developing countries." Consequently, "national interests, rather than friendships, have been the salient drivers of the growing presence of the BRIC countries in Africa", they "are not primarily driven by Africa's development concerns, but are seeking to fulfill their own commercial interests as well as use Africa as an avenue for shoring up their international legitimacy and credibility." Visentini (2009) concurs stating that "for many, the relations with Africa prove the solidarity dimension of the social program of President Lula, while others consider these only as prestige diplomacy, a waste of time and money. Finally, some just regard these relations as business diplomacy, a 'soft imperialism', which is only different from the Chinese presence in Africa by its form and intensity."

# Chapter 13

# Seeking Sino–India Development Coordination under the Belt and Road

Lin Minwang

*Institute of International Affairs, Fudan University, Shanghai, China*

## Coordination as a Method of Propelling the Belt and Road: Basis, Form and Content

In 2013, President Xi Jinping brought forth the "Silk Road Economic Belt" and the "21st century Maritime Silk Road" (the Belt and Road) proposals in Kazakhstan and Indonesia, respectively. The proposals were greatly welcomed both domestically and abroad and gradually developed into a national strategy. The central government especially established a Belt and Road construction leadership group and published the Vision and actions on jointly building Belt and Road (Vision and Actions).[1] In Visions and Actions, China brought forth the principles of joint establishment, which pointed out that "The Initiative seeks mutual benefit. It accommodates the interests and concerns of all parties involved, and seeks a conjunction of interests and the 'biggest common denominator' for cooperation so as to give full play to the wisdom and creativity, strengths

---

[1] China.com: "Pushing for joint construction of the Belt and Road Outlook and Action," http://news.china.com/domesticgd/10000159/20150328/19439017_all.html#page_2, Accessed on 22 April 2016.

155

and potentials of all parties."[2] This principle in fact makes up the basis of propelling the Belt and Road to coordinate with strategic development of all parties.

The earliest integration to the Belt and Road is the Eurasian Economic Union (EEU) led by Russia. In May 2015, when Russian president Putin was visiting China, China and Russia signed the Joint Declaration on integrating the development projects of the EEU and Silk Road Economic Belt, proposing that both sides will negotiate and try to integrate Belt and Road construction with EEU construction, making sure regional economy grows steadily, strengthens regional economic unification and maintains regional peace and development. Another important breakthrough is the joint integration sought by China, Russia and Mongolia. In July 2015, during the second meeting between Chinese, Russian and Mongolian leaders, they signed the Medium-Term Roadmap between China, Russia and Mongolia, declaring the outline of China–Mongolia–Russia Economic Corridor on the basis of integrating the Belt and Road and EEU construction, and the "Steppe Road".[3] After that, more than 30 countries along the Belt and Road gradually signed official documents with China, integrating into the Belt and Road, such as Kazakhstan's "Bright Road", Mongolia's "Steppe Road" and Indonesia's "Global Maritime Axis". Therefore, seeking strategic and developmental "integration" has become an important method of China pushing Belt and Road to countries along the line.

Judging from integration agreements already reached, to realize integration of two countries' development strategy, we have to search for meeting points of interest with the Belt and Road. Through demonstrating their own advantages and abilities, they can fully exert their potential and realize the goal of mutual benefit. Therefore, an important point in the integrating process is that both sides need to recognize where their interests meet and find the coherence among their goals. If such foundation is

---

[2]China.com: "Pushing for joint construction of the Belt and Road Outlook and Action, http://news.china.com/domesticgd/10000159/20150328/19439017_all.html#page_2, Accessed on 22 April 2016.

[3]Foreign Ministry: Medium-Term Roadmap between China, Russia and Mongolia, http://www.fmprc.gov.cn/web/gjhdq_676201/gj_676203/oz_678770/1206_679110/1207_6791 22/t1280229.shtml. Accessed on April 22 2016.

absent, then the possibility of integration is absent. In other words, the premise of participants integrating into the Belt and Road is that they acknowledge the Belt and Road can provide them development opportunities. Even though it might bring challenges, opportunities are always greater than challenges.

On the specific form of integration, the Vision and Action has pointed out that "China will take full advantage of the existing bilateral and multilateral cooperation mechanisms to push forward the building of the Belt and Road and to promote the development of regional cooperation." Main forms include the following: (1) Strengthen bilateral cooperation and promote comprehensive development of bilateral relations through multilevel and multichannel communication and consultation. Encourage the signing of cooperation MOUs or plans and develop a number of bilateral cooperation pilot projects. (2) Enhance the role of multilateral cooperation mechanisms, make full use of existing mechanisms such as the Shanghai Cooperation Organization (SCO), ASEAN Plus China (10+1), Asia–Pacific Economic Cooperation (APEC), Asia–Europe Meeting (ASEM), Asia Cooperation Dialogue (ACD), Conference on Interaction and Confidence-Building Measures in Asia (CICA), China–Arab States Cooperation Forum (CASCF), China–Gulf Cooperation Council Strategic Dialogue, Greater Mekong Sub-region (GMS) Economic Cooperation and Central Asia Regional Economic Cooperation (CAREC) to strengthen communication with relevant countries and attract more countries and regions to participate in the Belt and Road Initiative. (3) Continue to encourage the constructive role of the international forums and exhibitions at the regional and subregional levels hosted by countries along the Belt and Road, as well as such platforms as Boao Forum for Asia, China–ASEAN Expo, China–Eurasia Expo, Euro–Asia Economic Forum, China International Fair for Investment and Trade, China–South Asia Expo, China–Arab States Expo, Western China International Fair, China–Russia Expo and Qianhai Cooperation Forum. We should support the local authorities and general public of countries along the Belt and Road route to explore their historical and cultural heritage, jointly hold investment, trade and cultural exchange activities, and ensure the success of the Silk Road (Dunhuang) International Culture Expo, Silk Road International Film Festival and Silk Road International Book Fair. We propose to set up

## 158    Lin Minwang

an international summit forum on the Belt and Road Initiative. Therefore, the specific mechanisms of integration can be bilateral or multilateral;[4] it can be bilateral, or regional or global; it can be using existing mechanisms or establishing new platforms. Belt and Road has no particular requirements on specific forms of integration, but holds an open mind.

On the specific content of integration, it's concentrated on five coordinations: policy coordination, facilities connectivity, investment and trade cooperation, financial integration and people-to-people bond. Their contents and effects are as follows: (1) Enhancing policy coordination is an important guarantee for implementing the Initiative. (2) Facilities connectivity is a priority area for implementing the Initiative. (3) Investment and trade cooperation is a major task in building the Belt and Road. (4) Financial integration is an important underpinning for implementing the Belt and Road Initiative. (5) People-to-people bond provides the public support for implementing the Initiative.[5]

## Seeking Possibility of Sino–India Development Integration

India has great influence on China's construction of the Belt and Road in the south Asian region. The geographical structure has made India the center of the subcontinent and India's entire GDP is 80% of the region's, making it unmatched by any country of influence in South Asia. On the contrary, there's possibility for winning India on board because India has in fact stepped over the Belt and Road threshold: India has joined in Belt and Road financing mechanisms such as the Asian Infrastructure Investment Bank and the BRICS bank and is constructing the Bangladesh–China–India–Myanmar economic corridor with the three countries.

---

[4] China.com: Pushing for joint construction of the Belt and Road Outlook and Action, http://news.china.com/domesticgd/10000159/20150328/19439017_all.html#page_2. Accessed on April 22 2016 SOKO.indd 130 2017/8/18 14:51:06.

[5] China.com: Pushing for joint construction of the Belt and Road Outlook and Action, http://news.china.com/domesticgd/10000159/20150328/19439017_all.html#page_2. Accessed on April 22 2016 SOKO.indd 130 2017/8/18 14:51:06.

Despite India's position on the Belt and Road, both countries have a strong need of economic and trade cooperation. As early as May 2013, when Premier Li Keqiang visited India, he has called for the complement and integration of the Chinese and Indian markets. "Both the Chinese and Indian markets are markets with much potential, with a total population of over 2.5 billion. If everybody gets a new phone, then global IT manufacturers would be full of orders. The two countries have complementary industries. India has advantages in information technology and software and bio-pharmaceuticals, China is developing fast in electronics, textile and emerging industries. India is pushing for infrastructure construction, and China is experienced in this area. The integration of Chinese and Indian markets can have a superimposed effect of 1+1>2, which is beneficial to both economies' sustainable development and can motivate the global economy." Premier Li Keqiang said when summing up the fruits of his visit that China and India have made clear a new path for two markets with the most potential to integrate and complement. The two countries discussed trade and making investment convenient, came to terms on large projects such as industrial zones and railway, pushing bilateral trade balance and continued expansion of economic and trade cooperation. At the same time, the two countries explored new ways for two emerging economies to integrate, especially the proposal of the Bangladesh–China–India–Myanmar Economic Corridor, and strengthening of border trade, pushing it to form greater market and united development power.[6]

In other words, before president Xi Jinping put forth the Belt and Road, China and India have already been talking about market integration.

In September 2014, when President Xi Jinping visited India, he reevaluated the two countries' strategic partnership, saying China and India need to be closer partners in development, cooperation partners who promoted growth and global partners in strategic coordination. President Xi Jinping emphasized in a speech at the Indian Council of World Affairs that "China and India should become closer partners for

---

[6]Li Keqiang's Speech at the Indian World Affairs Committee, http://www.fmprc.gov.cn/web/gjhdq_676201/gj_676203/yz_676205/1206_677220/1209_677230/t1042441.shtml.

development who will jointly pursue their respective national renewal. Development is the top strategic goal shared by the two countries. Nothing is more imperative than to deliver a more comfortable, more secure and happier life to our peoples. For that, we both need to focus on development, share experience and deepen mutually beneficial cooperation, so as to achieve peaceful, cooperative and inclusive development for our two countries." He also mentioned that China and India need to have development integration, "Known, respectively, as the 'factory' and 'office' of the world, China and India need to enhance cooperation to tap into our mutually complementary advantages. China's westward opening-up should be geared to dovetail with India's 'look east' policy with a view to shaping the world's most competitive production bases, most attractive consumer markets and most powerful growth engines. The two countries also need to expand cooperation in investment, finance and other areas and pursue practical cooperation across the board."[7]

In May 2015, after Prime Minister Modi successfully visited China, the consensus on the two countries' development integration was further acknowledged. In November 2015, when Premier Li Keqiang met Modi during the East Asian summit, he pointed out that China and India's development strategies match. China is exerting strategies such as "Made in China 2025" and "Internet+", and India is pushing "Make in India" and "Digital India", etc. There's broad prospect for cooperation. China is willing to push for early fruits in the construction of the economic corridor, strengthen trade and investment, infrastructure and financial cooperation, widening space on cultural and people exchanges, stabilizing public opinion and support in both countries.[8]

To sum up, the integration of China and India during Belt and Road construction is not only possible but has also been launched before the Belt and Road was proposed, and the two countries are seeking deeper levels of integration.

---

[7] Speech by Xi Jinping at the Indian World Affairs Committee, http://www.fmprc.gov.cn/web/gjhdq_676201/gj_676203/yz_676205/1206_677220/1209_677230/t1192744.shtml.

[8] *Xinhua News*, "Li Keqiang Meets Indian Prime Minister Modi", http://news.xinhuanet.com/world/2015-11/21/c_1117216984.htm. Accessed on 22 April 2016.

## Basis and Content of Sino–India Development Integration

### *The real-world basis of Sino-India integration: "Make in India campaign"*

On 25 September 2014, Indian Prime Minister Modi proposed the Make in India Campaign, hoping to increase the proportion of manufacturing in India's GNP from 15% to 25% and create jobs for more than 12 million young people who enter the labor force every year, making India a global manufacturing center that can match China.[9]

"Make in India" campaign is made up of newly established national projects, with the goal of making investment convenient, promoting innovation, increasing technology development, protecting intellectual property and establishing high-level infrastructure in order to increase the proportion of Indian manufacturing in GNP and make cities centered around manufacturing as an important economic engine into sustainable, smart cities. Right now, the Department of Industrial Policy and Promotion is in charge of this plan and the Indian government has constructed five corridors in the shape of an octagon to develop manufacturing. The most important one is the Delhi–Mumbai industrial corridor. The Indian government approved it in principle in August 2007. The other four are the Amritsar–Kolkata industrial corridor, Bengaluru–Mumbai economic corridor, the Chennai–Bengaluru Industrial Corridor and the Vizag–Chennai Industrial Corridor.[10]

"Make in India" and China's Belt and Road strategies are high in coherence. India has become the prime destination for Chinese enterprises' industrial transfer, China needs the growing Indian market to relieve the production capacity surplus and reduce export pressure, and India can take the industrial transfer and rapidly develop its domestic industry in a short period of time.[11]

---

[9] *Financial Times*: Modi pushes for Make in India Campaign: http://www.ftchinese.com/story/001058406. Accessed on 20 November 2015.

[10] Make in India: http://www.makeinindia.com/live-projects-industrial-corridor/. Accessed on November 20, 2016.

[11] Liu Xiaoxue (2013), The complication of the Sino-India economic and trades. *China's Economics and Trade* **2013** (3), 24.

For Chinese investors, the Make in India campaign needs to be paid attention to in the following fields: (1) Exploitation and processing of minerals — India produces a total of 88 minerals, including four energy mines, 10 heavy metals, 50 non-metallic minerals and 24 sub-ores; (2) Construction, maintenance and upgrade of transportation and electric infrastructure and construction, upgrade, remodeling and maintenance of regular roads and high-speed roads, regular railway and high-speed rails, and oil pipes; (3) The automobile industry, the industry that Indian government gives special support to, including manufacturing of automobiles and tractors and auto parts, the market future of electric cars is also bright; (4) Development of new energy, including development of hydropower plants, construction of wind generating set, development of the photovoltaic industry and exploitation of bio energy (such as ethanol gasoline); (5) Navigation and shipbuilding industries, including port construction, remodeling and upgrade, construction of slipways and docks and technology upgrade, manufacturing and maintenance of civil transportation ships, special ships and ocean engineering equipment, training of shipmen and navigation managers and the development of maritime service; (6) Exploitation of tourism, including rural tourism and ecological tourism.

## *Main content of China-India integration*

Since Indian Prime Minister Modi brought forth the "Make in India" campaign on 25 September 2014, many projects welled up inside India, including India's industrial zone and economic special zone, energy resource, transportation infrastructure construction and shipbuilding, which means this is a time of opportunity and emphasis for Sino–India trade and economic integration.

First, there's investment in natural resources. India has abundant natural resources, with almost 100 types of minerals. It ranks first in the world in mica production and third in coal and barite production. India has huge mineral production potentials and can promise mine renting rights for as long as 20–30 years. Its demand for all types of metals and minerals will largely increase in the next 15 years. Besides, India's development of the energy and cement industries boosted the development of mineral and

*Seeking Sino–India Development Coordination under the Belt and Road*  **163**

metal industries, and its geographic location is beneficial for export. India ranks sixth in the world in aluminum ore reserves and fifth in iron ore reserves, taking up 5% and 8% of global production, respectively.

In oil and gas, India has 15 basins with oil and gas, with a reserve of 28.1 billion tons of oil equivalent, out of which 11.1 billion tons of oil equivalent have been discovered and 17 billion tons are waiting to be discovered, taking up 60% of the entire quantity of resources. The discovered oil and gas resources are located in Mumbai High Basin on the western sea and in the states of Andhra Pradesh, Gujarat, Odisha and Assam on the Bay of Bengal in the east. Seven of these basins already have oil and gas production activities.[12]

Second is the investment in India's special economic zones and industrial zones. Right now, India has 202 export-oriented special economic zones, located in Uttar Pradesh, Madhya Pradesh, Tamil Nadu, etc.[13] India's special economic zone policies are still in their beginning stages and most of such planned zones are quite small.[14] In recent years, many industrial parks established were dilapidated because industrial parks and their matching facilities could not satisfy the needs of foreign investment, and also because India's land law is not beneficial to foreign investment, making land requisition extremely difficult and the labor policies are quite harsh to large enterprises.[15]

Third is the shipbuilding industry. India is a large country on the South Asian subcontinent and along the Indian Ocean coast, with about 7,500 kilometers of coast line, with natural conditions for developing shipbuilding industry. India's shipbuilding industry experienced a rapid growth in 2002–2007, with an overall turnover of 259%, making India a main ship export country in the world. But during the following few years, the shipbuilding industry experienced a downfall because of

---

[12] Sedimentary Basins in India, Ministry of Petroleum & Natural Gas, http://www.oilobserver.com/tendency/ article/1504. Accessed on 20 April 2016.

[13] List of Operational SEZ of India as on 18.02.2016, http://sezindia.nic.in/writereaddata/pdf/ListofoperationalSEZs.pdf. Accessed on 20 November 2015.

[14] *Financial Times*: Modi pushes for Make in India Campaign: http://www.ftchinese.com/story/001058406. Accessed on 20 November 2015.

[15] Liu Xiaoxue,"There are potentials in the economic and trade between China and India", http://www.nbd.com.cn/articles/2014-09-11/862453.html. Accessed on 20 November 2015.

two reasons: the lack of government policies and lack of government support in tax and financing; the lack of skilled, experienced workers in the industry. Even so, India's shipbuilding industry has its advantages, including cheap labor prices, large domestic demand and its domestic industries can provide raw materials for shipbuilding, and 7,500 kilometers of coastline.[16]

Fourth, infrastructure construction. India's Twelfth 5-Year Plan Committee has planned to invest 1 trillion in infrastructure construction, out of which, investment on India's road and bridge construction was expected to be close to 19.2 billion USD in 2017, with the expectation of road and bridge infrastructure growing 17.4% from 2012 to 2017. In the 12th 5-Year Plan, about 20% of the investment is used in developing basic infrastructure such as national highways. In railway, the committee has approved an investment of 95.6 billion USD. With the joining of the private sector, in 2020 it's expected that investment in India's domestic railway net will reach 42 billion USD. India's civil aviation is also a rapidly growing industry. It is estimated that India will become the world's third largest civil aviation market in 2020 and the largest in 2030.[17] India's planning committee plans to invest 30.05 billion USD in ports as part of the 5-year plan. Right now, India has 13 main ports and 95% of its trade comes from sea transports. In electric infrastructure, Modi planned to have all families to "at least light one lamp" within his 5-year term, concentrating in thermoelectricity, hydroelectricity, solar power, etc.[18] India's domestic gas pipelines are mainly located in its northwest and northeast. The Indian government plans to add 18 million meters of natural gas pipelines and plans to construct multiple cross-border natural pipelines, such as the Turkmenistan–Afghanistan–Pakistan–India Pipeline.

---

[16] Indian Shipbuilding Industry: Poised for Take off, https://www.kpmg.com/IN/en/IssuesAndInsights/ThoughtLeadership/Indian%20Shipbuilding%20Industry-%20Poised%20for%20Take%20off.pdf. Accessed on 20 April 2016.

[17] India China Chamber of Commerce and Industry, http://ccei.org.in/infrastructure.html. Accessed on 20 November 2015.

[18] India China Chamber of Commerce and Industry, http://ccei.org.in/infrastructure.html. Accessed on 20 November 2015.

## Risks and challenges in Sino–India integration

To attract more foreign investment, the Indian government has made a policy beneficial to investors: in most departments and areas, the government allows an investment ceiling in the automatic route of foreign investment of 100%.[19]

The Indian government also released an Internet environmental approval mechanism, to speed up project approval and increase transparency. In some industries where the government encourages investment, which mainly includes infrastructure construction, projects with export potential, projects that can hire lots of labor, the government gives investors preferential policies on tariff and taxes. The special economic zone also has a series of preferential policies toward domestic and foreign investments, such as a 100% exemption of income tax on export earnings in the first 5 years after company establishment, and 50% exemption of income tax on export earnings in the next 5 years and 50% exemption of income tax on export earnings after reinvestment. The government also has no limit on foreign commercial loan less than 500 million USD, exempts central sales tax, Alternative Minimum Tax and service tax.[20]

To help remote areas with inconvenient transportation to industrialize, the central government tailored policies for India's eight northeast states. According to regulations of value add made by the Tax Bureau under the Finance Department, the policy provided enterprises in these regions with a series of preferential policies, including capital investment subsidies, interest subsidies, insurance reimbursement, exemption of 100% income taxes, consumption taxes, etc.[21]

At the same time, we need to recognize the risks and challenges of investing in India. In September 2014, President Xi Jinping visited India and in May 2015, Indian Prime Minister Modi visited China. China promised investment to India and India promised to keep improving investment environment and giving China more investment benefits.

---

[19]Ministry of Commerce and Industry of India: Annual Report 2014–2015, http://mhrd.gov.in/annual-report-2015-part-i. Accessed on 20 April 2016.

[20]*Ibid.*

[21]*Ibid.*

However, Chinese side still has many potential investment risks in India, such as many restrictions on Chinese investment in India; India has a serious corruption issue and complicated approval process; India has complicated and verbose laws, preventing foreign investments from entering the Indian market and bad infrastructure.

Because of a lack of political mutual trust between China and India, India has a lot of a restrictions on investment from China. The Foreign Exchange Management Act dictates that if citizens of Pakistan, Bangladesh, Sri Lanka, Afghanistan, Iran and China want to establish any commercial organizations in India, they need to have permission of the Indian Reserve Bank first. With regard to the visa issue, many citizens from restricted countries cannot apply for long-term visa and work visa and need to go back to their countries to renew their visas, which seriously hinders investment in India.

Investment risks in India include rampant corruption among domestic officials, and rent-seeking activities are widely prevalent. Corruption and low executive efficiency are publicly considered two stubborn diseases of the Indian government. When foreign companies apply for registration or project approval in India, they usually go on for more than half a year without hearing back. Even though India's legal system is relatively complete, the execution isn't good. It's extremely complicated to solve investment or cooperation conflicts through the judicial process and some conflicts are left for long terms without being solved.

Furthermore, India has complicated and various laws, placing lots of restrictions on foreign investment. In 2013, a new land law in India was regulated such that requisition parties need to pay a compensation that's four times and two times the land price to rural and urban landowners, respectively. Also, when joint state–private projects and private enterprises requisition land, they need to seek agreement of 70% and 80% of landowners in advance. Compared to other countries, India's Labor Law is strict and complicated; the 1947 Industrial Disputes Act dictates that enterprises with more than 100 employees need to have government permission between laying off people or closing business. Besides, India has complex types of taxes on foreign investment, with large tax rate fluctuations. Even though the Modi government brought forth a series of plans for reform, it received a lot of opposition from the Indian people and the opposition party, making it difficult to push forward reforms.

Besides the above investment risks, India's infrastructure lags behind, its regional infrastructure such as railway, road, airport and port are seriously lacking and inefficient. At the same time, India has a serious shortage of energy, especially oil and electricity. These elements greatly increased the cost of foreign investment. When Chinese enterprises are investing, they should be aware of such risks.

To sum up, India's economic foundation and Modi government's "Make in India" campaign have provided the joining of Chinese and Indian economies with an opportunity. This chapter emphasized on a few regions where they may possibly join. In fact, the content of Sino–India economic cooperation and range is far wider. In 2013, when Premier Li Keqiang visited India, China promised to take measures to deal with unbalanced trade issue, including establishing drug supervision (including registration) cooperation, strengthening the connection between Chinese enterprises and Indian information enterprises, and complete communications on plant quarantine of agricultural products. India, on the contrary, welcomes Chinese enterprises to visit the country and invest, participate in infrastructure construction and strengthen cooperation on project contracting. At the same time, both sides appointed a strategic economic dialogue mechanism to research macroeconomic policy coordinate and agreed to strengthen the cooperation on energy conservation and environmental protection, new energy and sustainable energy and high technology. The two sides also agreed to strengthen cooperation on railway, including heavy haulage and development of stations.

Since 2014, the two countries began cooperation in construction of industrial zones. China has already set up two industrial zones in India, setting up a platform for cluster-type development of Chinese enterprises in India. At the same time, the two sides discussed the strengthening of cooperation between financial supervision organizations in the two countries as well as cooperation of financial organizations in the two countries, to provide financing support of economic and trade cooperation projects. As one of the first countries admitted into the Asia Infrastructure Investment Bank, India has played an important part in the Belt and Road financing mechanism. Furthermore, in people-to-people exchanges, India has made a lot of adjustments in visa policy, making it convenient for Chinese to apply for business and travel visa in India. At the same time, in order to promote border trade and people-to-people exchanges and communication, China has provided more convenience for Indian pilgrims to pay pilgrimage to the holy mountains and lakes in the Tibet Autonomous Region.

# Chapter 14

# The Development and Future of BRICS Countries — BRICS: Toward Multipolarity and Global Governance

Bali Ram Deepak

*Center of Chinese and Southeast Asian Studies,*
*Jawaharlal Nehru University, Delhi, India*

## Introduction

We have witnessed the world moving away from unipolarity to bipolarity and now to multipolarity. The US is not declining; however, its clout is fading away as other countries such as China and India are rising. Multipolarity is reflected not only in the emerging economies but also in the organizations formed by the states and also those by the non-state actors. The heterogeneous multipolarity has called for a structural change.

Various scholars have tried to find out answers to these structural changes. Samuel Huntington (1999, p. 35) has coined the notion of uni–multipolar structure with the US in the core and various other countries extending diplomatic, economic and military support for its initiatives. Some of its representations have been obvious in the invasion of Iraq, Afghanistan, imposition of "no fly zone" in Libya, and its involvement in Syria. Such a structural arrangement is unsustainable in the long term, the Libyan and Syrian crises are demonstrative of this. With Donald Trump at the white house, the fissures between the US and its allies are too obvious

## 170  *Bali Ram Deepak*

and the inward thinking of Trump shows that the US as well as its allies will remain non-committal in shaping the future of global order. Richard Haass (2008, p. 44) has argued that "non-polarity" is the answer, where dozens of countries could have the capability of "exercising different powers". Giovanni Grevi (2009, p. 9), on the contrary, argues that the world is becoming increasingly "interpolar" which is "multipolarity in the age of interdependence". He puts the state at the center; however, he agrees that non-state actors could inflict a severe blow on the system. The 9/11 and 26/11 terror strikes in the US and India, respectively, are pointers to the capabilities acquired by the non-state actors and their disastrous consequences. Whatever may be the acronym, this is all a pointer to mutilaterism in the age of global interdependence. Multilaterism or multi-multilateralism is not necessarily an ultimate solution to bilateral or multilateral problem; however, it is extremely important for conflict resolutions and enhancing understanding and cooperation among the nations. The BRICS is just an example of that. The grouping accounts for 22% of the world economy, 19% of the global trade and contributes more than 50% to the world's economic growth. However, if we analyze China's GDP, it is bigger than the GDP of the remaining four, and its contribution to world economy is over 33%.

## BRICS 9th Summit in Xiamen, Fujian

Xiamen is one of the earliest SEZs of China. The city of 3.80 million people with over $13,000 per capita is one of the "pivot cities" for the construction of the Belt and Road Initiative. Together with two more pivot cities in Fujian, namely Fuzhou and Quanzhou, the pivots add $224 billion to $400 billion GDP of Fujian province, where Xi Jinping spent 18 years of his career. No wonder it is one of the "pilot free trade zones" of China, a "demonstration district for cross-strait emerging industries and modern service cooperation", an international shipping center in southeast China, a regional financial service center and trading center of the two sides of the Taiwan straits. Of late, Fujian has taken the lead in declaring three important projects funded by the China–ASEAN Maritime Cooperation Fund: China–ASEAN Marine Products Exchange, China–ASEAN Maritime University, and China–ASEAN Marine Cooperation Center.

In 2016, the province's total import and export trade with BRICS amounted to 67.9 billion yuan, accounting for 6.6% of the province's total foreign trade. Now, what are the likely themes of the summit and what are the themes that Fujian desires to reap the benefits from?

## Likely Themes of the Summit

### Globalization versus deglobalization

The retrenchment of the West led by the US, fissures in the Western alliance, doubts over the success of the European Union following the BREXIT and economic slump in most of the countries and the refugee crisis, etc., issues in the West, have increasingly made these countries protectionist, so much so the US has pulled out of the Paris Climate Change Agreement. On the contrary, the BRICS including many developing countries have remained committed to the globalization and connectivity initiatives in the region and beyond. The BRICS remains committed to the Paris Climate Change Agreement as well as multilateralism.

In the face of such a scenario, BRICS countries face new opportunities but entail greater responsibilities too. During the 9th BRICS summit in Xiamen, the BRICS made a high pitch for globalization and countered the deglobalization or protectionist tendencies of the West. Since the Belt and Road initiative (BRI) proposed by China remains a mammoth connectivity initiative of the century geared toward boosting regional as well as global growth, its endorsement by BRICS may be problematic as there are differing perceptions about some of the BRI corridors among the BRICS countries; however, BRICS countries may not be averse to cooperate on certain projects identified by them after mutual consultations.

### South–South cooperation

It is evident that the developing countries would like to break free from the subservient role they had with the industrialized economies and forge stronger economic and political relations among themselves, which are based on mutual respect, equality and win–win cooperation. The establishment of the BRICS and its affiliated institutions such as the BRICS

New Development Bank (NDB) and Contingency Reserve Fund should be seen in this light. China's connectivity initiative appears to offer such a model for cooperation, which is seen as less exploitative and more relevant to mutual development. No wonder, over 70 countries are on board China's BRI initiative, albeit some smaller BRICS countries have apprehensions about the ultimate goals of the connectivity. However, it is the fact that the BRICS countries, especially China has been instrumental in South–South finance flows; today China's policy banks lend more capital than any other bank in the world. The cooperation has resulted in foreign direct investment, trade, transfer of technology especially in mining, energy, infrastructure sectors, etc. Therefore, South–South Cooperation will be one of the major themes of the summit. Inviting investment from the BRICS and "Going out" to the BRICS would be the main focus of China, particularly Fujian. NDB is expected to make $2.5 billion in loans this year for such cooperation.

However, irrespective of the fact that Brazil is a huge commodity market, Africa and Russia are rich in natural resources, India the biggest agricultural economy, and China the largest exporter of commodities and production capacities, the intra trade between the BRICS countries remains abysmal. For example, in 2015 it stood at about $250 billion. Although Indian Prime Minister Modi called for doubling this number to $500 billion by 2020, if development strategies are incoherent this would be a far cry.

It must be understood by the member countries that unless and until they do not align their respective national development strategies, they cannot think of making their domestic drivers stronger. Hence, the alignment of each other's connectivity projects whether domestic or beyond will result in an enhanced level of engagement at intra BRICS or beyond, thus pushing an all-round growth in trade and investment, finance, tourism, and also people-to-people contacts. In the long run, we would be able to think of a better regional connectivity, intra-regional connectivity which will pave a way for regional or trans-regional economic integration.

Finally, it may seem logical to extend BRICS membership to other countries or at minimum to have a BRICS plus mechanism under the ambit of South–South cooperation; however, presently it is the general feeling of the BRICS countries that multiplicity of membership will make it difficult to prioritize BRICS goal and distribution of the resources.

## Global governance

The paradigm shift in the global economic and political structure has resulted in structural adjustment in the global governance system. The G20 demonstrated that the developed and developing countries could sit together at the high table, while the birth of various new mechanisms such as BRICS, SCO, NDB, Asia Infrastructure Investment Bank (AIIB), Silk Road Fund, etc. indicated that the emerging economies were capable of reshaping or willing to supplement the existing governance mechanisms with new ones. Being the founder members of many of these mechanisms, both India and China are playing a leading role and building bridges between the developed and developing countries and adding multitude of wealth to the global economy.

As China gathers confidence after leading and creating the above-mentioned institutions, a new institution that was likely to be created in the 9th BRICS summit was the establishment of an independent ratings agency. It was agreed during 8th summit in Goa, India that an independent BRICS Rating Agency would be established to transform global financial architecture based on the principles of fairness and equity. It has been believed by the member countries that the lead agencies in the West such as S&P, Fitch and Moody's that account for 90% of the rating market are biased toward the developing countries. For example in May 2017, Moody's ratings agency downgraded China's credit score, warning that economy-wide debt is expected to rise as potential economic growth slows over the coming years (PTI, 2017). Both India and China had slammed the Moody's "inappropriate methodologies" at that time.

There are voices that the establishment of these institutions including the NDB and AIIB has challenged in the post-World War II order. The fact remains that the establishment of these institutions is the outcome of the Bretton Woods System that has been on shaky grounds after the 2008–2009 financial crises as well as the Euro crises, a reminder that if the institutions like IMF, the WB and ADB continue to attach strings to the developmental aids and loans, there is going to be a serious demand for alternative institutions. Especially when the global economic recovery is weak, the establishment of such institutions will promote infrastructural as well as social and economic development in the regions. Even if AIIB does not challenge the existing financial institutions, it would be seen as complementing the existing order.

## Counter terrorism

BRICS countries remain committed to combat terrorism in any shape and form and believe that there is a need to expand practical cooperation in intelligence sharing, capacity building and providing security to their sprawling interests abroad. In this context, a Counter-Terrorism Working Group was established during the 8th summit in Goa and held its first meeting. The group agreed to expand counter terrorism cooperation further to include measures for denying terrorists access to finance and terror hardware such as equipment, arms and ammunition. The second meeting was held in Beijing on 17 May 2017 and conducted extensive discussions on the issue affecting the region and beyond. India has been urging the BRICS nations to back its efforts for the adoption of a comprehensive convention on terrorism at the UN and shed the ambiguity on "good" and "bad" terrorists.

## Combat global warming

At a time when President Donald Trump is withdrawing the US from multilateral arrangements such as the Paris Climate Change Agreement, the BRICS countries have repeatedly expressed their commitment toward the Paris deal and the emission cuts they have undertaken for combating the global warming. No one denies the fact that the combined population of 3 billion people and a GDP of $16 trillion will have a huge impact on global emissions; however, can the BRICS initiate joint research and development into new energy technologies? This has been expressed by some of the BRICS countries like Russia and Brazil that they do not want to be seen as exporters of their natural wealth.

### *People-to-people exchange*

People-to-people exchanges are the pillar of all bilateral and multilateral exchanges. It is the cultural capital of a country that has attraction and lays foundations of understanding between the people. As regards the people-to-people exchanges between the BRICS nations, I believe, even if there are various exchanges such as cultural festivals, media and film exchange, BRICS scholarships programs, etc., however, there is a huge scope to strengthen and broaden the scope of these exchanges. The establishment of BRICS University League is an excellent example. There is a need to institutionalize these mechanisms and establish even more mechanisms at various levels.

## What India and China Can Do

At the outset, the economic and political clout they will exert on the mechanisms of global governance hinges upon their domestic drivers. Therefore, the greatest contribution they can make to the G20 or other new mechanisms is by maintaining a robust domestic growth and regional peace and stability. It is for this reason that the emerging economies have been able to inject billions of dollars into the existing institutions of global governance and push for their reform and ask for greater representation.

Second, it is owing to these strong domestic drivers that emerging economies would be able to support the ideas such as global infrastructure hub and global infrastructure fund mooted by the 2014 G20 Brisbane summit and the World Bank. President Xi Jinping has supported such moves and has rendered support for the same through the "Belt and Road" initiative, the AIIB, the Silk Road Fund mechanisms, etc.

Third, domestic growth could be stimulated in various ways as both India and China have unfolded ambitious connectivity projects which could be docked together by way of consultation and coordination at the provincial as well as national level. For example, Prime Minister Modi's pet project, the National Perspective Plan of the Sagarmala Programme, which aims to modernize India's ports and integrate them with Special Economic Zones, Port-based Smart Cities, Industrial Parks, Warehouses, Logistics Parks and Transport Corridors could be docked to China's

"Belt and Road" initiative notwithstanding with the fact that India has expressed its strong dissatisfaction over the China–Pakistan Economic Corridor on the issue of sovereignty. As far as the regional connectivity is concerned, India's "Bharatmala" plans to connect the entire Himalayan belt of Indian states through a network of rails and roads and could be docked to China's Northwest and Southwest regional plans. In eastern India, the BCIM economic corridor could revolutionize the overland connectivity and facilitate not only domestic but also the regional growth with ASEAN. Similarly, India and China could negotiate a larger economic corridor running through Northwest China and Northern India, which could easily be connected through a network of roads, railways and oil and gas pipelines. Needless to say, in order to materialize these projects, both need to take a holistic and long-term view of their relations as well as the global shift from the Atlantic to the Pacific. The BRICS will cease to exist if India and China cannot hold together. Can they coordinate their policies *vis-à-vis* millennium development goals and sustainability, thus setting example to other BRICS countries?

Fourth, in order to push the transformation of the global governance structure, both India and China need to become partners in each other's development. There have been positive changes in the bilateral security as well as business environment; however, given the potentials of both, there is a huge scope. In order to tap this potential, both need to initiate innovative developmental plans and policies and initiate structural reforms in areas such as taxation, investment, finance, labor, etc. Besides, the macroeconomic policies should be in sync with the social policies, which will ensure stability in society and acceptance of the government planning.

In conclusion, even though the paradigm shift in the global governance has given India and China a bigger say as well as responsibility in the evolving global ecosystem, there remains huge asymmetries in their power and economic structures *vis-à-vis* the developed economies. Rather than challenging the existing system, they need to bide their time, innovate new ones and become partners in each other's development by docking their developmental strategies. It is natural to have differences between two big neighbors; nevertheless, these could be mitigated if a holistic view of the relationship is taken. Therefore, the momentum of the high-level visits and people-to-people exchanges need to be heightened.

# References

Grevi, G. (2009) The Interpolar World: A New Scenario. Occasional Paper 79, Paris: EU Institute for Security Studies, June 2009, p. 9.

Haass, R. N. (2008) The age of nonpolarity: What will follow US dominance. *Foreign Affairs* **87** (3), 44–56.

Huntington, S. P. (1999) The lonely superpower. *Foreign Affairs* **78** (2), 35–49.

PTI [Press Trust of India] (2017) Moody's Cuts China's Rating on Debt Concerns. *The Hindu*, 24 May 2017.

Renard, T. (2009) A Brick in the World: Emerging powers, Europe and the world order. Egmont paper, The Royal Institute for International Relations, Brussels.

# Chapter 15

# The BRICS: An Attractive and Compelling Alternative to Global Governance

Tony Karbo

*Centre for Conflict Resolution, Cape Town, South Africa*

## Introduction

The Brazil, Russia, India, China and South Africa partnership association is the brainchild of Goldman Sachs, an Investment Company that coined the term. At first it was viewed as a meeting of four of the most vibrant economies (emerging economies) in the world at the turn of the century. The growth of South Africa as the foremost economy in Africa accorded it the privilege of membership into the loose grouping of countries that share interests in particular areas (economy, development). What started as sidelines meetings during the UN General Assembly in New York quickly grew into a multilateral alternative force for global development. It is now an established fact that the Brazil, Russia, India, China and South Africa (BRICS) platform represents one of the most significant developments in global governance in the 21st century. The block brings together significant members of emerging powers from the global south, each playing significant regional roles in South America, South Asia, Eurasia and Africa.

**180** *Tony Karbo*

Within a very short period of time, the BRICS platform has brought together powers that have become strategic in global discourses, taking significant international decisions and playing a pivotal role in the negotiation of major global affairs. Individually, BRICS states bring economic and political stature to international partnerships during a period when the old western-world system is under pressure to transform. What brings the BRICS together is a desire to change the world system to one that reflects the diversity of world power, cultures, economies and societies. They share this reformist agenda and the determination to exercise relevance in the hope of a just and fair world system. This is facilitated by the fact that the five BRICS countries make up about 25% of the global GDP and host more than 40% of the world's population, a population which is spread across five continents.[1]

The end of the Cold War and the beginning of the 21st century ushered in a shift in global power distribution giving credence to a broader alliance of states in the global South to address the issues of global economic inequality that the UN has been debating since the 1960s. At issue is whether or not the BRICS have sufficient collective power to influence global affairs including decisions in the UN Security Council and other global institutions (WTO, IMF, WB).

To address the question of relevance of BRICS in the second decade of the 21st century, one needs to answer the following questions:

- Is the BRICS a community of states or is it simply a group of solidarity between member states?
- What are the criteria for inclusion?
- Are the criteria still relevant today?
- Is expansion possible and if so how do we bring in new members?
- Have the developmental needs of the people of BRICS countries been addressed? In other words, are the citizens of BRICS part of the processes of association?
- What are the processes used in BRICS development?

---

[1] Centre for Conflict Resolution (2014), Concept Paper for a Policy Advisory Group Seminar on South Africa and the BRICS: Progress, Problems and Prospects, Cape Town, South Africa.

The reality on the ground has been that while BRICS pronouncements hint at a broader conception and indeed understanding, the realities of the forms of engagement still resonate with more traditional forms of alliance building that are aimed less at transformation than at coordinating individual national self-interests.

While the transformation from a sidelines meeting of foreign ministers at the UN General Assembly into a Head of State meeting was quick, the more substantive cooperation and the development of pathways toward integration of policies has been incremental. We have seen some positive movements in certain areas of economic cooperation, academic and intellectual cooperation (this Think Tank Summit is one such example) and finance and banking. A web of networks has been created with a view to build consensus on important issues and to encourage heads of state to include those issues at larger global fora such as the G20 and indeed the UN. This approach is a marked departure from the top-down approach of traditional multilateral cooperation led by the more developed states of Europe and America.

## BRICS Coordination: What Do We Mean?

The term coordination is used loosely and means different things to different people, so the first step in assessing coordination in this chapter was to adopt an operational definition of the term to use as a framework. There are at least three closely interlinked yet slightly different dimensions of coordination that have to be considered. The first dimension is Aid Coordination which refers to the established mechanisms and management that member governments and their external partners have agreed to in order to maximize the effectiveness of external aid for development at the national and sectoral levels.

The second dimension is a subset of aid coordination and refers to specific mechanisms and arrangements agreed to by partners on how to improve their effectiveness in the process of development. Finally, the third dimension, development coordination, refers to specific mechanisms and arrangements agreed within and among the community of development partners to improve their effectiveness as partners in the development process. This third dimension of coordination is what this chapter will attempt to address as it relates to the BRICS.

The importance of development coordination and sector coordination — both of which go beyond mere aid or donor coordination — has been highlighted in recent years and heavily influenced the 2016 BRICS summit. To be effective, BRICS countries need to recognize the fact that efforts at coordination will not achieve significant improvements unless and until they are effectively integrated within national development planning, governance structures and systems. To be precise, achieving effective coordination of BRICS cooperation agenda must be integrated into national governance structures of BRICS. This means that BRICS governments must increasingly take a leading role in policy formulation and implementation, combined with strategic mechanisms for management of resources and engagement between the government and the community of development partners; in this case — BRICS countries.

Five years ago, the rapid rate at which Brazil, Russia, India, China and South Africa (BRICS) have been closing the gap with the developed world was breathtaking. The popular BRICS acronym referring to these rising powers was at least up until 2015 an indication of the shifts in global economic and political relations. We have witnessed, however, in the last few years a reversal of gains in three of the BRICS member countries (Brazil, Russia and South Africa) due to political and economic reasons prevailing in the last few years. Brazil on its part has witnessed an impeachment of a sitting president; Russia is facing excruciating economic sanctions from the west and involved in at least two fronts of wars — Syria and Ukraine; and, South Africa is reeling from domestic scandals of corruption, state capture by business associates of the sitting president and economic downturn. China and India are still growing though at a much slower pace than the above 10 percentile range 15 years ago.

Other obstacles include the threat of political and social instability arising from extreme social inequality and rampant corruption, as well as problems caused by an inadequate infrastructure unable to keep apace of the rapid economic growth seen in recent years. Further obstacles include massive environmental problems and the weight of demographic pressures on labor markets and education and social welfare systems.

As has been seen already, the maintenance of economic growth does not guarantee social equality and environmental sustainability. Indeed,

BRICS countries already marked by regional and social disparities will likely see problems associated with social inequality and environmental sustainability further exacerbated. Experience shows that only the right policy choices at the right stage in the economic development of BRICS will support and sustain growth. The choices that BRICS have to make include among others a clear definition of their identity (defining who they are), what their *modus operandi* would be and how the objectives of BRICS will be achieved. At the moment, it appears that BRICS is like the African Union (AU) — an organization that meets twice every year to make plans which will never see the light of day. Coming up with policies is not enough to bring results. Steps must be taken to implement the policies. Without a BRICS secretariat, this cannot be realized. This should be established within certain legal parameters that will layout operational frameworks for BRICS. Only then can coordination be made efficient.

These challenges have aptly demonstrated the considerable obstacles to development. Liberal economies as we know them go through periods of boom and bust, and for BRICS to be able to deal with these challenges, they need to identify unambiguously who they are and what the purpose of their coming together speaks to.

## The Evolution and Pathways to Integration

As stated previously, the promotion of national interests by each BRICS member country is the biggest threat to the loose alliance. The evolution of the BRICS can be divided into four distinct epochs or eras. The first era is the era of formation (2006–2008). This era marked the beginning of informal meetings on the sidelines of the once a year UN General Assembly when initially four countries (Brazil, Russia, India and China) would meet at the ministerial level to explore possibilities and areas of collaboration. By 2009, the four countries (BRIC) met in Russia and established BRIC. Each country was pushing for its own agenda with significant risks.

The second era was the Expansion Era (2009–2011). This era marked the beginning of deeper discussions around issues of economic collaboration and the invitation of South Africa, the largest economy on the African continent at the time to join the association. The loose grouping by now is

**184** *Tony Karbo*

spread across four continents with five members with different strategic interests in international relations and diplomacy. For example, whereas South Africa has significant energy-related interests with China, India is perhaps more interested in attracting Chinese investment for job creation, economic growth and a reduction of pressures related to climate change. The spread of member countries across five continents makes it difficult to align these divergent interests in a coordinated manner.

The third era is the Era of Institutionalization (2013–2016). This era marked the setting up of various structures including the New Development Bank (NDB) and the Contingent Reserves Arrangement (CRA). The NDB and CRA were established as an alternative financial facility that will assist members absorb developmental needs in addition to other traditional mechanisms of national resource mobilization. The establishment of the BRICS Business Council (BBC) and the information-sharing platform to include education, culture and environmental engagement in 2013 was a signal to the rest of the world about the seriousness with which the BRICS states intend to move to propel the alliance into global significance. The NDB is seen as representing an alternative to the World Bank and IMF, with an initial capital commitment of $50 Billion US dollars and a CRA amounting to $100 billion US dollars.

The fourth era is the Era of Transformation and Recoupling. In the face of the growing backlash in globalization and the rising nationalist sentiments in Europe and the election of Donald Trump in the United States, the international community was compelled to rethink global governance issues and examine alternatives to globalization. The BRICS which has by this time become increasingly visible on the global stage had to quickly adapt to the new global realities, thus, the urgent call as we write this chapter for more pragmatic approaches to dealing with global problems such as climate change, migration, energy crises, transnational crime, etc. The original objective of economic collaboration has quickly been transformed into taking a leadership role with China in the lead of these global problems.

Member countries are scattered across four continents. This expansive nature of the alliance makes it impossible to have a strategic security alliance from the block. It will be difficult to imagine Russia and India going into a security partnership with China; the three countries are nuclear powers, with two of them (Russian and China) having permanent seats at the Security Council. China sees the BRICS as a channel through which South–South cooperation can be promulgated. South–South cooperation is a conduit to global peace and security. If China continues to take a lead role in the block, the BRICS will certainly come to play a key role in global governance.

## Alternative Solutions to Development

The BRICS alliance is seen by many as an alternative solution to global development challenges. The formal structures established are designed to facilitate engagement including organizing annual Heads of State Summits. Scholars such as Thakar suggest that the BRICS as a group was not created out of political negotiations but created out of shared values or common economic interests.[2] Thakar believes that such a basis for coming together poses a fundamental problem since all five BRICS countries also have deep and specific ties with the pivotal developed countries in the western world.[3] The significance of BRICS in the international system will be measured by the influence of its members individually and collectively on the international political system. In other words, the relevance of BRICS will depend not simply on the growth trajectories of individual group members but also on the extent to which, in global discourse and decisions, they can individually and collectively represent the interests, worldviews, and policy priorities of the mass of developing countries.[4] In terms of identity and direction, it can be argued that BRICS remains a community of states based on sovereignty and non-interference in the internal affairs of another sovereign state. The alternative to traditional top-down partnerships is embedded in the BRICS principles of openness, solidarity, equality, mutual understanding, inclusivity and mutually beneficial cooperation.

---

[2]Thakar (2014, 1792–1793).
[3]*Ibid.*
[4]*Ibid.*

## Strategies for Deepening Cooperation

The adopted strategies for incrementally developing BRICS as a global player that promotes South–South cooperation are enshrined in two primary pillars including:

- coordination in multilateral fora with a focus on economic and political governance
- cooperation among members.

Intra-BRICS cooperation has been gaining traction in the areas of finance, agriculture, trade transnational crime, education and health. Of these, the financial sector receives a special focus as a new front of cooperation. At its 6th Summit, the BRICS established the NDB, aimed at financing infrastructure and sustainable development projects in the BRICS and other developing countries. The new institution will initially have a combined subscribed capital of 50 billion USD.

Similarly, the BRICS have also concluded the agreement that creates the CRA, a fund with an initial investment sum of 100 billion USD, which the BRICS countries will be able to use to forestall short-term liquidity shortfalls. One of the objectives of the CRA is to contribute to international financial stability, by providing an additional line of defense to the BRICS. The establishment of the Bank and the CRA conveyed a strong message on the willingness of BRICS members to deepen and consolidate their partnership in the economic-financial area.

Deepening the focus on social inclusion and sustainable development gave visibility to policies implemented by member countries and to the contribution of the BRICS' economic growth to poverty reduction. Social policies regarding inclusive growth and sustainable development were carved out to tackle pressing social problems not only in BRICS member countries but global challenges as well. The BRICS played a key role in the formulation of Agenda 2030 (The Sustainable Development Goals).

The BRICS agenda is deliberately designed as a South–South cooperation agenda. Therefore, the establishment of the NDB has been portrayed as the most vivid illustration of that process. The NDB can serve a dual purpose including a financial mechanism for BRICS countries as well as a tool to coordinate cooperation with other developing countries to finance their development projects.

## BRICS Challenges

Before it was plagued by political and economic scandals, Brazil had the most promising prospects for implementing key policy areas regarding BRICS cooperation. With the largest economy in South America, Brazil was poised to play a strategic role in regional development. However, inadequate infrastructure and high levels of inequality have hampered prospects for Brazil to take off. Reforms adopted in recent years to address social inequalities were positive steps in the right direction.

What could have been one of the most vibrant of all BRICS economies is almost stagnant due to sanctions imposed by the EU and the US for Russia's involvement in the Ukraine and Syria. BRICS countries have been ambivalent about Russia's involvement in Ukraine and Syria despite international condemnation of its activities in these sovereign states. Russia's strategic interests at the international level are at odds with the strategic interests of China and other BRICS countries. BRICS must align their strategic interests in order to have impact on the global stage.

India has one of the most unequal societies of all the BRICS countries. Its growth projections can only be sustained, if it can positively address the enormous social inequality and improve its infrastructure. There is a need to modernize the education and health systems in India. There is commendable strategic capacity in policy development and implementation. This puts it much higher along the spectrum when compared with the other BRICS countries.

China has the largest economy and the most diverse demography in the block. It also has the greatest potential to lead the block in the formulation and implementation of strategic policies that will spur the BRICS to take on global leadership on several global issues including climate change, migration, achieving sustainable development goals and global trade. China has the most stable political and economic system, and yet, like its counterparts in the block, this system is put at great risk due to the high levels of inequality in the country. However, China over time will be in a better position to apply sound long-term solutions to the problems outlined above, as the country's performance in the area of governance structures is aligned with its economic system.

Recent events in South Africa pose a great threat not only to the BRICS alliance but also to South Africa's regional role in Southern Africa and the African continent. Although South Africa has institutional capacity in the areas of policy formulation and implementation, the split in the ruling party and the apparent economic decline is putting into question the gains that the country has made since the end of Apartheid in 1994. The South African government requires significant improvement in the areas of effective inter-ministerial coordination, policy implementation and communication policy. Among the greatest challenges faced by the BRICS today is the levels of inequality and social exclusion in all five countries. Economic inequality is rising across the BRICS countries. South Africa is punted as the most unequal country in Africa with a majority of the black population living in poor conditions and not taking part in the formal economy. Steady economic growths in China and India have not translated to improved standards of life for a majority of the people. Significant gains in GDP have not translated into commensurate improvements in living standards. With the exception of the NDB and the CRA, the BRICS framework has not proven very efficient or substantive in bridging the inequality gap with BRICS countries.

A second and perhaps a more pressing challenge is how BRICS can manage multiple multilateral members. All five members belong to the G20 and G77 Global Governance Frameworks. The BRICS interests will be better secured if the larger global governance frameworks are used to promote strategic interests. For example, a more representative framework that can do more for BRICS is the G20. To compete with the G20 for global dominance, using the BRICS will not achieve intended objectives.

There seems to be some improvement in terms of dialogue between and among BRICS leaders. Dialogue must take place on important issues before policy prescriptions are offered. BRICS leaders must overcome the challenge of promoting individual interests and should strive to support the collective interests of members. At the ministerial level, dialogue is more substantial. Representatives can prepare agendas and policy options ahead of time so they can be discussed at the meetings. But those options may just be suggestions or advice, not formal policy adjustments.

Seen as an alternative voice for the developing countries, BRICS can turn themselves into an alliance that will speak for the poorer countries of the world. But will this be a panacea to the problems of the developing world. BRICS should entertain the idea of seeing itself as an entity that could offer relief to poorer countries in cases where the global instruments such as WB, IMF and WTO have failed to deliver solutions.

## Recommendations

Over the years, BRICS have developed specific strategies to tackle development problems in each member state. Collectively, the results of these strategies are at best mixed. This is not surprising due to a large extent in the disparities in economic, political and other considerations. Whereas the largest economy of the BRICS, China has maintained and sustained economic growth of 10%, other members have remarkably different results. With the exception of India which, like China has also maintained a relatively stable growth pattern for the last 10 or so years, Russia, Brazil and South Africa are not so fortunate. Economic sanctions imposed on Russia by the EU and the United States because of its involvement in Ukraine have thwarted Russian economic growth for several years. Brazil is not only reeling from low economic outputs but also dealing with a plethora of political scandals that have led to the impeachment of one president and the successor now facing repeated calls for his impeachment. This does not bode well with the market performance and economic growth.

South Africa is no different as the current president is under pressure to resign because of what some scholars have called "state capture" by the president's close business associates. South Africa is officially in recession. With three out of five struggling economically and politically, the BRICS can hardly be seen as an organization that is ready to take on leadership of global challenges in the 21st century.

A fundamental value for the BRICS states is the shared desire for a more equitable and fairer world. This value is more pronounced in the block's desire for peace, security and development of the developing world through South–South cooperation. The framework of cooperation is to enhance economic growth through greater engagement with one another as well as with the rest of the developing world.

Specifically, BRICS should take note of the following:

- Establish a set of institutions with sound legal frameworks and infrastructure that guarantee enforcement of private contracts and provide adequate protection of property rights. An important step in improving the quality of institutions is to establish corporate governance arrangements that ensure independence from government.
- BRICS countries can make their financial systems more balanced and growth-friendly by helping diversify funding sources away from excess reliance on banks. According to OECD, high reliance on bank lending slows growth and widens inequality. The establishment of the NDB is a welcome step in that direction.
- Income inequality has increased among the BRICS countries. Reducing inequalities and strengthening social cohesion through inclusive growth is one way of addressing the problems of inequality. BRICS should establish social safety policies as a requirement for access to loans from the NDB.
- Devise policies that consider the multidimensional nature of prosperity and how various well-being outcomes are distributed in the population. The benefits of increased prosperity and globalization must be shared more evenly across social groups.
- Make sure that voices of all citizens are heard by promoting wide participation to political and economic decisions, in particular, from less engaged groups.
- Harmonize the Strategic Planning Capacities of BRICS countries with a view to strengthen institutional capacity for development cooperation among BRICS countries. Improve inter-ministerial coordination and policy steering function of BRICS countries. This is of particular importance when it comes to social financial and industrial policies.
- Policy design and implementation should involve an active and vibrant civil society. Sustainable governance institutions must demonstrate inclusivity of citizens of BRICS countries and this includes the participation of civil society groups. Civil society does have the

*The BRICS: An Attractive and Compelling Alternative to Global Governance* **191**

potential to actively engage in the fight against inequality, social exclusion and poverty.

- Harmonize the fields of education and labor market policies.
- BRICS should facilitate greater cooperation in the area of trade, especially in goods and services, toward strengthening partnerships for development and industrialization. They should engage in further discussions on the feasibility of implementing preferential trade agreements among themselves. In addition to the BRICS Development Bank established in 2016, BRICS should establish deliberate mechanisms that discriminate in favor of the least developed of the BRICS countries in industrialization and infrastructure loans.
- Recognizing the shared objective of progressive and democratic transformation of the institutions of global governance, BRICS should strive to enhance the voice and representation of emerging economies and developing countries in multilateral forums. BRICS should actively explore innovative and complementary partnerships for sustainable and equitable development.
- In peace and security, BRICS cannot create a viable peace and security architecture capable of dealing with security issues of individual and collective security problems. BRICS should therefore continue to promote the United Nations as the legitimate and central international agency responsible for the maintenance of peace and security at the global level. The UN is the only global institution with the credibility, infrastructure and trust by members of the international community. China and Russia should use the Security Council leverage to push for more support of the UNDPKO and the UN PBF (United Nations Peace Building Fund). Contemporary global issues such as nuclear proliferation, refugees, migration, climate change and human and drug trafficking can only be tackled by a global body such as the UN. BRICS should strongly support the work of the UN in these issues.
- BRICS should intensify its support for collaboration between academics and scholars through a variety of institutions, networks and programs that advance education, research and skills development. Joint research should be conducted by BRICS Think Tanks to further the collaborative objectives of BRICS in the areas of scientific research and technology transfer.

- Lift the quantity and the quality of jobs and address labor market insecurity and segmentation. Policy reforms should aim at creating quality jobs while integrating specific socio-demographic groups that are underrepresented in the workforce, most notably young people and women and preserving the inclusion of senior workers. BRICS must minimize the risk of vulnerable youth — such as early school leavers who are neither employed nor educated or trained.

## References

Daniel, R. and Virk, K. (2014) (Rapporteurs); Africa and the BRICS: Progress, Problems and Problems. Policy Advisory Group Seminar Report: Tshwane (Pretoria), South Africa, November, 2014.

Dzinesa, G. A. and Masters, L. (2009) (Rapporteurs); Taming The Dragon? Defining Africa's Interests at The Forum on China-Africa Co-operation (FOCAC). Policy Advisory Group Seminar Report: Premier Hotel, Tshwane (Pretoria), South Africa, May 13–14, 2009.

Sidiropoulos, E. (2017) Emerging Powers, Clubs and Equality. In *Perspectives: Political Analysis and Commentary: Africa: South Africa: Emerging Power or Fading Star*. Heinrich Boll Stiftung, Issue 1, January 2017.

# Chapter 16

# Policy Suggestions on the Coordination of BRICS Strategies*

### Renato Galvao Flores

*International Intelligence Unit and Graduate School of Economics, FGV, Rio de Janeiro, Brazil*

## Introduction

The suggestions made here are not aimed at coordination alone. We believe it is high time that a more effective role and substance be given to the BRICS. Without extending coordination to address themes like the ones proposed here, a very light and powerless BRICS, as nowadays perceived, will continue to be the main traits of this ever odd, though not unreasonable, association. Indeed, after having made a fuss in the international scenario, the group has somewhat been subsumed under the fast, unexpected and fairly disturbing changes in the scenario, losing momentum and purpose, in spite of recent achievements like the New Development Bank.

A new push is needed.

Fully aware that there exist forward-looking agendas, with some of their items in progress, our departure point is an ideal one: the thoughts shared here suppose that, apart from positive will from the five members,

---

*The author is solely responsible for the views expressed here; and doesn't commit anybody else or represent, in any way whatsoever, ideas or positions of his institution.

**194** *Renato Galvao Flores*

there are no major constraints to their implementation. They also underline a plea for more focus on realistic BRICS actions, avoiding either too general statements or the vapid desire to address all the present world problems.

Notwithstanding, focused actions need not deal with concrete or specific themes alone. The suggestions made here may be divided into two classes: one comprising general issues where specific problems or areas must be tackled and another addressing well-characterized sectors where selected projects and targeted measures apply. Focus is inherent to both, and both demand wise coordination efforts.

The structure of the chapter is as follows: After a preliminary discussion on the different merits of cooperation and coordination, and the present relevance of the latter, two sections introduce the proposals, one for each class. A final one concludes the argument.

## A Preliminary Comment: Coordination Versus Cooperation

In nearly all BRICS fora and debates, one clearly perceives confusion between cooperation and coordination, the former, though with qualities of its own, is to a certain extent easier to be achieved and does not necessarily need the existence of the very association. Particularly, when it evolves within a bilateral framework, something that may indirectly strengthen relations inside the group but in reality lacks a BRICS character.

In the absence of actual "BRICS achievements", many researchers and policymakers raise a list of bilateral initiatives, comprising the different pairs of members, implicitly exhibiting those as evidence of a solid group character.

Nobody denies the fact that an environment with plenty of important bilateral relations is a fertile ground for broader, more encompassing endeavors among all countries involved. However, this is a second-order, indirect effect and does not stand as real proof that the (potential) underlying association is driving the plurilateral initiatives.

Coordination is more subtle and harder to achieve. It requires and effectively translates the very essence of the group, even if loose and practically non-institutionalized like the BRICS. Confounding it with cooperation is unfortunate because both their origins and ways of operating are different.

Coordination is the outcome of joint debate and plans and aims at using the unique synergy of the combined assets — soft and hard, psychological or reputational and material — of all members in order to induce a specific change or acquire a new common status. Its *modus operandi* can involve synchronized diplomatic efforts within a global strategy that may or may not call for individual measures by specific members.

BRICS have till now spent much time and energy in either impact or cliché statements, and in the identification of areas of cooperation, but sufficient attention has not been paid to coordinated strategies.

Perhaps an example, close to our host's policies, may help perceiving the nuances between the two concepts.

China has been pursuing the (One) Belt and (One) Road Initiative — OBOR, an encompassing mega-project launched in 2013 by General Secretary Xi Jinping.[1] OBOR will give rise to a myriad of endeavors, joint works and cooperation activities; China having, in many of them, a main role as partner and sponsor (Linggui and Janglin, 2017).

Nevertheless, OBOR — or B&R — also brings forth, sometimes implicitly, the necessity of coordinated efforts along the belt and the road, in order to turn it into a true and bigger New Silk Road. Coordination, to a certain extent, is the ultimate goal, and it will signal to a more mature stage for the whole initiative.

This is also what the BRICS must pursue.

## The Four Suggestions — I: On General Issues

Both the International Financial System (IFS) and the Foreign Affairs realm are a sort of taboo for the group; it intentionally avoids questions related to them. We believe it is time to face these two dragons.

### *Finance*

BRICS countries are not particularly short of funds — thanks mostly to China — but their impact on the procedures and control of the

---

[1] See, for a general introduction, Lei and Liqiang (2017).

international financial system is disproportionately small, or rather, close to zero. The reasons for this are historical, as the five members have been either hostages or marginal to the system, never decisive actors.

China still displays, nowadays, a weak and incipient financial system; India is even more poorly developed, lacking important basic features; Russia remains insulated from the world system, using mostly indirect ways to interact with it and looking for gateways that would lead it to relevant parts of the system. Brazil and South Africa, thanks to unfortunate macroeconomic policies, remain as peripheral nodes still fighting for domestic stability.

Broadly, all five systems are inwardly oriented and, in different instances, hostages of the IFS. None of their currencies is internationally convertible, in spite of intermittent efforts in this direction by China.

Without a coordinated footprint on the IFS, the BRICS is nothing.

How to build up presence and relevance? A series of measures can be envisaged, exploiting existing gaps or occupying empty spaces often related to a regional dimension.

Why not creating a BRICS credit card?

Think of the credit area of the OBOR Initiative, of the innumerable financial banks in Southeast Asia, even as well in South America, not to mention the underdeveloped market of the very members like India and Russia. A carefully designed popular card, backed by selected private banks, could be a game changer for several populations and a vector for better positioning in the IFS.

Innovative alternative domains — inspired and supported by disruptive technologies — have been created at the margins of the system, like the bitcoin revolution or microfinance and creative, novel credit structures. What is the position of the BRICS toward bitcoin? How could we profit from it, or from similar innovations?

In the areas of infrastructure and climate change, new instruments, boosted by the New Development Bank and the AIIB — Asia Infrastructure Investment Bank — could be designed under a BRICS seal.

Many other initiatives, producing a BRICS ever-spreading spot on international finance, could be conceived; the combined size of the members would nearly assure their success.

*Policy Suggestions on the Coordination of BRICS Strategies* **197**

## Foreign policy

This theme reappears frequently in every BRICS seminar, but usually lacks a proper framing. We explicitly aim here at two objectives.

First, we do not advocate a full BRICS Common Foreign Policy, something so farfetched that it can be considered impossible in the foreseeable future. However, there are a few selected points that the BRICS might — or must — face. This would give them a more coherent and assertive position in the international scene, showing that, beyond the rhetoric, the group moves in a coordinated way in key world affairs.

Some, or all, of the points would involve or rather interact with specific members' policies; an important breakthrough since, until now, each country has cultivated a polite silence on other members' conflicts or ticklish issues. Examples are easy to mention, from Crimea to the India–China border, the South China Sea and even as regards a common policy toward Africa.

Of course, this is a too broad and difficult agenda, but the rewards of a careful choice would be immense. A united BRICS view on global issues akin to their world perspective and affairs would strengthen cohesion, improving the image of the group and enhancing each member's standing.

However, there is nothing against to assert a position about problems outside the five countries' territory either. An explosive exercise would be to fashion a joint standing on the Middle East.

The second line, still within this suggestion, is to continue to pursue a joint, coordinate activity in the face of the international organizations.

In this case, perhaps the great initial success in altering the weighting system for the IMF votes, followed by the stalemate created by the refusal of the US Congress to ratify the decision by the US delegation, had a negative impact on the appeal of this sort of strategy. The impulse gained seems to have evaporated, only a bunch of intentions remaining.

Notwithstanding, this is a key effort that must be pursued at all cost, being closely related to a main goal of the BRICS: to bring, in a peaceful way, but forcefully, deep changes in the existing international order.

## The Four Suggestions — II: On Concrete Areas

Among the several sectors and concrete activities or needed tasks figuring in the international development agenda, we have selected two of foremost relevance.

### *Infrastructure*

Actually, we feel somewhat uncomfortable in raising this suggestion as, from the beaches of Durban to those of Copacabana, from the Kremlin to the Taj Mahal, passing through the Forbidden City, infrastructure is the buzzword of the day, the new miraculous elixir for launching and oiling the development process.

In spite of the monotonous repetition of this mantra, nobody mentions crucial aspects of infrastructure development such as the optimal sequencing and the time lag of the required works, the dire need of adequate planning for the developing and revamping projects and the several associated risks and their proper management, just to mention a few. Too much emphasis is being put on the financing side and related entities, engineering and public policy constraints being usually neglected.

Initiatives then oftentimes result as individual pursuits with low synergy and poorly matched spillovers.

Moreover, infrastructure efforts *per se* are risky — as seen many times in developing countries — building roads that lead to nowhere, raising housing complexes that remain empty, and pursuing urban improvements that create new problems, like traffic increases or overburdens on the city energy sources or its sewage system.

A threading line should orient BRICS policies in this area: coordination, in our view, should come via the sustainability link.

The recent retrenchment of the US from the political arena in the climate change issue opens up a fantastic opportunity for the whole group. Progressively, a BRICS sustainability imprint should be imposed on all infrastructure projects conducted by each member country, aiming at turning BRICS into a model group in the infrastructure debate.

The five countries could become pioneers in setting standards for such endeavors, something that could be greatly helped by its already existing network of influence. In fact, it comprises fund providers like the New Development Bank and the Asia Infrastructure Investment Bank, together with domestic sponsors like Brazil's powerful BNDES (National Bank for Economic and Social Development), encompassing projects like OBOR and proposed energy integration initiatives in Africa, South America and Southeast Asia, and — finally yet importantly — their notorious influence in their respective neighborhoods.

A further important instance in a coordinate sustainability effort is the United Nations Sustainable Development Goals — SDGs. Though too broad by themselves, a subset more related to all activities and impacts associated with infrastructure development could be extracted to serve as a guiding framework for the formulation of the standards. A dialogue between such goals and the various kinds of infrastructure works would be universally welcome.

This attitude and ensuing measures also bear on the energy matrix of each member, an ultimate objective of the coordination effort being the achievement of as clean as possible energy matrices in the BRICS space.

## The electromagnetic spectrum and its myriad applications

This suggestion touches different aspects of the several uses currently — top industries, commercial and daily life applications — which rely on electromagnetic waves.

We begin with the major communication power of television.

Russia and China have important international channels, as Russia Today and the array of channels under the powerful CCTV label. Brazil, through its modern and well-managed GLOBO organization, as well as one or two less big channels, also has an international presence, though more modest. Notably through GLOBO, it is a major provider of content, basically in the form of its world-renowned soap operas. The same applies to India, where Bollywood movies attract a wide, internationally spread audience. South Africa, even if in a lesser scale and spread, has also interesting and relevant content.

Why not create a BRICS channel, coordinated by the five members?

It could have a BRICS News program, focusing on news and views from the five countries and, at the side of the information segments, it would broadcast select emissions from each of the five members. Brazilian soap operas and music would follow Bollywood movies and Chinese and Russian historical productions. The unique character of the channel, pooling together the best and more attractive in each country, would guarantee its worldwide interest, making for a major highway for connectivity and cultural exchanges and an invaluable soft power instrument for the group.

The second point relates to Internet governance, still heavily in the hands of Western powers. In the last multilateral forum for telecommunications, sponsored by the International Telecommunications Union — ITU — the internationally accredited institution for the world governance of all usages of the electromagnetic spectrum — Brazil, China and Russia led a position that envisaged to actually accruing ITU's (notional) powers on the governance of the Internet. This clashed with fierce opposition from the US and Europe, favorable to maintaining the present status quo. The meeting ended in a stalemate, no concrete decision having been achieved.

A coordinated front and ensuing actions in the ITU and the several instances related to Internet governance are essential for shaping a strong and united BRICS image.

In a broader dimension, coordination should aim at the cyberspace policy in general, in order to protect a BRICS' common space and offer a joint alternative of a secure, democratic but realistic cyber policy.

Until about 2 or 3 years ago, China, Russia and Brazil were close to roughly aligning their policies in this issue, with prospects of India following suit. Unfortunately, this welcomed convergence lost impetus; distances increased again and China advanced to newer developments at a fast pace. This mindset must be reverted, and the efforts to achieve something more than a minimal commonality of views resumed. They will be surely rewarding as new uses of the cyberspace are created nearly every quarter.

Cloud policy is a good example of such uses. With its simple, multipurpose technology, its demand is becoming widespread, and one facility could be developed under a BRICS perspective, without closing the door to significant partners, like the EU.

The upcoming implementation of the G5 technology, drastically providing major changes in industrial production, Internet of things and diversified digital techniques, will require, beyond a substantial amount of funds for updating the telecoms infrastructure, major changes in the existing regulatory framework. This opens another challenging opportunity for a BRICS-coordinated action in the adoption and sharing of this disruptive new communication mode.

Again, China stands as the most forward-looking and active member in these topics, but concerns regarding the other members' standing should not be dismissed.

## Conclusion

For at least five years, we have been arguing that, without innovation and more than a grain of salt of daring, the BRICS — this strange animal — will progressively move to irrelevance (Flôres, 2013). The time of surprise and curiosity has long passed. Forgetting its anecdotal beginning, together with standard ideas on regional integrations, is a pre-condition for the group to engage in a virtuous process that will eventually forge a new, never before seen identity in the world of international relations (Flôres, 2017).

Uncompromising, within this idea, is the practice of coordination: of plans, actions, projects and visibility measures. Without inhibiting the cooperation activities already in progress, their furthering and increase, more coordinated policies are necessary. The title of the present Forum could not have been more adequate to the present reality of the group.

We have outlined in the two previous sections, four suggestions of relevant coordination endeavors. They show that both concrete domains as more elusive fields, like foreign policy, offer opportunities for this unavoidable exercise. Nothing will be either simple or immediate; this chapter has outlined broad, possible strategies; as usual, tactics is now required.

However, we hope the main message stands clear: the special character of the BRICS requires specifically tailored, non-traditional advances and projects; this, in turn, will only be feasible through coordinated actions, when the capacity and desire to survive and prosper will be effectively tested for the whole group.

## References

Flôres, R. G., Jr. (2013) International innovation and daring: The BRICS. *Global Dialogue Review* **1**(1) New Delhi.

Flôres, R. G., Jr. (2017) BRICS: Approaches to a dynamic process, in BRICS — Studies and Documents, several authors. Brasília: Funda.o Alexandre de Gusm.o, Itamaraty. In Lei, W. and W. Liqiang (eds.), *The Belt and Road towards Win-Win Cooperation* (Social Sciences Academic Press, China).

Linggui, W. and Jianglin, Z. (eds.) (2017) *The Belt and Road Initiative in the Global Context: International Joint Study Report, No. 1.* National Institute for Global Strategy, CASS (Social Sciences Academic Press, China).

# Chapter 17

# Soft Power, Inter-cultural Communication and Inter-civilizational Dialogue as Main Strategies of Development of International Cooperation

Guseynova Innara Alyevna

*Moscow State Linguistic University, Moscow, Russia*

## Introduction: Theoretical Remarks

Since prehistoric times and to the present day, in the center of humanitarian space has been the human — a local system comprising two sides: the corporeal and the spiritual. This ambiguous unity, indeed, should be analyzed within philosophical and theological conceptions, but the development of the cognitive paradigm in modern scientific knowledge allows for studying humans not only as an ambivalent entity but also as a unity of the emotional and the rational components (Kubryakova, 2004; Nechayeva, 2013; Schwartz-Frizel, 2007). Such an approach discovers a prospect of researching humans in a new format, as complex programmable systems, which generate cognitive dissonance (Festinger, 2000) and a cognitive conflict (Frygina, 1980).

We believe, following Nechayeva (2013), that a cognitive conflict is a result of collision between the emotional and the rational components of a person's cognitive system that arises during the perception and mental processing of incoming information. Cognitive dissonance, as opposed to cognitive conflict, is a result of a person's mental collision with events happening in the outside world. It also embraces several stages of information processing: emotional perception, intellectual assessment and the analysis of the outcome that needs to be verbalized in either the native or a foreign language.

At the foundation of both cognitive dissonance and the cognitive conflict lies a basic emotion: fear. In other words, any collision with something new and unknown implies experiencing the numinous, i.e. something terrifying and frightening. Each person requires a different amount of time to overcome their fear before the new and unknown. A rich cultural background and the knowledge of the foreign culture's unique characteristics help in overcoming the fear. Lack of such knowledge, however, makes it more difficult to overcome fear and regain self-control. In this context, it is necessary to work out strategies that help overcome cognitive dissonance and cognitive conflict.

## Main Strategies of Development of International Cooperation

### *The soft power strategy*

One of the contemporary strategies is the so-called soft power strategy. It permeates the whole of institutional communication and is meant at the same time to overcome the negative stereotypes based on cognitive dissonance and cognitive conflict.

It is generally accepted in the humanities that it was Joseph Nye,[1] an American political scientist, who first introduced the term soft power as he identified the two strategies for state-level operation: "hard power" and "soft power". According to Nye (2004), "hard power" means the ability to promote the country's foreign policy interests by means of military and

---

[1] Nye is the author of 13 books, among them are *Bound to Lead: The Changing Nature of American Power* (1990), *Governance in a Globalizing World* (2000), *The Paradox of American Power* (2002), *Soft Power* (2004), etc.

economic power of the country, while "soft power" means the ability of the state to attract people with its culture and its social and political values.

Let us recall that the term power is polysemic and can mean such things as authority, force, influence and so on. Such ambiguity of the term allows us to subdivide the soft power (Nye, 2004) strategy into at least three components: the cultural component (the system of basic values shared by all members of the society); the ideological component (a set of beliefs in a variety of fields, from scientific knowledge to religion and everyday notions of good conduct adopted in the society); and the foreign policy component (diplomacy in its broadest sense and use). The cultural and ideological components embody the stable side of the soft power strategy, while the foreign policy component is dynamic and variable and can be used to overcome negative stereotypes.

We would like to stress that the soft power strategy facilitates overcoming all kinds of stereotypes, including ethnic stereotypes, and stimulates sociocultural cooperation. Within the framework of cross-cultural communication, the soft power strategy encourages a mediating process aimed at building partnership relations between representatives of different cultures, thus constructing a multipolar environment.

The soft power strategy embraces the strategies of cultural management, which includes three factors described in detail in Ageeva's study — the role of "soft power" tools in the foreign policy of the Russian Federation in the context of globalization (Ageeva, 2016). The author refers to them as "economic success, ideological persuasiveness and cultural attractiveness of the country" (Ageeva, 2016, p. 3). These factors are also factors aspiring for world domination in the social and humanitarian spaces. This involves, above all, communicative technologies, which enable partnerships with countries belonging to different cultural phenotypes. Second, this could lead to a system of soft impact on all participants of inter-cultural dialogue, which is achieved through a display of a country's cultural and technological achievements through literature, art, modern industrial technologies, innovations, etc.

The three-fold construction of the soft power strategy (with its cultural, ideological and foreign policy components) makes it possible to apply it not only as an instrument of political and ideological nature but also as a marketing and management tool in various types of discourse that advance culture in a society.

## Inter-cultural communication (approach)

The second tool could be called the inter-cultural approach connected with the inter-cultural communication. We see inter-cultural communication as communication of linguistic identities belonging to different linguistic and cultural communities (Gudkov, 2003).

The modern inter-cultural/geopolitical space is characterized by two opposite trends: "On the one hand, there are integration processes uniting people and populations of the planet. On the other hand, there are disintegration ones" (Global Challenges of the XXI Century, 2012, p. 9). It is necessary to take into account the fact that global world politics, economy and culture are based on coordination of activities of many participants. In this regard, culture becomes a geopolitical factor that can serve as a force for unification and at the same time as a means of national and cultural presentation of the country in the context of globalization.

It is generally accepted that geopolitical, ideological and economic factors are influenced by a number of other factors, the significance of which varies with, and depends on, specific cultural and historical circumstances. At the same time, the preservation of the cultural and historical heritage is closely tied to preserving and promoting the national language in the context of globalization. This makes it possible to consider language as a "mirror" reflecting the geopolitical processes that are typical for a globalizing world. With this in mind, analysis of borrowed vocabulary, described by modern researchers, and the key words that determine the branch-wise specificity of different types of discourse produce what can be called "fashion" in languages and countries.

Inter-cultural communication is based on awareness of the image of a country: foreign, or one's own. Each organization aims to develop communicative strategies designed to ensure external communication, and the inter-cultural approach helps consolidate efforts to ease cross-cultural communication and overcome negative stereotypes.

It should be emphasized that in the institutional sphere, fashion in languages and relevant countries is regulated at the level of governmental and public organizations and of various social institutions that determine the behavior of a person in an ethnosocium. The operation of these institutions results in the emergence of various political and economic unions, organizations and associations, for example, the Shanghai Cooperation Organization (SCO), BRICS, etc. It is necessary to develop a set of measures to provide systematic cultural and discursive space for their sustainable functioning.

## *Inter-civilizational dialogue*

The third contemporary strategy, inter-civilizational dialogue, at present is realized in institutional, professional and daily environments, both in social and virtual spaces. This means that any country is interested in a positive image, both in physical socio-cultural interaction and on the Internet. Thus, real geopolitical changes find their expression in all institutions: in the media, in marketing, advertising, education and others. All this is achieved through language, which is regarded as an "institution of institutions", since language enables all forms of human activity, whether cognitive, practical, communicative, or others. Inter-civilizational dialogue is aimed at building a common communicative space and finding the intersection points of practical interests of all the parties. The joint communicative space builds a positive image of every country. In our view, inter-civilizational dialogue today is to be based on the locus brand, or the "good name of the country", usually associated with a certain locus (administrative unit, geographic feature, territory, place, city, region, etc.). Notably, the concept of locus branding was largely formed under the influence of studies on national identity and the so-called "country of origin effect" (COE) (Parshin, 2015, p. 29). To a large extent, this was facilitated by the reference to the place of origin of the goods "Made in ...." Inter-civilizational dialogue serves to build affinity for the country. Researchers say that the brands of countries and states are very stable: the composition of the top 10 locus brands has remained unchanged for many years; they are the USA, Germany, Great Britain, France, Japan, Canada, Italy, Australia, Switzerland and Sweden. Some of the main attributes of inter-civilizational dialogue are the national cuisine, drinks, architecture, commercial brands, etc. Certain commercial brands may be almost the main attributes of the country, such as IKEA and Absolut for Sweden or Samsung for South Korea. The countries of Eastern Europe and the Baltics brand themselves by distancing themselves from the Soviet/ communist past. According to the author, the countries of East and Southeast Asia seek to overcome their simplified, unilateral brand image: either purely as tourist destination countries (Malaysia, Singapore) or as workshop countries (Taiwan, South Korea). Countries such as Iraq, Colombia, Romania, Kosovo and Southern Sudan are also concerned about their locus branding.

Locus branding in Russia has its own characteristics and consists in promoting the national brand of Russia as a country with unique potential as producer of goods and services based on its scientific and educational potential, on cultural traditions and on natural and recreational resources.

At present, inter-civilizational dialogue manifests itself in excessive use of lexical borrowings and foreign words. To quote, the article by Mazurova published in Literaturnaya Gazeta under the title Foreign as Russian (Mazurova, 2016) where the author harshly criticizes this phenomenon: "Near the Kremlin there are signboards in Latin script: "Luxury Nikolskaya Plaza"; "Fashion Brand"; "Persona Beauty Salon"; "Republika Fitness Club"; "Audi City Moscow" show-room (Mazurova, 2016, p. 18). Undoubtedly, these are signs of globalization, which are indicative of erasing borders and bringing closer various people.

## Conclusion

In conclusion, we would like to stress that all the strategies mentioned above contribute to building a multipolar world and are necessary for the development of international cooperation.

## References

Ageeva, V. D. (2016) Rol instrumentov "myagkoy sily" vo vneshney politike Rossiyskoy Federacii v kontekste globalizacii: avtoref. diss. cand. polit. nauk -Sankt-Peterburg/SPbGU, 29 s.

Festinger, (2000) *Cognitive Dissonance Theory. Transl. From English.* Spb: .Rech., 320 p.

Soft Power, Inter-cultural Communication and Inter-civilizational Dialogue **209**

Frygina, N. I. (1980) Factory prevrascheniya kognitivnogo konflikta v mezhlichnostny konflikt v situatsiyakh gruppovogo obsuzhdeniya: dis. – M. (1980), 149 p.

Globalnye vyzovy XXI veka — geopoliticheskiy otvet Rossii. – M. (2012), 318s.

Gudkov, D. B. (2003) *Theory and Practice of Cross-cultural Communication*, (ITDGK, Moscow) "Gnozis", 288 p. (in Russian).

Kubryakova, E. C. (2004) Yazyk i znaniye. M.: Ros. Akademiya nauk. Institut yazykoznaniya, M.: Yazyki slavyanskoy kultury, (2004), 560 p.

Mazurova, L. (2016) Inostranniy kak russkiy. -Litereaturnaya gazeta. -№39 (6569), 5 -11 oktybrya 2016 g, s.18.

Nay Dzh. S. (2004) Myagkaya sila: Slagaemye uspekha v mirovoy politike -Nyu York, 2004, 192s.

Nechayeva, V. S. (2013) Upravleniye konfliktami v elektronnoy kommunikatsii (na material elekronnykh delovykh pisem)/Psykholingvistika: [sb. nauch. trudov GVUZ .Pereyaslav-Khmelnitsky gosudarstvenny pedagogichesky universitet imeni Grigoriya Skovorody.], # 14, Pereyaslav-Khmelnitsky: FLP Lukashevich A. M., pp. 261–274.

Nechayeva, B. C. (2013) Sposoby obyektivatsii kognitivnogo konflikta v elektronnoy nemetskoyazychnoy delovoy perepiske/Semioticheskaya geterogennost yazykovoy kommunikatsii: teoriya i praktika. Vestnik MGLU, # 15 (675), M.: FGBOU VPO MGLU (2013), pp. 153–163.

Nye, J. S. (1990) *Bound to Lead: The Changing Nature of American Power* (Basic Books, New York), 307 p.

Nye, J. S. (2004) *Soft Power: The Means to Success in World Politics* (Public Affairs, New York), 192 p.

Parshin, P. B. (2015) Territoria kak brend: Marketingovaya metaphora, identichnost i konkurentsia, M. (2015), 195s.

Schwarz-Friesel, M. (2007) *Sprache und Emotion* (Tübingen: Narr Francke Attempto Verlag), 401 S.

# Chapter 18

# A New Type of South–South Cooperation and BRICS New Development Bank

Zhu Jiejin

*The Center of BRICS Countries Studies, Fudan University,*
*Shanghai, China*

As a carrier for the development strategy of BRICS, the establishment of the BRICS New Development Bank signals that the cooperation in developmental affairs between the five countries has entered a new stage, and this also transcends the traditional South–South cooperation between developing countries. We call it a new type of South–South Cooperation. In the past 10 years, how did the BRICS countries innovate South–South cooperation through the establishment of the New Development Bank? What types of new developmental cooperation concepts belong to the BRICS countries? I think the concept is innovated in these three areas:

The first area is development and cooperation on the basis of respecting sovereignty and mutual benefits. When we talk about South–South cooperation, we think about the Asian–African Conference, or the Bandung Conference, in 1955. The Bandung Conference began the history of South–South Cooperation. When we say the spirit of the Bandung Conference built the foundation of South–South Cooperation, we are talking about two core concepts: One is economic cooperation should be built on the foundation of respecting sovereignty.

211

Respecting sovereignty refers to considering all countries as equal regardless of size or financial status. In the language of the BRICS Summit, it is expounded as follows: "all countries should enjoy due rights, equal opportunities and fair participation in global economic, financial and trade affairs, recognizing that countries have different capacities and are at different levels of development". The second concept is economic cooperation should be mutually beneficial. If we compare South–South cooperation with South–North cooperation, especially cooperation led by OECD, you will find they differ greatly. South–South Cooperation has achieved brilliantly in the 1960s and 1970s, such as the birth of the Non-Aligned Movement in 1961, the establishment of Group of 77 in 1964 and the declaration and action plan of establishing a new international order passed at the sixth special session of the United Nations General Assembly. But since the 1980s and 1990s, we heard more about neoliberalism and the Washington Consensus, but South–South cooperation has fallen into a slump.

In a new historic period, after we entered the 21st century, thanks to the economic growth of the BRICS countries, there has been a new revival of South–South cooperation. BRICS countries established their own development bank, realizing the actual spirit of South–South cooperation. In the new development bank, a new principle of share allocation is used that's different from the existing multilateral development banks. The bank follows a principle of equality, instead of allocating share according to GDP. The five countries allocating shares equally show the principle of equality. At the same time, the operation of the bank follows a marketization principle. The Charter talks about a steady operation principle, but in fact it's a mutually beneficial principle. The principles of quality and mutual benefit are shown in the BRICS new development bank.

The second area is "the theory of economic growth first". There's a debate in development economics on how to promote development of the developing countries. One theory is through economic growth while the other through poverty reduction. The theory of economic growth believes development of a developing country is the prime responsibility that a country needs to take on and this depends on endogenous economic growth. The biggest bottleneck restriction element to endogenous economic growth is the lack of basic infrastructure. How to help developing

A New Type of South–South Cooperation and BRICS New Development Bank **213**

countries to improve their infrastructure is what this theory has always advocated. The other theory has a different view, it believes the nature of development is the reduction of the population of the poorest people in the poorest countries, and it doesn't necessarily have to be realized through economic growth. In many countries, the economy might be growing, but the gap between the rich and the poor is increasing; the poor aren't benefiting from the economic growth and poverty isn't reducing. So, this theory advocates direct "poverty reduction", through point-to-point help to the population in poverty, such as in education, medical care, social security and gender equality.

In fact, it's hard to say which theory is better, the poverty reduction theory or the economic growth theory. The key is which theory's hypothesis is more suitable for the developing countries' reality. The poverty reduction theory believes that more private investment needs to be drawn in to invest on infrastructure and multilateral banks should exist in this field, so we can see multilateral banks such as the World Bank or Asian Bank used to have lots of programs concerning infrastructure, but now the programs are focusing more and more on education, medical, etc. and less on infrastructure. However, the economic growth theory believes in many developing countries because no effective market mechanism has been established; on the one hand, it's difficult to attract enough private capital into the field of infrastructure, and on the other hand, benefit generated by having multilateral banks focusing on society cannot spread to other fields and cannot turn into economic growth. Therefore, BRICS New Development Bank focuses on infrastructure, emphasizing on economic growth first. This reflects the difference between theories and concepts.

The last area is "development-oriented global economic governance". According to UN definition, economic governance means the role global multilateral organizations and processes play in shaping global economic policies, regulations and rules. What's the goal and core of global economic governance? In other words, why should we have global economic governance? For developed countries, the goal and core is to popularize the Washington Consensus and promote developing countries to become marketized, liberalized, privatized and rid of government restriction. This can be shown from IMF, World Bank and WTO.

IMF requires many developing countries to open up capital market and let capital flow freely, removes restrictions on foreign exchange and uses this as a condition to loan to developing countries. It's controversial whether this is beneficial for developing countries' development. The World Bank transited from focusing on programs that help developing countries to focusing on development policies that help developing countries and then to focusing on pushing for governmental changes in developing countries. It became more and more involved in fields such as governance and anti-corruption, public administration and development of civil society and has become more and more separated from its developmental role. WTO has always made it its goal to push for trade liberalization and doesn't pay enough attention to the development needs of developing countries. Since the Uruguay Round, developing countries were all dissatisfied toward it and forced WTO to open a new round of negotiations — the Doha Round, demanding to put developing countries' development benefits first, and called it the Doha Development Round. But a troubling matter is right now the future of the Doha Development Round is uncertain.

What's different is that the BRICS countries emphasize that the goal and core of global economic governance should be helping developing countries to solve their development issues. Developing countries have their own development strategies, the international multilateral organizations and processes should think of a way to respond to their development strategies, instead of changing the policies or changing the governments. This is a concept that's development-oriented in global economic governance. The New Development Bank established by the BRICS countries does not have additional policies and political conditions in its loan programs and relies on the borrowing country's own environment and societal standards to evaluate projects, which speeds up the examination and approval process of the projects and can be a real, equal developing partner to developing countries. While the World Bank and Asian Bank transfuse the developed countries' standard to you through loans, money and projects, the BRICS countries respond to your own standards and undertake anegotiation process on how to raise your standards and abilities.

At the same time, it shouldn't be overlooked that the nature of the new South–South cooperation has brought challenges to the operation and future development of the new development bank, such as: (1) International rating — South–South cooperation means being led by developing countries and this will result in no developed countries to participate, which will reduce capital scale for the bank and will lead to West-led international rating organizations such as Fitch, Standard & Poor's and Moody's to have bias on the New Development Bank. At the same time, South–South Cooperation means total equality between the five countries, which restricts the abilities to contribute for countries with greater power in the BRICS, and will have a disadvantage for the bank's rating objectively. (2) Financing cost — The bank, being misunderstood by the West on the issue of international rating would have bad influence on the bank's financing cost. In 2016, the new development bank issued the first green bond worth 3 billion RMB in the Chinese inter-bank bond market, with the nominal interest rate of 3.07%. In the same year, the 3-year bonds worth 500 million SDR issued by the World Bank in China as a trial has a nominal interest rate of 0.49%. (3) Expansion — In order to persist on the new style of South–South cooperation, when thinking about expansion, the New Development Bank should choose developing countries that have rather good governing systems, most of which should be emerging market countries. This by itself is a paradox because low-income developing countries who wish to receive bank loans have stronger wills to enter the bank, but in the short term, new emerging market countries should receive the priority consideration for bank expansion rather than low-income developing countries.

# Chapter 19

# The Coordination of BRICS Development Strategies: Way to Common Prosperity — Sum of 2017 BRICS Think Tanks Forum and International Conference

Wei Siying

*National Institute for Global Strategy, Chinese Academy of Social Sciences, Beijing, China*

## Introduction

From 8 to 9 June 2017, the National Institute for Global Strategy (NIGS) of the Chinese Academy of Social Sciences (CASS), the Guangming Think Tank and the University of International Relations (UIR) jointly held a 2017 BRICS Think Tanks Forum in Beijing. The forum was titled "The Coordination of BRICS Development Strategies: Way to Common Prosperity" and more than 40 government officials and experts from nearly 40 organizations in the BRICS attended the conference.

Wang Linggui, Executive Vice Chairman of Board of Directors and Secretary of NIGS, hosted the opening ceremony. Cai Fang, Vice President of CASS and Chairman of Board of Directors of NIGS, Shen Weixing, associate managing editor of *Guangming Daily*, Tao Jian, President of UIR, and Lu Zhongwei, Former General-Director of the China Institutes of Contemporary International Relations attended the opening ceremony and gave speeches. In the 2-day meeting, the officials and experts from five countries held dialogues on key issues of BRICS development and cooperation, ran through background, condition, content, method and experience for the development and cooperation, as well as root questions faced and possible challenges in the future, attempted to bring forth new ideas, structures, concepts and methods that might promote strategic integration among the BRICS, in order to realize BRICS countries' common interest, steady development and harmonious multilateral cooperation and contribution to regional peace and prosperity. In September 2017, the BRICS leadership summit was held in Xiamen and this conference provided preheat and outlook for the Xiamen summit. The speeches and discussions at the conference were in-depth and fruitful.

## Origin of BRICS: Concept, Goal and Position

Participants discussed the definition of BRICS and analyzed its reason of formation, looked back on the development process of BRICS and brought forward the goal and position for future BRICS cooperation. The views were diverse and abundant.

As to the concept of BRICS, Alexander Lukin, Director of the Center for East Asian and Shanghai Cooperation Organization Studies at the Moscow State Institute of International Relations, believes BRICS is a political group or organization launched by political elites. Ana Flávia Barros-Platiau, Director of the Graduate Studies of the International Relations Institute of the University of Brasilia, believes that in the past BRICS used to be an alliance against the West. But as international situation changes, the concept of BRICS is also changing. BRICS has become an institutionalized platform, through which broader international affairs can be dealt with. Boris Guseletov, Senior Fellow at the Institute of Europe of Russian Academy of Sciences, believes BRICS was formed based on changes in international relations, it used to be a group formed out of political interactions, but later on expanded to cooperation in economy, trade, finances, etc. The five countries have the will and resources to cooperate and formed a mutually dependent relationship. Wang Yiwei, Professor at the School of International Relations of Renmin

University, called BRICS a community with shared fortune. Paulo Esteves, Supervisor of the BRICS Policy Center in Brazil, defined BRICS from a unique point of view. He sees BRICS as a club, with members not only from participating countries, but the entire international society. They are both policymakers and policy benefiters. He Wenping, Director of the Division of African Studies at the Institute of West-Asian and African Studies in CASS, believes whether as an organization or a type of club, BRICS countries have economic responsibilities, as well as political and diplomatic responsibilities. In the future, some military targets can be added as well, they can emphasize more on cooperation in international security.

Participating experts believe the goal of BRICS is to participate in financial system reform, participate in global governance and fight for more say in international, political and economic new orders. Vinod Kumar Anand, Senior Fellow and Research Coordinator of the Vivekanand International Foundation in India, has higher expectations. He believes the development strategy of BRICS should be kept the same as UN's future goals. These sustainability goals are also the key issues in BRICS development. Hu Shisheng, Director of the Institute of South Asian, Southeast Asian and Oceanian Studies at the China Institutes of Contemporary International Relations, points that the goal of BRICS countries is to pursue fairness, to obtain the same competition advantage as developing countries and that's the reason for unity of the five countries. Zhu Jiejin, Senior researcher at the Center for BRICS Studies of Fudan University, brings out a consensus BRICS made on the development goals. He calls in a new development mindset: South–South cooperation and South–North cooperation; the dialectical relationship between economic development and poverty reduction; seeking development and trying to participate in global economic governance.

On the category of BRICS, experts all agree the countries can be divided into three categories: the first category is South Africa and Brazil: high proportion of European immigrants, the influence of slavery still exists, serious social injustice; the second category is China and India: relatively long experience of colonization, the two most populous countries, in similar development stage; the third category is Russia: never went through exploitation and is one of the Western imperialist powers, with advanced technology development.

On the development process of BRICS, Vasily Mikheev, Deputy Director of the Institute of World Economy and International Relations at the Russian Academy of Sciences, said BRICS development experienced three main phases: market development, political development and pragmatism. Paulo Esteves divided BRICS into four phases from the angle of development procedures: the first three are acceptance, reorganization and financial cooperation, now the countries are in phase four: since the 2016 Goa Summit, the international situation has changed and BRICS countries are seeking to shoulder new responsibilities. To this, Tony Karbo, Executive Director at the Centre for Conflict Resolution in South Africa, has different views. He believes the second phase began with South Africa joining the BRICS and it's the expansion phase. During this phase, BRICS was formed and made great achievements in cooperation.

## Development Strategy Integration in a Global Governance Viewpoint

Former Ambassador to China Nalin Surie said in his keynote speech that BRICS will contribute new powers to future global governance and international governance structure reform, as well as play an influential role in many international affairs waiting to be solved. Right now, there's necessity for BRICS to actively participate in global governance.

Neelam Deo, Director of Gateway House, believes right now global governance is dominated by the western world and developing countries are in minority. BRICS includes the main developing countries and it's crucial to the five countries that they exert influence in global governance. Huang Maoxing, Director of School of Economics at Fujian Normal University, agrees with his viewpoint. He believes developing countries should actively participate in global governance, break away from a passive state and increase discourse power. Vinod Kumar Anand points out that, as US leans toward conservatism, BRICS countries face an important opportunity to increase international power of discourse and they should seize the opportunity and push for effective policies and methods in south-south cooperation. Tao Jian points out that BRICS countries have the responsibility to actively participate in global governance, maintain and develop an open global economy, pushing for construction of a just, logical and transparent international economic and trade investment regulation system and provide more public products for developing countries. Dong Manyuan, Vice President of the China Institute of International Studies, points out that BRICS should shoulder a leadership role through global governance, so that developing countries can rise as a whole. Georgy Toloraya, Director of the Asian Strategy Center at the Institute of Economics of the Russian Academy of Science, Russia, thinks the five countries can increase their perspective statuses in global governance affairs, increase discourse and play a more and more important role in global order. Boris Guseletov points out the five countries also think BRICS should enjoy more say in international society.

On how BRICS should participate in global governance, Chen Zhongwei believes BRICS development bank should be taken full advantage of to participate in global governance, increase the sway of emerging economies and developing countries, make up for the supply shortage of World Bank and Asian Development Bank. Roberto Abdenur, Member of Board of Trustees at the Brazilian Center for International Relations and former Brazil's ambassador to China, points out that when BRICS countries are cooperating within, if they cooperate with other countries with BRICS member's identity, they can bring more possibilities to the world. Therefore, in protecting multilateralism, BRICS countries should shoulder more responsibilities. BRICS countries not only need to strengthen communication in academic, commercial and diplomatic aspects but also need to increase collaboration in social areas. Paulo Esteves especially emphasizes on BRICS cooperation on the climate issue. He believes that on this issue, BRICS countries should extend to developed countries and European countries. Sanusha Naidu, Senior Research Fellow of the Centre for Chinese Studies in South Africa, believes it's important that BRICS should seek the backbone and blank areas of global governance, such as ocean control, ocean economy, Internet governing, etc. Zhu Jiejin believes BRICS should pay more attention to and extend help to developing countries in global governance. Wang Yiwei believes BRICS countries come from different continents and should have parallel cooperation between emerging countries under the global governance framework. Georgy Toloraya believes BRICS countries should strive to change the political and economic foundation of the world, promote independence of international law and policy, as well as its status in other international organizations. Bali Ram Deepak, Professor at the Center of Chinese and Southeast Asian Studies at Jawaharlal Nehru University, points out that BRICS countries should have a connecting and integrating mindset, to connect BRICS countries with globalization, and fight for advantages brought by this connection. Renato Galvao Flôres, Director of the International Intelligence Unit (FGV), points out that BRICS countries should try to change the status of international organizations through peaceful and harmonious ways, no matter what the reason may be.

## Deepening Cooperation: Fruits and Challenges

Since BRICS countries launched cooperation, they've achieved greatly through economic, political, diplomatic, trade and security cooperation. Experts' sum and commentary on cooperation fruits are as follows: first, BRICS countries have established an all-aspect, wide-region, multilayered partnership covering political, economic and cultural exchanges and cooperation, using economic cooperation as the main line. The Goa Summit brought forth that in 2020, the overall GDP of BRICS countries will reach 500 billion USD. Second, there's breakthrough in mechanism construction. The BRICS Development Bank and BRICS emergency reserve arrangement have been established, providing new sources of finance to meet the need of developing countries during transition era. After only more than 1 year of establishment, the BRICS new development bank has granted multiple projects close to 1 billion USD in value. The emergency reserve arrangement is helpful for the stability of global finance system. Third, eight summits were successfully held and the ninth one was held in Xiamen in 2017. More than 400 conferences and other forms of dialogues were held. Fourth, great achievements were made in pushing for global economic and finance governance reform, realizing transition of international politics and economic scale, a transition from north to south.

While achieving fruits, BRICS countries are faced with challenges of future development at the same time. Experts' viewpoints can be summed as the following: first, security challenges caused by new changes in international environment. At present, the influence of global financial crisis lasts till today and the economic resurgence is slow and lacks power; countries have inward policy tendencies with increase of protectionism, there are complicated elements of geopolitics; traditional and untraditional security risks are intersecting; global challenges such as terrorism, infectious diseases and climate change are becoming more apparent; there's increase of uncertain and unstable elements. In recent years, there's a trend of deglobalization, some former leaders have become opposition power, with the Trump government's conservatism tendencies, the situation is difficult. The US' backing out of the Paris Climate Change Agreement and Brexit are two big global events in 2016, climate change and global governance took huge hits, and former developing countries are beginning to lose their leadership position internationally.

Second, a structural challenge faced by the countries' domestic development dilemma. BRICS countries are all faced with their unique challenges. Russia faces transition of resource and economic structure and politics, and it relies too much on its advantageous areas. There's too much executive interference and monopoly in its domestic political and economic rule, which is not beneficial to the formation of a free market and competitive environment. India has long-term bipolar structural problems with urgent need for infrastructure construction. South Africa has excessive high reliance of the outside world, diminishing its economic development independence. Its key difficulty is transitioning from natural resource export to manufacturing. Brazil needs adjustments in its governance system, its series of political issues lead to uncertainty in Brazil's future economic development. China is facing systematic obstacles in supply structural reform, its cost of human resources, land and environmental protection is on the rise and it is losing its labor-intensive industrial advantage. BRICS countries need to solve their domestic issues before they can discuss future integration.

Third, the differences between BRICS lead to integration challenges. Politically, BRICS countries are unequal in status, with different domestic and international environments and huge differences in legal system. Economically, differences in financial system cause differences in the countries' outward economic strategies, demands and priorities. On security, members have compatibility obstacles and different ideas of future development of the world system and many are strategic components in many affairs, bringing uncertainty to BRICS. Culturally, the ethnicities differ greatly, increasing the difficulties in integration. Geographically, differences have negative influence on the future development of the whole organization: the countries are situated in three continents, causing logistic and trade obstacles. The five countries should coordinate together and make up their differences, this process is long term, and the countries need to help each other and jointly solve the issues.

## Response and Future BRICS Cooperation

Even though BRICS is faced with severe challenges, experts are optimistic about BRICS countries' ability to cope with issues. Nalin Surie points out that BRICS can be a bridge between north and south, east and west, and the five countries have the ability to rise up to international challenges and achieve more. The specific policies brought forth by experts can be categorized as follows:

First, increase macro policy coordination. The five countries should pay more attention on how to solve differences and strengthen cooperation from within. This can be realized in these aspects: first, seeking commonalities and common interests in global affairs setting aside differences and having strategic integration. Second, actively exploit advantages from these countries, complement advantages and mutually benefit. Alexander Lukin points out there's an adverb in China, "harmonious but different". The countries need to strive to create harmony while keeping their own characteristics. Facing the challenges alone can make the five countries competitors instead of cooperators. Third, seeking common development. They should together cultivate three types of ability: integration ability, production ability and consumption ability, forming great competition advantage. Fourth, increase strategic communication and dialogue; strengthen strategic mutual trust; making the people and enterprises in the five countries more adapted to and understand each other's strategic roles, legal systems and working mechanism; ensure tolerance, transparency and mutual benefits; realize a harmonious and mutually beneficial cooperative partnership. Fifth, emphasis on soft power strategy, suggesting BRICS countries to form a cross-cultural intersection and launch dialogue

The Coordination of BRICS Development Strategies    225

between civilizations, to find common ground in viewpoint debate. BRICS countries must improve their relations with each other and set BRICS development as a priority of consideration in political life.

Second, push for cooperation in key areas and seize emerging cooperation opportunities. The countries need to run through their economic agendas and keep expanding integration in trade areas and increase cooperation level in key areas. At the same time, the five countries need to continue strengthening cooperation of supervision organizations, respect each other's supervision organizations and acknowledge each other's supervision standards. Bai Ming, Vice Director of International Market Research Bureau at the Chinese Academy of International Trade and Economic Cooperation of the Ministry of Commerce, points out that there are three levels of benefits in BRICS' development-based cooperation: outward benefits, mutual benefits and domestic increasing benefits. Through five-country cooperation, there can be push of member states' mechanism reform and industry restructure. Furthermore, the countries should seize cooperation opportunities in emerging regions and cultivate new cooperation growing points. At present, new cooperation areas BRICS countries need to seize include sustainable development, such as new energy, circular economy, etc.; electronics, such as media and Internet; military technology, such as helicopter and missile construction, and nuclear industry; high technology, such as high-tech products and robots.

Third, actively fight for mechanism innovation. BRICS is an informal organization form of international forum and should keep improving the cooperation mechanism, transitioning from a loose organization to a specific institution, such as making the organization official and regulated by establishing a secretariat and an executive organization, or start with setting up smaller organizations to deepen mutual influence. Besides, some of the participants agreed to a "BRICS+" expansion mode, suggesting increasing more member states, expanding the BRICS friend circle. Some experts oppose to the expansion, such as Paulo Esteves, who believes the BRICS countries have already formed an existing mechanism and the countries should keep steadying and strengthening this mechanism. Boris Guseletov believes right now the group is already representative enough,

226  *Wei Siying*

and impertinent expansion might lead to imbalance and invalid integration. The countries think and reconsider after ensuring standards of development and accepting new members and their demands to standards. Ana Flávia Barros Platiau points out that the countries can hold an open attitude. Right now, there are lots of questions that need to be discussed and pondered; this question can be left for the future.

Fourth, hold wide exchanges and think tank cooperation. Think tank exchange is the window through which BRICS countries can increase understanding and acts the bridge to increase mutual trust and cooperation. Vasily Mikheev points out that BRICS countries have intersecting responsibilities and might lead to conflicts within, so think tank cooperation is especially important. Zhang Yuyan, General-Director of the Institute of World Economics and Politics of CASS, points out that think tanks play an important role in the platform of BRICS, especially in reducing cost of question and stabilizing the countries' future expectations. On the topic of think tank exchanges, Cai Fang brought forth five propositions: first, plan topics together and launch joint research projects. Second, share academic fruits and information. Third, cultivate academic talents jointly. Fourth, jointly release periodic or topical research results that are influential. Fifth, jointly hold periodic meetings.

At present, under the new global scale, BRICS countries have huge development potential in the future. Zhu Caihua, Dean of the School of International Economics of China Foreign Affairs University, points out that the new age is an age of reglobalization, an era of fourth industrial revolution and an era of new energy revolution. On the future of BRICS in the new age and new global situation, experts brought forth some ideas. Vasily Mikheev believes the Belt and Road Initiative can bring more opportunities to the countries. Georgy Toloraya points out that BRICS will become the catalyst of international order. In the future, BRICS can propose some new mechanisms led by the government; some new mechanisms can exist independent of the present western mainstream global governance framework. Paulo Esteves brings forth some goals BRICS countries can fight for in the future: making sustainable development mainstream, paying attention on development of children and youth, reform of WHO, etc. and also bring up a new concept: climate adaptation, everybody is talking about prolonging climate change, but only few are talking about adapting to the climate change. For developing countries, adapting to climate change is the most important because we must face the consequences of climate change. Sanusha Naidu points out that BRICS doesn't want to replace any international organization. The five countries hope to form a united group and coexist in peace with the so-called western economy.

# Index

**A**

Asian Infrastructure Investment
  Bank, 25

**B**

Belt and Road, 155
Brazil, 8, 77
BREXIT, 22
BRICS, 1

**C**

China, 8
cooperation mechanism, 77
Corporación Andina de Fomento,
  25
counter terrorism, 174

**D**

deglobalization, 171

**F**

finance, 195
FMI, 21
foreign policy, 197

**G**

G20 group, 38
G7 partners, 38
global governance, 169
global warming, 174
globalization, 35, 171
Goa Summit, 69

**I**

India, 8
industrial revolution, 46
infrastructure, 198
inter-civilizational dialogue, 207
inter-cultural communication,
  203
International Monetary Fund, 3

**N**

NAFTA, 21
New Development Bank, 26
new energy revolution, 49

**P**

President Xi Jinping, 1

## R

Regional Comprehensive Economic Partnership, 25
reglobalization, 45
Russia, 8, 132

## S

Sino–India Development, 158
soft power, 203
South Africa, 135
south–south cooperation, 14, 171
structural reform, 57

sustainable development goals (SDGs), 101

## T

Transnational Organized Crime, 147

## U

UN, 21

## W

World Bank, 21

CPSIA information can be obtained
at www.ICGtesting.com
Printed in the USA
JSHW021736260919
1611JS00002B/2